$ 37.50
21.50
Δ= 16.00

Crutches _____ 5
Open stairs _____ 77

Design
for
Accessibility

Design
for
Accessibility

Robert James Sorensen / architect

McGraw-Hill Book Company

New York St. Louis San Francisco Auckland
Bogotá Düsseldorf Johannesburg London
Madrid Mexico Montreal New Delhi
Panama São Paulo Singapore
Sydney Tokyo Toronto

To my children, Elise, Kristin and Mark,
who remind me to care.

Library of Congress Cataloging in Publication Data

Sorensen, Robert J
  Design for accessibility.

  Bibliography: p.
  Includes index.
  1. Architecture and the handicapped — United
States. I. Title.
NA2545.A1S67   720   78-11801
ISBN 0-07-059680-8

1234567890 HDHD 7865432109

The editors for this book were Jeremy Robinson and Joseph Williams,
the designer was Naomi Auerbach, and the production supervisor was
Sally Fliess. It was set in Avant Garde Book by University
Graphics, Inc.

Printed and bound by Halliday Lithographics, Inc.

Contents

Preface

Having been involved over the past few years in several building projects for facilities for the disabled, I have had occasion to refer to various standards and codes on accessibility for the handicapped. In using these standards and references, it was impressed upon me forcefully (and annoyingly) that while many or most of the various standards had been set, they seemed to be scattered in a multitude of pamphlets and publications.

This situation impressed me in three ways: first, there seemed to be no one source for all the information I required; second, much good information and many excellent recommendations appeared only in local or little-circulated publications; third, almost invariably the information appeared largely or only in verbal form, not easily referred to by the busy architect, designer, or draftsperson.

All of this finally led me to the conclusion that a single nationally distributed volume that graphically displayed the current standards and recommendations would be an extremely useful reference for the working architect or designer.

In researching and reviewing standards for handicapped access, I came to realize much more than before the multitude of even minor things which, when overlooked or incorrectly designed, make the everyday life of the handicapped person unnecessarily difficult.

I feel certain that as more architects and designers become aware of what they can do — easily — to provide accessible building and facilities, they will remove the unnecessary burdens which have been unknowingly placed on the lives of the handicapped for too long.

In the drawn portion of the book which follows, I have given all dimensions in both the U.S. Customary and metric systems. In general conformance to recommendations for the use of SI (Système Internationale, the modernized metric system), most linear measurements are given in centimeters without the designation "cm." All other dimension designations are given.

Part One
Considerations

Approximately 10 percent of the population of the United States has some degree of physical handicap. The physical handicaps which afflict people can generally be divided into three types: vision, hearing, and movement. Handicaps of movement are the most prevalent and in their most extreme forms can create an absolute barrier to building access.

An estimated 22 million persons in the United States suffer some limitation of movement, about 400,000 of them being permanently and totally confined to wheelchairs. In addition to those with limitations of movement, there are about 5½ million blind or sight-impaired persons and 8 million deaf or hearing-impaired persons in the United States.

The most difficult handicaps are perhaps those which permit mobility only by the use of various appliances. Such disabilities include paraplegia (paralysis of the lower half of the body), quadriplegia (paralysis in all four limbs), hemiplegia (paralysis in the entire right or left half of the body), loss of joint mobility (arthritis and rheumatism), motor incoordination (multiple sclerosis), loss of control of movement (spastic condition), amputation, loss of nervous system control (brain or spinal cord injury or disease), loss of muscular strength (muscular dystrophy), extreme aging, accident, or surgery.

There are other handicaps not as dramatic as paralysis or the loss of a limb which permit movement only by use of a mechanical aid but which make access difficult, time-consuming, and in some cases impossible. The handicaps which permit mobility with aid, less extensive appliances, or prosthetic devices include loss of stamina, incoordination, diabetes and heart disease, arthritis and rheumatism, high blood pressure, reaching disability, and reduced grasping and manipulative ability.

The disabilities of blindness and deafness are different from the impairments of physical movement in that they are sensory deficiencies, which the designer must allow for by providing additional or alternate information systems or sources.

In some cases the different kinds of physical impairments require identical, sometimes conflicting, considerations. For example, the person confined to a wheelchair can generally operate best in spaces which are open and larger than average, while the blind person may be most comfortable in smaller spaces, where most elements are within touch. Both are somewhat better able to function in a space with hard surfaced floors (the wheelchair-bound person for traction, the blind person for sound). An acoustically "live" space is better for the blind person, while such a room may make things much more difficult for the hearing-impaired person. The good designer will make himself or herself aware of conflicting requirements and will attempt to balance them in the best way possible.

The following general observations regarding special considerations for the different types of handicaps should be kept in mind by the designer:

- Slopes, reach distances, and forces should be reduced below those shown wherever possible, since many persons will be smaller or weaker than the average.
- Many persons forced to use wheelchairs or appliances may have secondary disabilities in addition to their major handicap; these especially include difficulty in grasping, pinching, and twisting.
- Most persons born blind know *only* braille; most persons blinded later in life do *not* know braille.
- While small groups of raised letters and numbers are easily "read" by touch (such as room numbers), larger groups of letters and longer text are very difficult for the blind to read.
- Because of the danger of confusion, too many tactile signals for the blind should be avoided.
- Because tactile signals and signs are useful only if perceived, their locations should be carefully considered and made uniform throughout a building or complex.
- Audible signals for the blind should be in the lower frequencies, since the elderly have difficulty hearing higher-frequency sounds.
- Many legally deaf persons can hear somewhat in a favorable environment (low uniform background noise level, in moderate to slightly acoustically "dead" surroundings).
- It is generally desirable to provide both visual and aural signals where possible to accommodate both the deaf and the blind.

Many persons plagued with disabilities of movement also suffer increased sensibility to cold. Temperatures may need to be kept higher in spaces for these persons, and surfaces which come in contact with their bare skin should not be naturally cold to the touch, such as enameled cast iron and ceramic tile.

Some persons with disabilities of movement also suffer partial or complete loss of feeling. Such loss can be dangerous where they may be subject to being burned without sensing it. This is especially true around cooking appliances and sources of hot water.

A deaf or blind person can move in exactly the same manner as a nonhandicapped person if given the necessary data. However, those with a functional disability in most cases can move about only with an appliance or a prosthetic device and in many cases, again, only in an environment which makes allowance for the disability.

The following comments refer to and explain the diagrams given in Part 2.

WHEELCHAIR

The most difficult appliance in bulk, weight, and spatial requirements is, of course, the wheelchair. In general, where spaces and clearances are designed to allow for the use of wheelchairs, the spaces will be usable by persons using all the other devices, and by the general public also.

The person confined to a wheelchair may be able, within the physical and spatial limitations of the chair, to operate much as a fully ambulatory person. Others, however, because of the nature of their handicap, may be able to approach or use facilities *only* from a certain direction or only by a certain process or approach.

The basic maneuver in using a wheelchair is the procedure of getting into or out of the chair. The methods are:

Frontal: The chairbound person approaches and positions the chair in front of and facing the new seat, and sets the brake on the chair. Setting his or her feet on the floor and using the chair arms and adjacent grab bars, the person stands upright. Using the grab bars at the sides of the new seat or location, the person turns his or her body 180 degrees, still standing, and lets himself or herself down onto the new seat.

Diagonal: This is essentially the same as the frontal approach, but with the chair at an angle to the new seat. Since the body needs to be turned through a smaller angle, this is a slightly easier operation than the frontal approach, but requires sufficient room for the chair to stand at an angle to the new seat.

Lateral: The wheelchair is brought alongside the new position, facing in the direction the person will be seated in when finished. The brakes are set, the arm of the chair is collapsed, and the person slides sideways out of the chair onto the new seat.

Reverse: The chair is turned around and backed up to the new seat and the brakes are set. The back of the chair is collapsed and the person, again using the chair seat and grab bars, slides himself or herself out of the back of the chair onto the new seat.

Since most models of wheelchairs are available with collapsible arms and since the lateral approach does not require the wheelchair user to reach a standing position, this method is generally preferable where possible. The reverse approach is not generally desirable because it requires the user to drag his or her feet and lower body out over the back of the chair. Because of spatial limitations, the frontal approach is the one most usually provided for, even though it is not the preferred one. In some cases, for example at waterclosets, where the wheelchair user must make a frontal approach but cannot stand up, he or she must slide forward to straddle the fixture, while facing backwards, which is a highly uncomfortable position.

Whenever possible, space should be provided for a lateral approach, preferably for both a right and a left approach (since some persons can operate on only one side of their body).

Some sources show or recommend diagonal grab bars. Generally these should be avoided, since they are basically a compromise between a horizontal grab (with which one *lifts* the body), and a vertical grab (with which one *pulls* the body up). For a diagonal bar to be usable, it must be long enough to be grasped with the hand, while bracing the elbow on the bar at the other end, and pulled with the hand, while pushing or lifting with the elbow. This process is difficult for the weak and the elderly. If diagonal bars must be used, they should *never* be used singly, but always in pairs on either side of the body. The use of a single diagonal bar may cause a person's body to rotate as it rises, making him or her lose balance and fall.

Where wheelchairs can approach various fixtures and machines head-on only, the 3'-4" (102) maximum height for any operating mechanism or opening must be observed. Where the chair can approach the fixture alongside, the maximum height may be increased to 4'-0" (122) if necessary.

The maximum distances which can be reached over obstacles such as cabinets and up or down to shelves are well documented and are shown on the diagrams in Part 2.

The size of the wheelchair, along with the strength limitations of the average person using the chair, determines the restrictions of size and height clearances and openings which can be passed over or through. The width of the chair, with clearance for the user's arms propelling the chair, determines the 2'-8" (81) minimum clear opening (*not* door size) which a wheelchair can pass through.

While an average-to-strong male or a strong female can, with some practice, lift himself or herself with the wheelchair up one step or curb, smaller, weaker, and older persons cannot.

For a wheelchair to be lifted up a step, it must approach the step backwards with the large driving wheel going up the step first and with the user's body tipped backward, balancing over the center of the drive wheel. Because of the strength and agility required to lift up a step and the difficulty of forcing the smaller leading wheels over anything but the smallest rise, the highest step or bump or the widest gap which should exist in an accessible pathway is ½" (1.25).

The direction of travel of the standard user-driven wheelchair can be reversed by either one of two pivoting maneuvers. The *one-wheel pivot* involves holding one wheel still in place while turning the other wheel, pivoting the chair around the stationary wheel; this maneuver requires a space 6'-0" × 6'-0" (183 × 183). The other, called the *center pivot*, is accomplished by turning one driving wheel forward while the other, at the same time, is turned backward, thus rotating the chair about its centerpoint. The center pivot requires a space 5'-3" × 5'-3" (160 × 160).

The one-wheel pivot, although it requires more space, is more easily accomplished by those who are weaker or less dexterous. Space should be allowed for the one-wheel pivot rather than the center pivot wherever possible.

At all locations where a wheelchair user must open a door which swings toward him or her, a space of at least 1'-0" (30.5) should be provided at the latch edge of the door. This enables the wheelchair user to position the chair in such a location that he or she can reach and operate the latch and pull the door open with the door clearing the chair. This space enables the door to be opened without the necessity of maneuvering the chair to clear the door while at the same time pulling the door.

WALKER, CANE, AND CRUTCH

In facilities in which spaces have been sized to allow for wheelchair access, it will be found that access for persons using walkers, canes, and crutches will be facilitated. All these ambulatory aids require the user to have slightly more space for movement than a "normal" unaided person needs. Persons with canes and crutches are somewhat flexible in their space requirements, especially over short distances. The space required by a person in a walker, while inflexible, is adequately provided for by wheelchair allowances.

Many persons who require crutches or walkers are also required to wear leg braces which enable the foot and leg to be moved as a unit. Because of the linkage of the foot and leg, the foot cannot flex vertically as for a person without the braces; the foot is held almost rigidly parallel to the ground. For this reason, stairs with open risers or overly deep toes below the treads must be avoided, since these configurations will trap the person's foot as he or she ascends.

THE BLIND

Most blind persons who use a cane rather than a guide dog are taught to find their way using the "long cane" technique. This is a method of swinging the cane side to side to search an area approximately 1½' (46) in front and approximately 1' (30) to either side of them at ground level. The cane is swung back and forth with each pace taken. It is important therefore that nothing project more than about 1' (30) out from a wall or post, which can be detected by the cane at ground level.

Part Two
Basic Dimensions

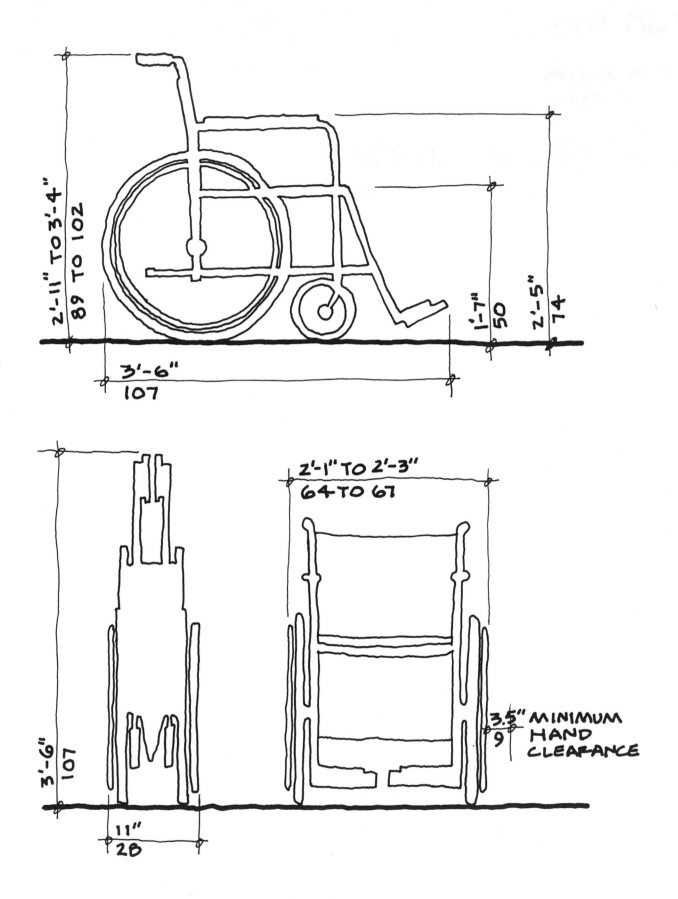

DETAIL 2.1   "Standard" collapsible wheelchair

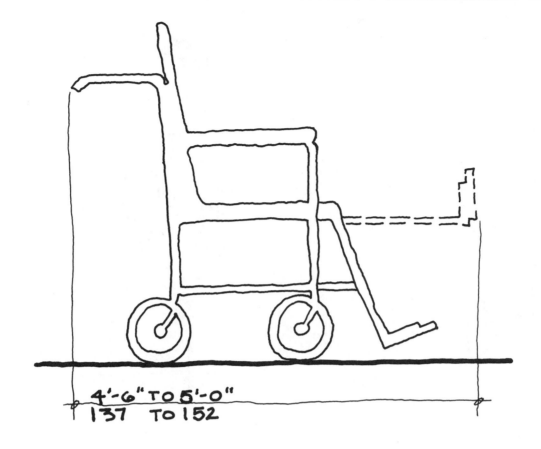

4'-6" TO 5'-0"
137 TO 152

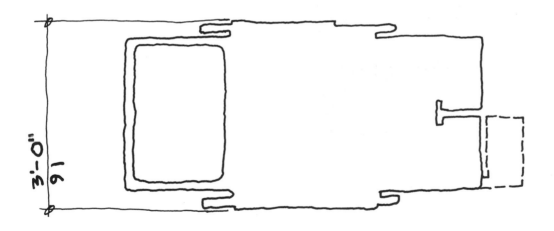

3'-0"
91

DETAIL 2.2   Attendant-powered (hospital type) wheelchair

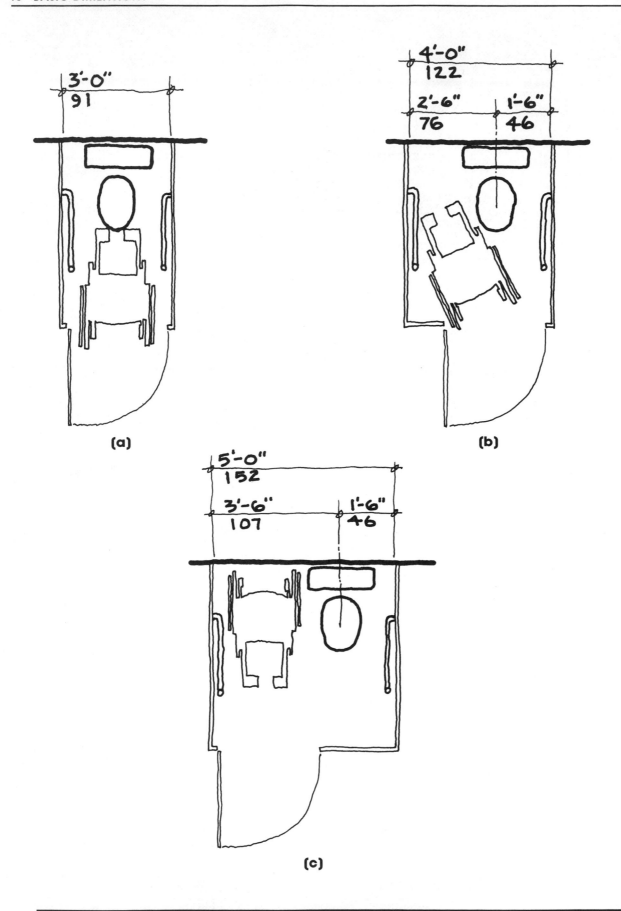

3'-0"
91

(a)

4'-0"
122

2'-6"   1'-6"
76   46

(b)

5'-0"
152

3'-6"   1'-6"
107   46

(c)

DETAIL 2.3a   Minimum-width toilet — frontal approach only
DETAIL 2.3b   Intermediate-width toilet — diagonal approach
DETAIL 2.3c   "Ideal" width toilet — lateral approach possible

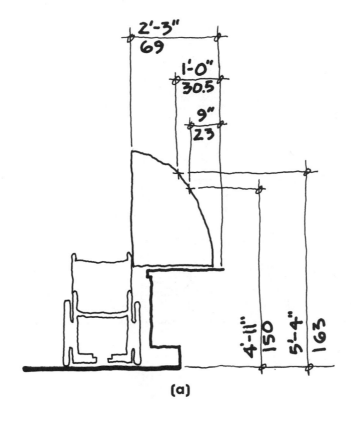

(a)

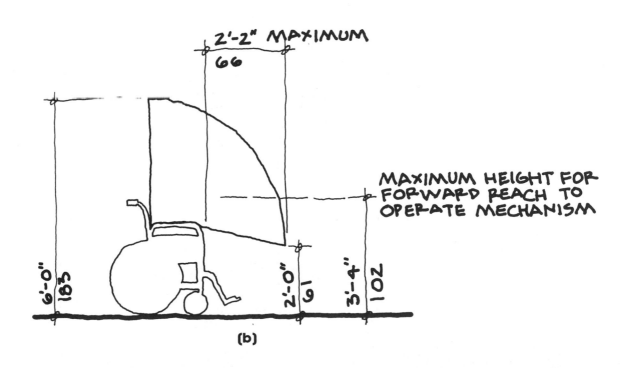

(b)

DETAIL 2.4a   Maximum reach over 2'-9" (84) high obstruction
DETAIL 2.4b   Maximum forward reach

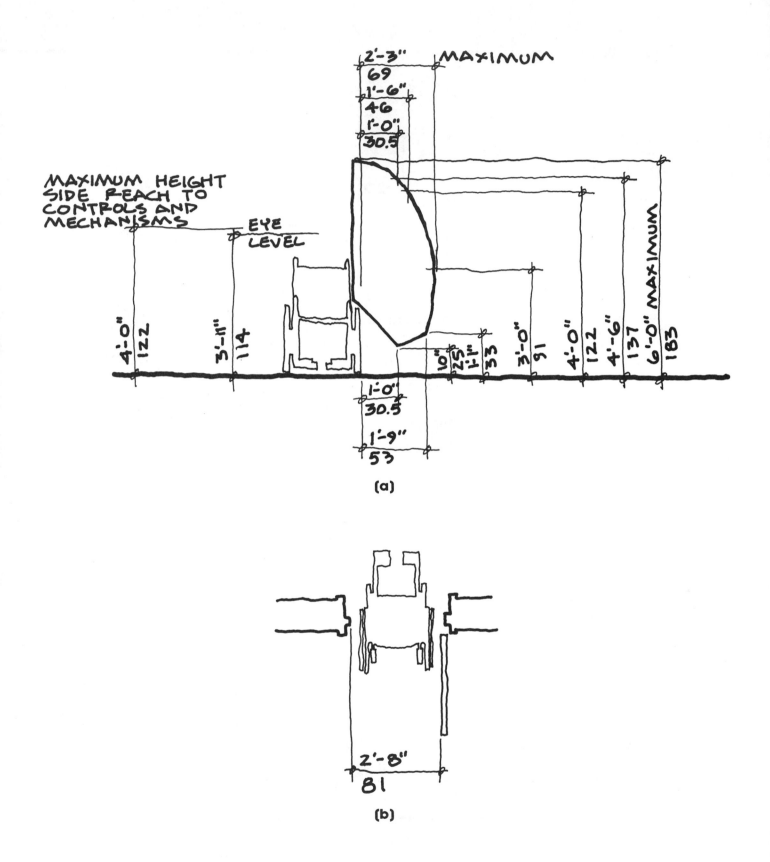

(a)

(b)

DETAIL 2.5a   Side reach

DETAIL 2.5b   Minimum clearance through door or between obstructions

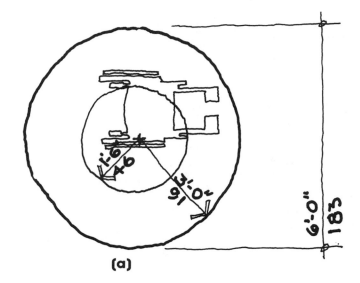

(a)

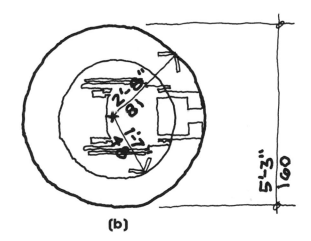

(b)

DETAIL 2.6a   One-wheel pivot
DETAIL 2.6b   Center pivot

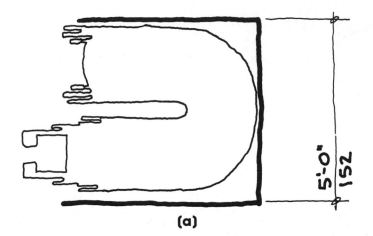

(a)

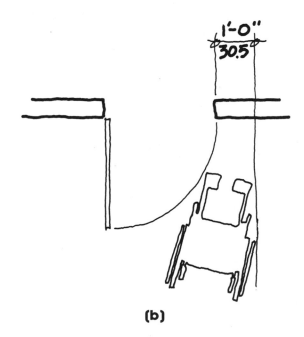

(b)

DETAIL 2.7a   Minimum 360° turn space
DETAIL 2.7b   Minimum latch side clearance to open door without maneuvering

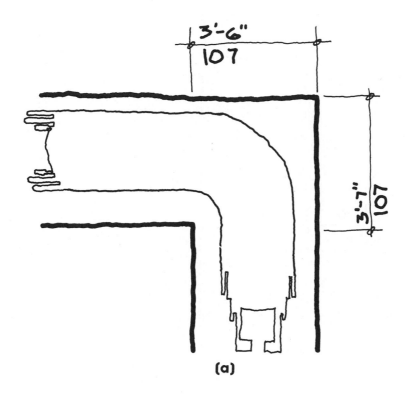

(a)

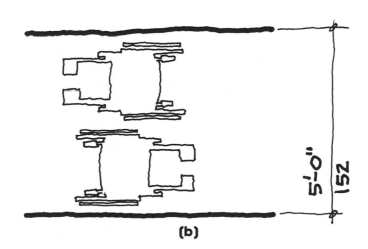

(b)

DETAIL 2.8a   Minimum 90° turn space
DETAIL 2.8b   Minimum passing space

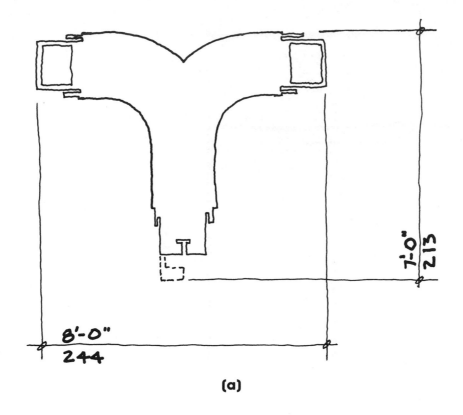

8'-0"
244

7'-0"
213

(a)

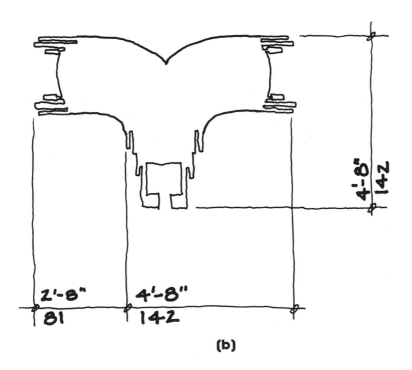

2'-8"
81

4'-8"
142

4'-8"
142

(b)

DETAIL 2.9a   Hospital-type wheelchair — three-point turn (pivot not possible)

DETAIL 2.9b   Standard wheelchair — three-point turn

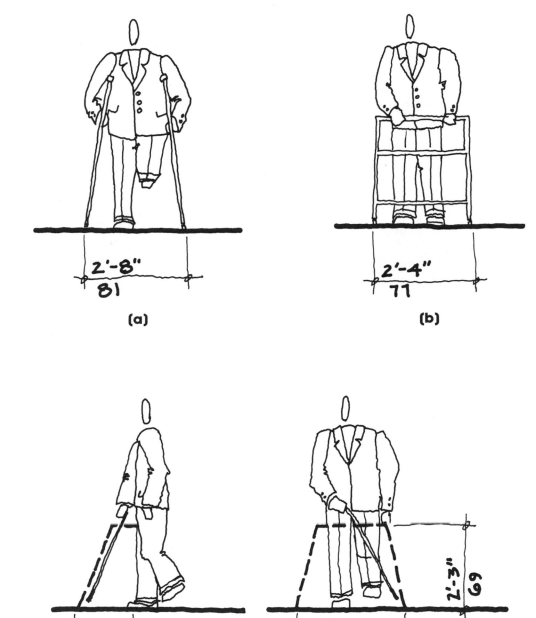

(a)

(b)

(c)

DETAIL 2.10a   Crutches
DETAIL 2.10b   Walker
DETAIL 2.10c   Approximate search volume with long-cane technique

Part Three
Exterior Elements

Accessibility to a building does not ordinarily begin at the entry door. The initial approach to most buildings is made from the exterior through a site developed in some manner. For this reason site layout design and detail presents the first challenge to accessibility.

For the person with limited mobility, impediments to movement must be avoided; for the blind, orientation and direction must be provided. While these needs are similar to those within buildings, the forms which barriers (and opportunities) take are different.

The point of vehicular arrival is the beginning of most people's route of travel over the site. The arrival point at a parking space or along a street must provide sufficient room for an automobile door to be opened fully, out of any vehicular travel path or between parked cars. Because of the low height of a person in a wheelchair, the route from the vehicle to a sidewalk or path must not, in any case, require travel behind a parked car or into any vehicular travel path.

Ramps should be provided from street to walk level as well as at all other locations where the path of travel changes elevation. The designer must consider several elements in providing exterior ramps:

- Ramps which extend down to street level must have some indication for the blind of the point at which the ramp reaches the line of the street or traffic way.
- The ramp, while lightly textured for wheelchair traction, should not be grooved in such a way that it holds water, which in cold climates may freeze into ice on the ramp.

- The vertical offset at the bottom of a ramp through a curb from street to walk level must not exceed ½" (1.25).
- Ramp surfaces should be non-slip for security of footing and wheelchair traction. Plastic "indoor-outdoor" carpet should be avoided since it tends to be slippery and contributes to the development of ice in winter.
- In climates where freezing temperatures may occur for more than a few hours, exterior ramp slopes should not exceed 1:20. (This is a code requirement in some northern states.)

Grilles, grates, bars, manholes, and other such rough (and for the blind, disorienting) elements should not occur in walkways for the handicapped. Wherever an elevation change must occur, it should be accomplished with a ramp; steps and any vertical offset greater than ½" (1.25) must be avoided. Loose, movable, overly rough, and uneven walkway surfaces must be avoided since they make wheelchair movement generally difficult or impossible, and may be a source of confusion or apprehension to the blind and elderly.

The use of plants which throw off large seeds, pods, or other debris should be avoided near walkways. Plantings which characteristically grow with spurs, thorns, and low or trailing branches should also be avoided near walks and seats. Of course, signs, mailboxes, and other obstacles should not project into or over the path of travel. Obstacles which must project into the volume of travel should not project more than 1' (30.5) past their ground-level support location; if projections into a walkway are supported from above or far away, a cane-detectable post or bollard should be placed below it as a warning to the blind.

In portions of the site developed for outdoor recreation, the designer should consider guide railings, chains, or textured guides for the blind, with recorded or braille information points. Wheelchair table and sitting locations should be provided. The designer should remember and consider the viewpoint of the handicapped person in planning views and viewing locations. Raised planting beds, sand play areas, and garden plots can make outdoor relaxation areas much more rewarding for the handicapped.

LOCATE HANDICAPPED PARKING SPACES
AS NEAR BUILDING OR FACILITY ENTRANCES
AS POSSIBLE

PROVIDE DOUBLE RAMPS TO PROVIDE
ACCESS TO BOTH SIDES OF AUTOMOBILE

PROVIDE 2% (MINIMUM 2 SPACES) AS
HANDICAPPED SPACES

HANDICAPPED SPACES MUST BE WITHIN
200' (610M), (100' (305M) IF ROUTE INCLUDES
A RAMP IN ADDITION TO THE CURB RAMP)
OF THE BUILDING OR FACILITY ENTRANCE

AVOID THE NECESSITY FOR WHEELCHAIRS
TO WHEEL BEHIND PARKED CARS OR
WITHIN A TRAFFICWAY

DETAIL 3.1   Notes

Parking

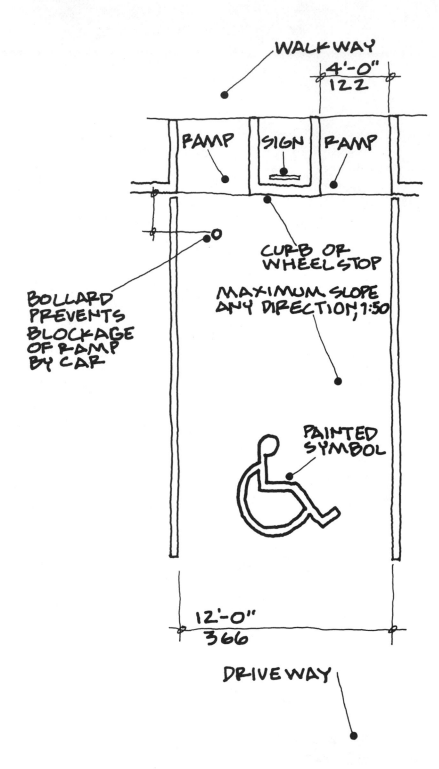

WALKWAY

4'-0"
122

RAMP   SIGN   RAMP

BOLLARD
PREVENTS
BLOCKAGE
OF RAMP
BY CAR

CURB OR
WHEEL STOP

MAXIMUM SLOPE
ANY DIRECTION, 1:50

PAINTED
SYMBOL

12'-0"
366

DRIVEWAY

AVOID NECESSITY FOR WHEELCHAIR TO WHEEL
BEHIND PARKED CAR, OR INTO TRAFFIC
WAYS

DETAIL 3.2 Typical parking space

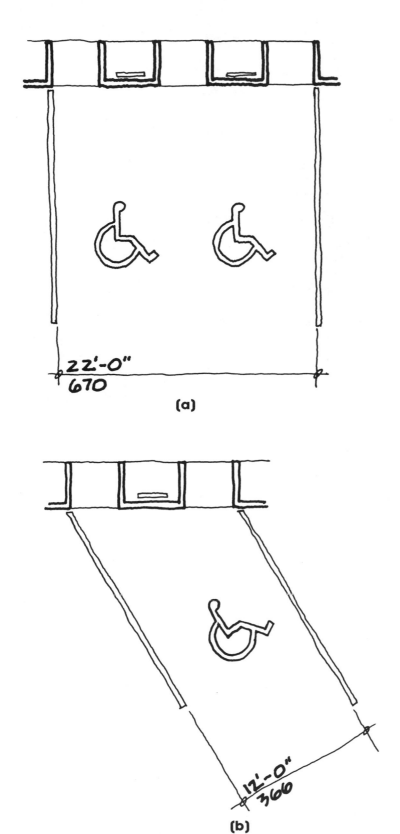

(a)

22'-0"
670

(b)

12'-0"
366

DETAIL 3.3a   Double parking space
DETAIL 3.3b   Angle parking space

Parking

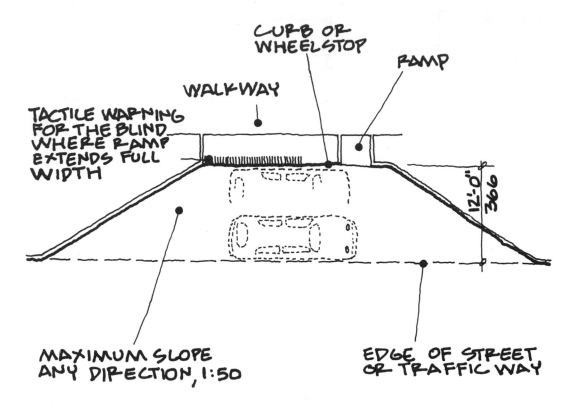

CURB OR
WHEEL STOP

RAMP

WALKWAY

TACTILE WARNING
FOR THE BLIND
WHERE RAMP
EXTENDS FULL
WIDTH

12'-0"
366

MAXIMUM SLOPE
ANY DIRECTION, 1:50

EDGE OF STREET
OR TRAFFIC WAY

DETAIL 3.4   Pedestrian drop

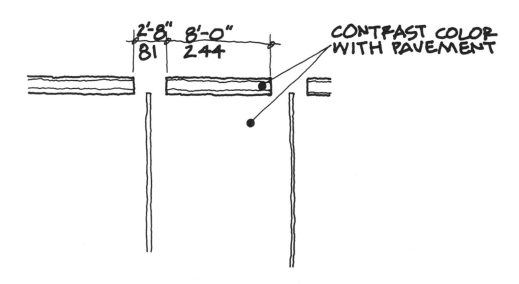

2'-8"   8'-0"
81   244

CONTRAST COLOR
WITH PAVEMENT

DETAIL 3.5   Parking space, standard wheel stop, handicapped access between stops

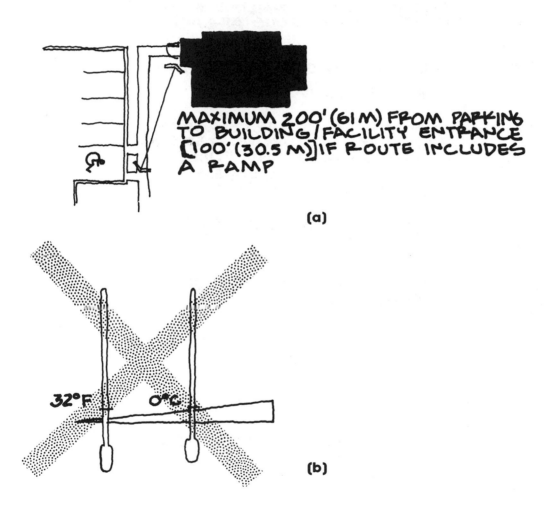

MAXIMUM 200' (61 M) FROM PARKING
TO BUILDING/FACILITY ENTRANCE
[100' (30.5 M)] IF ROUTE INCLUDES
A RAMP

(a)

32°F   0°C

(b)

DETAIL 3.6a   Distance to parking

**DETAIL 3.6b   Avoid exterior ramps (slopes steeper than 1:12) where
winter temperatures fall below freezing.**

Walks

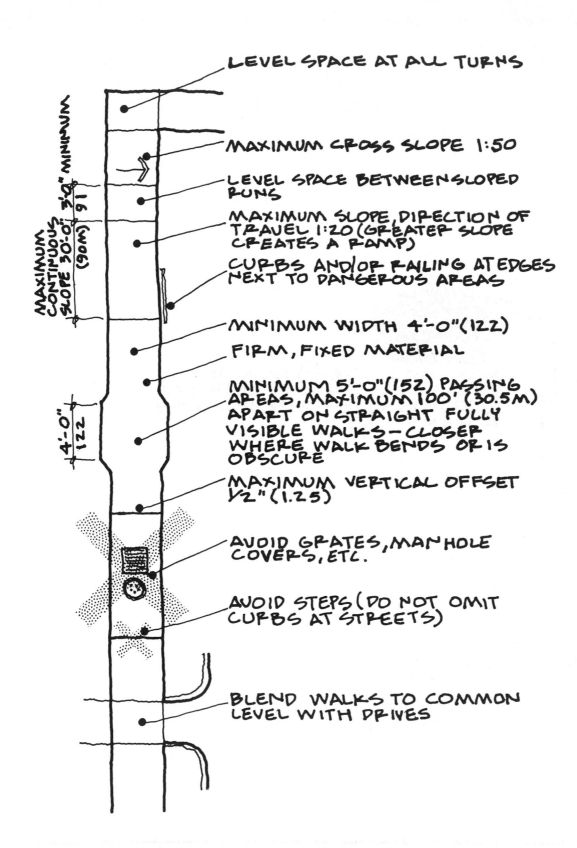

LEVEL SPACE AT ALL TURNS

MAXIMUM CROSS SLOPE 1:50

LEVEL SPACE BETWEEN SLOPED RUNS

MAXIMUM SLOPE, DIRECTION OF TRAVEL 1:20 (GREATER SLOPE CREATES A RAMP)

CURBS AND/OR RAILING AT EDGES NEXT TO DANGEROUS AREAS

MINIMUM WIDTH 4'-0" (122)

FIRM, FIXED MATERIAL

MINIMUM 5'-0" (152) PASSING AREAS, MAXIMUM 100' (30.5M) APART ON STRAIGHT FULLY VISIBLE WALKS — CLOSER WHERE WALK BENDS OR IS OBSCURE

MAXIMUM VERTICAL OFFSET ½" (1.25)

AVOID GRATES, MANHOLE COVERS, ETC.

AVOID STEPS (DO NOT OMIT CURBS AT STREETS)

BLEND WALKS TO COMMON LEVEL WITH DRIVES

MAXIMUM CONTINUOUS SLOPE 30'-0"; 3'-0" MINIMUM
91
(90M)

4'-0"
122

DETAIL 3.7   Sidewalk

WHERE GRATES OR GRILLES MUST OCCUR
WITHIN WALKS, SPACE BETWEEN BARS
MAXIMUM 1/2" (1.25); ORIENT BARS
PERPENDICULAR TO DIRECTION OF TRAVEL

PROVIDE SLIGHTLY TEXTURED (NON-SLIP)
SURFACE

CARBORUNDUM FOR NON-SLIP SURFACE
SHOULD NOT PASS #12 TO 30 MESH;
APPLY AT 2 1/2 LB/SQ.YD. (1.1 KG/SQ. M)

SUITABLE SURFACING MATERIAL IS
CONCRETE, ASPHALT CONCRETE,
MORTARED LEVEL BRICK OR TILE

AVOID LOOSE MATERIALS (STONE OR
GRAVEL, BARK CHIPS, SAND BEDDED
PAVERS)

DETAIL 3.8   Notes

Walks

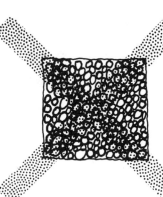

EARTH, GRAVEL, CRUSHED STONE, BARK

AVOID SOFT SURFACES IN PATHS OF
TRAVEL, UNLESS EQUALLY SHORT,
HARD SURFACED PATHS ARE
AVAILABLE

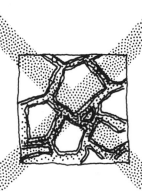

FLAGSTONE, COBBLESTONE, WOOD ROUNDS,
LOOSE LAID BRICK, EXPOSED AGGREGATE
CONCRETE

AVOID IRREGULAR AND ROUGH SURFACES
IN PATHS OF TRAVEL, UNLESS EQUALLY
SHORT, SMOOTH PATHS ARE AVAILABLE

DETAIL 3.9   Path surfacing

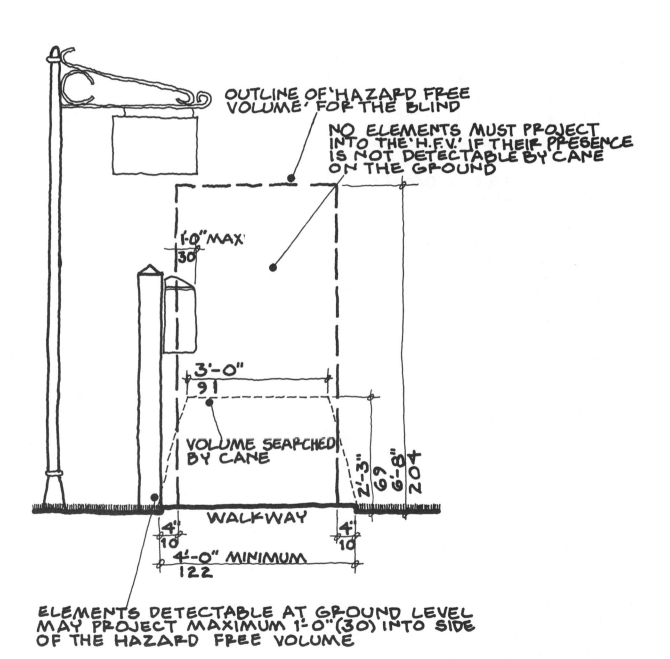

OUTLINE OF 'HAZARD FREE VOLUME' FOR THE BLIND

NO ELEMENTS MUST PROJECT INTO THE 'H.F.V.' IF THEIR PRESENCE IS NOT DETECTABLE BY CANE ON THE GROUND

1'-0" MAX 30

3'-0" 91

VOLUME SEARCHED BY CANE

2'-3" 69

6'-8" 204

WALKWAY

4" 10

4" 10

4'-0" MINIMUM 122

ELEMENTS DETECTABLE AT GROUND LEVEL MAY PROJECT MAXIMUM 1'-0"(30) INTO SIDE OF THE HAZARD FREE VOLUME

DETAIL 3.10   Hazard-free volume

Walks

LEVER OPERATED LATCH

VERTICAL GRAB ON ONE SIDE OF GATE
WITHOUT CLOSERS (PULL TO CLOSE
GATE)

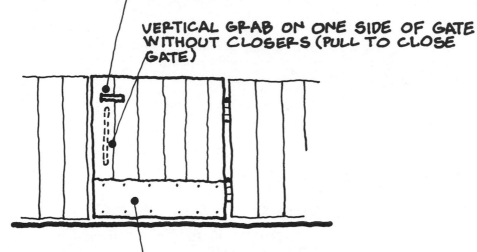

10"(25) HIGH KICKPLATE BOTH SIDES
OF HEAVY USE GATES

PROVIDE CLEAR OPENING WIDTH OF
2'-8"(81) MINIMUM
MAXIMUM FORCE TO OPEN GATE -
8 LBF (35 NEWTONS)

(a)

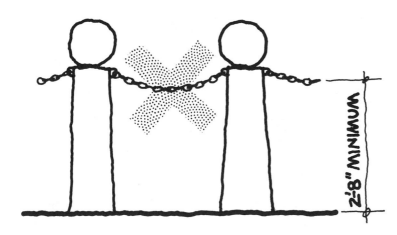

2'-8" MINIMUM

AVOID CHAINS AS BARRIERS ALONG
PEDESTRIAN WAYS: TOO FLEXIBLE FOR
SUPPORT, CREATE HAZARD TO THE
BLIND AND PARTIALLY SIGHTED

(b)

DETAIL 3.11a   Gate
DETAIL 3.11b   Automobile barriers

2'-0" MINIMUM 61

2'-8" MINIMUM 81

MAINTAIN MINIMUM HEIGHT FOR
VISIBILITY FROM AUTOMOBILES

MAINTAIN MINIMUM CLEARANCE FOR
WHEELCHAIRS

1'-0" (30) TOP DIMENSION ALLOWS
USE AS A SEAT

DETAIL 3.12   Automobile barriers

Lighting

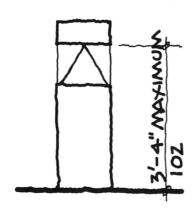

3'-4" MAXIMUM
102

AVOID LOW LEVEL LIGHT SOURCES WHICH
ARE HIGH ENOUGH TO PROVIDE GLARE TO
WHEELCHAIR USERS

DETAIL 3.13   Site lights

	FOOT CANDLES	LUMINOUS FLUX (LUX)
COMMERCIAL		
BUILDING ENTRANCE	5.0	54
ATTENDANT PARKING	2.0	22
PEDESTRIAN WAY	2.0	22
SELF PARKING	1.0	11
BUILDING GROUNDS	1.0	11
LOCAL ACCESS STREET	0.9	10
SIDEWALK	0.9	10
ALLEY	0.6	7
INDUSTRIAL		
BUILDING ENTRANCE	5.0	54
ATTENDANT PARKING	2.0	22
SELF PARKING	1.0	11
PEDESTRIAN WAY	1.0	11
BUILDING GROUNDS	1.0	11
LOCAL ACCESS STREET	0.6	7
SIDEWALK	0.6	7
ALLEY	0.4	4
RESIDENTIAL		
BUILDING ENTRANCE	5.0	54
SELF PARKING	1.0	11
BUILDING GROUNDS	1.0	17
PEDESTRIAN WAY	0.5	5
LOCAL STREET	0.4	4
SIDEWALK	0.2	2
ALLEY	0.2	2

BASED ON I.E.S. LIGHTING HANDBOOK, 4TH EDITION

DETAIL 3.14   Exterior illumination levels

Curbs and Crossings

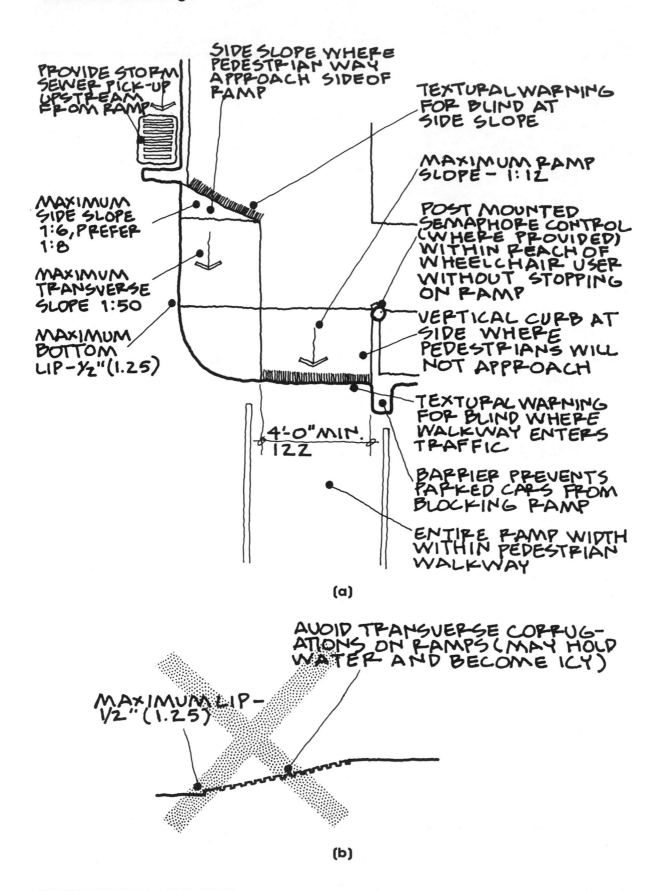

PROVIDE STORM SEWER PICK-UP UPSTREAM FROM RAMP

SIDE SLOPE WHERE PEDESTRIAN WAY APPROACH SIDE OF RAMP

TEXTURAL WARNING FOR BLIND AT SIDE SLOPE

MAXIMUM RAMP SLOPE - 1:12

MAXIMUM SIDE SLOPE 1:6, PREFER 1:8

POST MOUNTED SEMAPHORE CONTROL (WHERE PROVIDED) WITHIN REACH OF WHEELCHAIR USER WITHOUT STOPPING ON RAMP

MAXIMUM TRANSVERSE SLOPE 1:50

VERTICAL CURB AT SIDE WHERE PEDESTRIANS WILL NOT APPROACH

MAXIMUM BOTTOM LIP - ½"(1.25)

4'-0" MIN. 122

TEXTURAL WARNING FOR BLIND WHERE WALKWAY ENTERS TRAFFIC

BARRIER PREVENTS PARKED CARS FROM BLOCKING RAMP

ENTIRE RAMP WIDTH WITHIN PEDESTRIAN WALKWAY

(a)

AVOID TRANSVERSE CORRUGATIONS ON RAMPS (MAY HOLD WATER AND BECOME ICY)

MAXIMUM LIP - ½" (1.25)

(b)

DETAIL 3.15a   Curb cuts
DETAIL 3.15b   Curb conditions

Curbs and Crossings

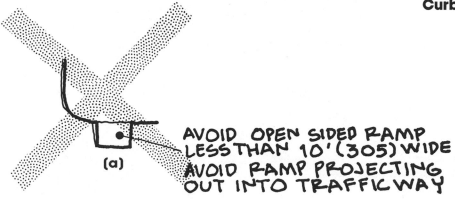

AVOID OPEN SIDED RAMP
LESS THAN 10' (305) WIDE
AVOID RAMP PROJECTING
OUT INTO TRAFFIC WAY

(a)

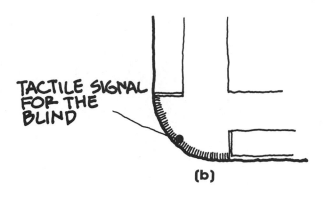

TACTILE SIGNAL
FOR THE
BLIND

(b)

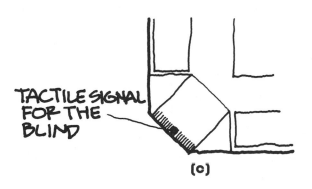

TACTILE SIGNAL
FOR THE
BLIND

(c)

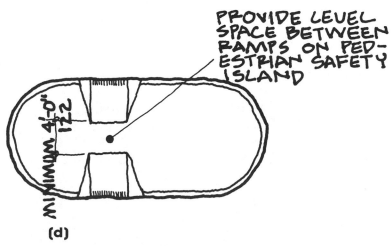

PROVIDE LEVEL
SPACE BETWEEN
RAMPS ON PED-
ESTRIAN SAFETY
ISLAND

Minimum 4'-0"
122

(d)

DETAIL 3.16a   Projecting ramp   **DETAIL 3.16c**   Corner ramp

DETAIL 3.16b   Ramp entire corner   **DETAIL 3.16d**   Pedestrian island ramp

Curbs and Crossings

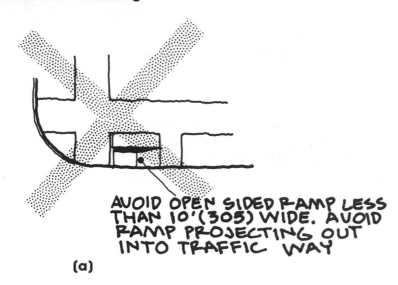

AVOID OPEN SIDED RAMP LESS THAN 10'(305) WIDE. AVOID RAMP PROJECTING OUT INTO TRAFFIC WAY

(a)

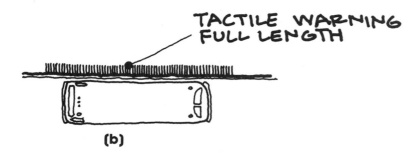

TACTILE WARNING FULL LENGTH

(b)

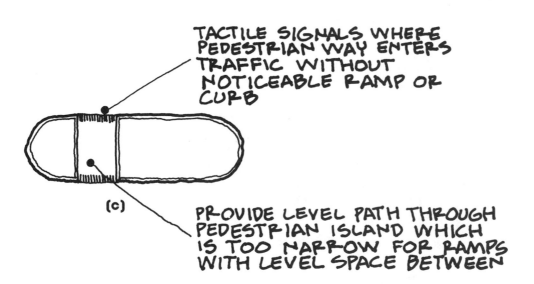

TACTILE SIGNALS WHERE PEDESTRIAN WAY ENTERS TRAFFIC WITHOUT NOTICEABLE RAMP OR CURB

(c)

PROVIDE LEVEL PATH THROUGH PEDESTRIAN ISLAND WHICH IS TOO NARROW FOR RAMPS WITH LEVEL SPACE BETWEEN

DETAIL 3.17a   Open side ramp   **DETAIL 3.17c   Pedestrian island**
DETAIL 3.17b   Transit loading platform

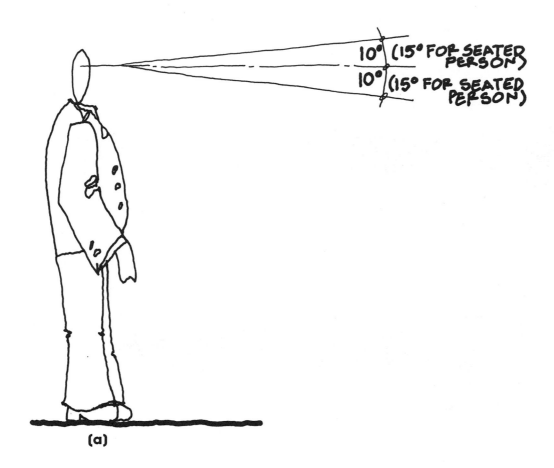

10° (15° FOR SEATED PERSON)
10° (15° FOR SEATED PERSON)

(a)

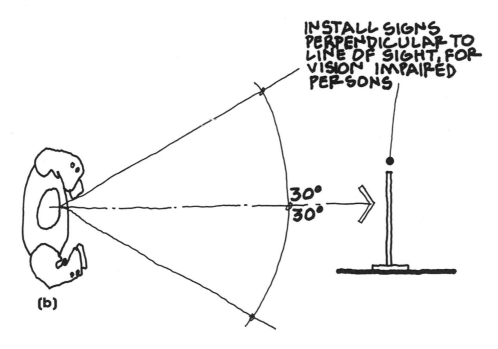

INSTALL SIGNS PERPENDICULAR TO LINE OF SIGHT FOR VISION IMPAIRED PERSONS

30°
30°

(b)

DETAIL 3.18a   Vertical angles of vision
DETAIL 3.18b   Lateral angles of vision

Signage

 PREFER WHITE LETTERS ON
BLACK BACKGROUND FOR
BETTER CONTRAST/LEGIBILITY

 PLACE BRAILLE EXPLANATORY
STRIPS ON UPPER LEFT CORNER
OF LONG TEXTUAL SIGNS

 AVOID GRAPHIC SYMBOLS AS
THE ONLY FORM OF SIGNAGE—
THEY ARE CONFUSING, HARD TO
'FEEL' FOR THE BLIND

DETAIL 3.19   Signage criteria

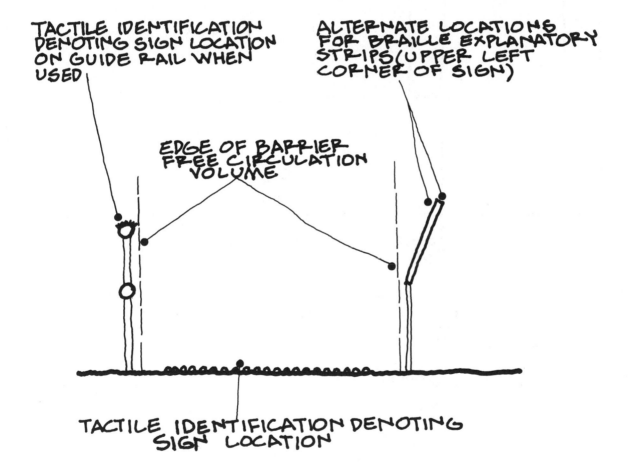

TACTILE IDENTIFICATION
DENOTING SIGN LOCATION
ON GUIDE RAIL WHEN
USED

ALTERNATE LOCATIONS
FOR BRAILLE EXPLANATORY
STRIPS(UPPER LEFT
CORNER OF SIGN)

EDGE OF BARRIER
FREE CIRCULATION
VOLUME

TACTILE IDENTIFICATION DENOTING
SIGN LOCATION

DETAIL 3.20   Site signage

Miscellaneous

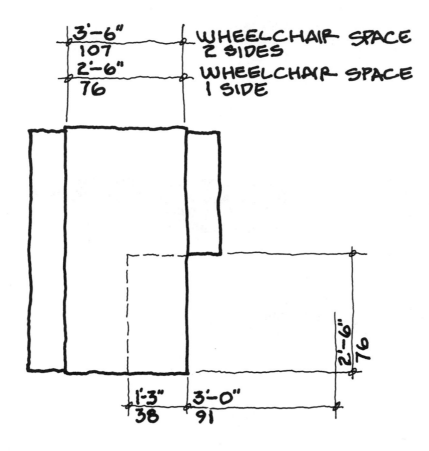

3'-6"
107
WHEELCHAIR SPACE
2 SIDES

2'-6"
76
WHEELCHAIR SPACE
1 SIDE

2'-6"
76

1'-3"
38

3'-0"
91

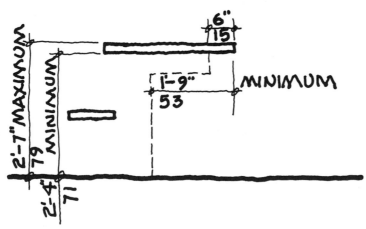

6"
15

1'-9"
53

MINIMUM

2'-7" MAXIMUM
79

MINIMUM

2'-4"
71

DETAIL 3.21 Picnic tables

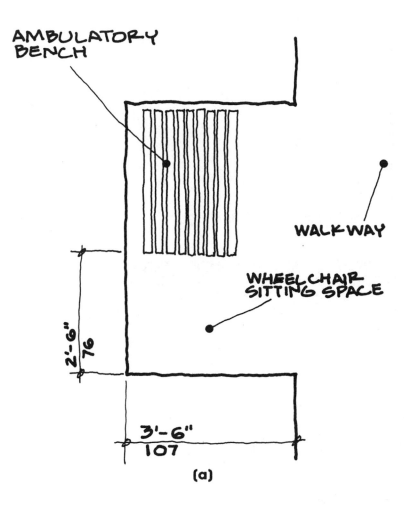

AMBULATORY
BENCH

WALKWAY

WHEELCHAIR
SITTING SPACE

2'-6"
76

3'-6"
107

(a)

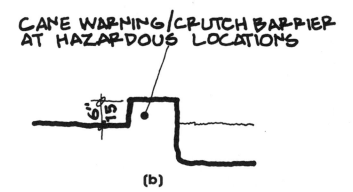

CANE WARNING/CRUTCH BARRIER
AT HAZARDOUS LOCATIONS

6"
15

(b)

DETAIL 3.22a   Site benches
DETAIL 3.22b   Warning barriers

Miscellaneous

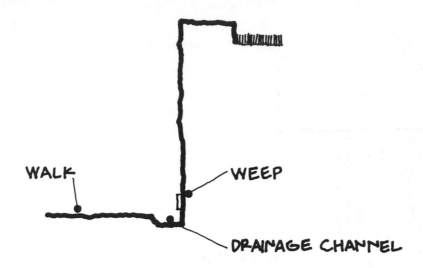

WALK

WEEP

DRAINAGE CHANNEL

WHERE RETAINING WALL, WEEP MUST DRAIN
ONTO WALK, PROVIDE A MEANS TO AVOID
DRAINAGE FREEZING ON WALK

(a)

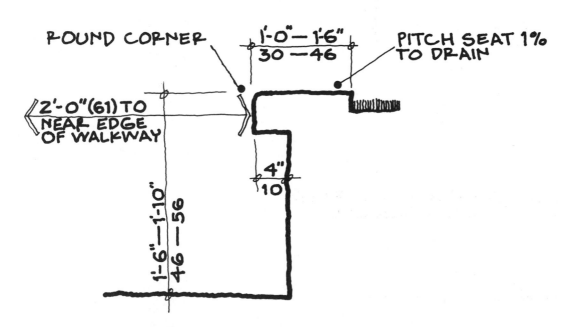

ROUND CORNER

1'-0" — 1'-6"
30 — 46

PITCH SEAT 1%
TO DRAIN

2'-0" (61) TO
NEAR EDGE
OF WALKWAY

4"
10

1'-6" — 1'-10"
46 — 56

LOW RETAINING WALLS CAN BE DESIGNED FOR
USE AS SEATS OR REST STATIONS

(b)

DETAIL 3.23a   Retaining wall
DETAIL 3.23b   Site seat

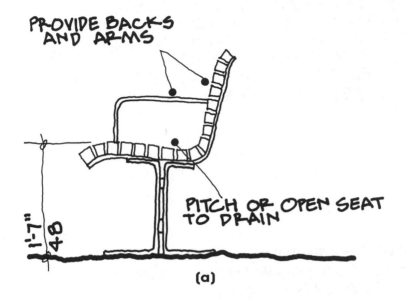

PROVIDE BACKS
AND ARMS

PITCH OR OPEN SEAT
TO DRAIN

1'-7"
48

(a)

TRASH   DEPOSIT

3'-4" MAXIMUM
102

PREFER OPEN RECEPTACLE, OR THOSE OPERABLE
BY ONE HAND - LIGHTLY SPRING LOADED DOORS
ARE ACCEPTABLE

AVOID DOORS REQUIRING TWO HANDS TO
OPERATE, OR FOOT OPERATION

(b)

DETAIL 3.24a   Bench
DETAIL 3.24b   Waste disposal

Miscellaneous

AVOID PLACING TREES OR SHRUBS WHICH LITTER BADLY NEAR WALKWAYS AND SEATING AREAS: BIRCH, BOX ELDER, CHERRY, CHESTNUT, CRAB APPLE, FIR, GUM, HEMLOCK, HICKORY, HONEY LOCUST, LARCH, LONDON PLANETREE, MAPLE, OAK, PINE, PLUM, SYCAMORE, SPRUCE AND YELLOW BUCKEYE

(a)

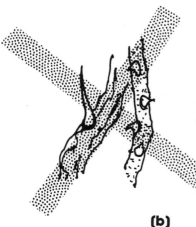

AVOID THORNED OR SPINEY PLANTINGS NEAR WALKWAYS AND SEATING AREAS: BARBERRY, BUCKTHORN, HAWTHORNE, ROSE, QUINCE

(b)

DETAIL 3.25a   Plant litter
DETAIL 3.25b   Thorned plantings

DETAIL 3.26   Wheelchair-accessible planting bed

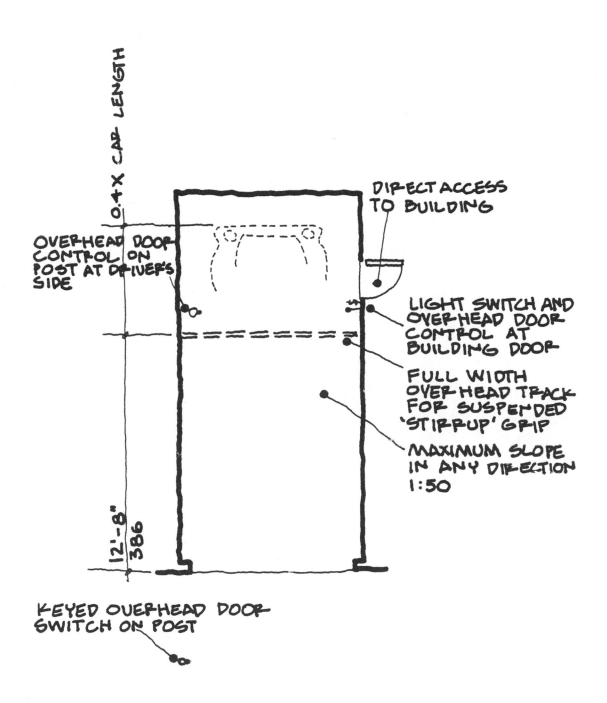

DETAIL 3.27   Private garage

Garages

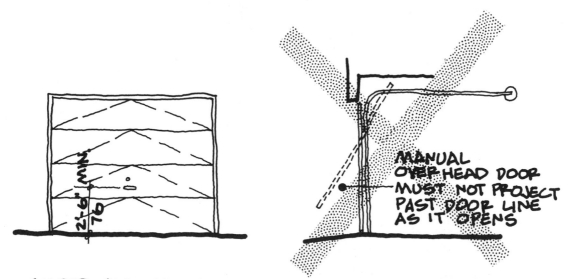

AVOID MANUAL OPERATED DOORS IF POSSIBLE
SWITCH FOR GARAGE LIGHTS INSIDE DWELLING
UNIT ALSO

DETAIL 3.28   Garage doors

Part Four
Building Areas

Generally, building areas will require somewhat more detailed consideration than will site areas to assure full accessibility. Of course, this is because of the need for a much closer "fit" between the handicapped person and the physical surroundings. Accessibility within spaces must be planned with relatively close tolerances between the person and the interior environment; the person must fit through, around, between, over, and below various obstacles and building elements.

General comments are in order concerning each of the building areas considered in this part.

ENTRY

Accessible entries for the handicapped should be placed (at least in new buildings) at each location where entrance is normally provided. "Back door" or service-entry locations must be avoided since they usually require farther travel and create the unacceptable image of "second-class citizenship." Many building codes require at least one accessible entrance, while requiring two or more fire exits. It seems that at least two and possibly more accessible *exits* should be provided. Entry points should be located with an eye toward accessibility to both general and vertical circulation and to all public areas. Access to and exit from buildings by the handicapped in the case of power failure (lighting and elevators) should be taken into account.

CIRCULATION

Circulation spaces must provide sufficient room both for the movement of the handicapped person individually and for clearance between opposing flows of traffic. As with exterior circulation paths, interior circulation must be carefully considered to avoid projection of any hazardous elements into any circulation path.

Open stairs in or near circulation paths must be carefully located and indicated to avoid hazard to the blind.

STAIRS, RAMPS, AND ELEVATORS

Vertical movement within buildings is most easily accomplished by the handicapped by elevator. Ramps, which must not exceed 1:12, require a great amount of space for any significant vertical rise; stairs are not accessible to those in the wheelchair. Most elevators as currently built are at least minimally accessible to and usable by wheelchair users. The major thrust of "providing accessibility" in elevators is the provision of informational elements for the blind and the location of operating and information elements for ease of use by the wheelchair user.

TOILET, BATH, AND SHOWER

Toilets, baths, and showers are generally relatively small spaces in which the location of, and clearance past, all elements must be carefully considered. Space to turn a wheelchair 180 degrees must be maintained in order to avoid the necessity of backing out of the room (with the great difficulty of opening the entry door behind the wheelchair). Clearances for access at various heights should be noted, with clear floor space at least 10" (25) high. Floor-set vanities and floor-mounted toilet partitions should be avoided. Clearance in both width and height for access to lavatories must be provided. In private toilets, location of the lavatory next to the watercloset permits the user to wash his or her hands before getting back into the wheelchair. Because of the insensitivity of some handicapped persons to extremes of temperature, hot water lines which may exceed 120°F (49°C) must be insulated.

Since most wheelchair users will use the watercloset in preference to a urinal, toilet stalls should be built with a width of at least 3'-6" to allow for easy access.

The inability of many handicapped persons to move quickly to change faucet settings or to move out of a stream of water makes the use of thermostatic (not volume) temperature-limiting devices on lavatories and showers mandatory.

Because of the presence of soap and water, all flooring and standing areas in and around tubs and showers should be nonslip.

KITCHEN

The presence of high-temperature elements and open flames in the kitchen necessitates a high degree of care in laying out the elements of this space. The relatively small size of the typical residential kitchen requires a high degree of organization of its elements in order to assure access within a reasonably functional layout.

The controls for all heating elements must be located to avoid the need of reaching over any heating element. Ideally it would be possible to slide utensils from a range along countertops to the table without a break, to avoid the need of lifting and carrying hot pans, especially those containing hot liquids. Because of the danger of scalding, contrary to some recommendations *no* kneespace for wheelchairs should be provided below cooktops. Pullout lap boards facilitate mixing foods in a wheelchair, while pullout boards at the refrigerator, and especially at the oven, ease the need to lift and carry heavy, and hot or cold, dishes for any distance before they can be set down on a counter. Where possible, it is desirable to provide space for eating within a kitchen to avoid the need to carry dishes and food both to and from a remote eating space.

Excess storage space in the kitchen, to minimize the difficulty of frequent shopping trips, should include excess refrigerator and freezer space where possible, as well as excess dry goods storage volume.

BEDROOM

Regardless of whether the bedroom is built as a small sleeping area or as a combined sleeping/sitting area, sufficient space must be provided for clearance in front of closet doors and alongside the beds. Sufficient room for access to both long sides of beds is desirable for bedmaking in the case where the homemaker may be in a wheelchair. Closets should be laid out to be shallow and able to be fully opened and accessible from the front, with bifolding doors preferably, or with sliding doors.

DINING ROOM

The larger dining room with multiple tables and chairs may become a quite congested space and difficult to move through for the handicapped person. At least one route of entry into the room for the handicapped, with sufficient width for passage by a wheelchair behind a wheelchair at a table, should be allowed for. Main and secondary general access and fire exit lanes will facilitate such passage.

Dining tables should preferably be the center-pedestal type for wheelchair clearance. The centerfoot should be heavily weighted to resist overturning if elderly or handicapped persons use the table edges to aid themselves in rising. The use of dining chairs with arm rests will greatly assist aged and infirm persons in rising.

ASSEMBLY AREAS

The entire route of access from entry to seating location in a place of assembly should be checked to assure accessibility. In such buildings, ramps and floor slopes especially should be checked. It is desirable that at least two of each type of handicapped seating arrangement be provided together so that friends may be seated together. Each type of handicapped seating should be located in several "representative" locations in each assembly area ("down front," in the middle, etc.). The designer should provide excess-width seats, with extra space or legroom in front of them so that those in walkers or on crutches can maneuver to be seated and to rise.

POOLS

Pools for the handicapped should provide a larger than normal shallow area [3' to 4' (91 to 120)], with no diving board if possible. There should be several "sit down" locations at the shallow end of the pool with raised seat and grabs to enable a person to transfer from a wheelchair to a seat and let himself or herself down to the pool edge, and from there into the water. Gutters are undesirable at these locations. Where pools are to be used predominantly or to a large extent by the handicapped, provision should be made to heat the water to a higher temperature than usual.

LAUNDRY, SEWING, AND WORK AREAS

Where equipment cannot be set upon permanent tabletops but must be folded out of the way, it is desirable to have a folding leg or "prop" at the free end of the worktop in case the top is used by the handicapped to help lift themselves up. Side-folding or rising worktops should be used for those in wheelchairs who may not be able to reach or hold an element which folds down from above them. Those on crutches or in walkers should have fold-down elements since they cannot so easily bend down to lift. Outlets and other utilities should be located high enough for crutch and walker users to reach them easily.

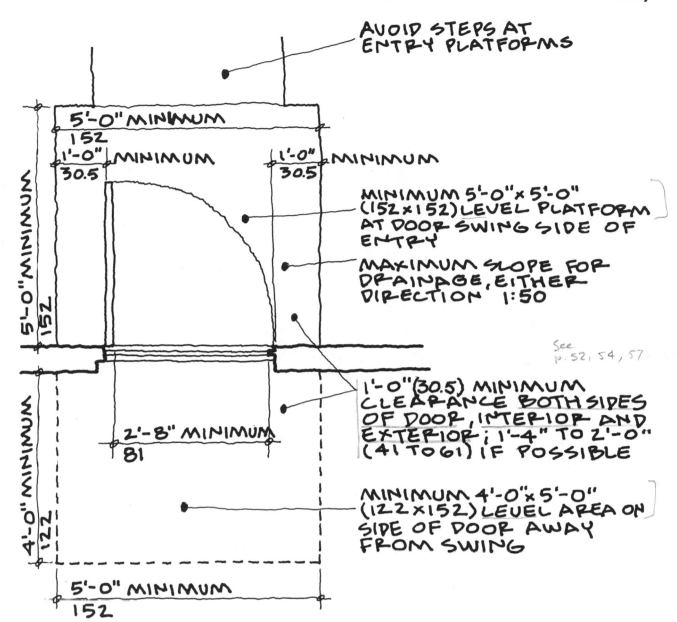

AVOID STEPS AT ENTRY PLATFORMS

5'-0" MINIMUM
152

1'-0" MINIMUM
30.5

1'-0" MINIMUM
30.5

5'-0" MINIMUM
152

MINIMUM 5'-0"x5'-0" (152x152) LEVEL PLATFORM AT DOOR SWING SIDE OF ENTRY

MAXIMUM SLOPE FOR DRAINAGE, EITHER DIRECTION 1:50

See p. 52, 54, 57

2'-8" MINIMUM
81

4'-0" MINIMUM
122

1'-0"(30.5) MINIMUM CLEARANCE BOTH SIDES OF DOOR, INTERIOR AND EXTERIOR; 1'-4" TO 2'-0" (41 TO 61) IF POSSIBLE

MINIMUM 4'-0"x5'-0" (122x152) LEVEL AREA ON SIDE OF DOOR AWAY FROM SWING

5'-0" MINIMUM
152

ENTRY/EXIT DOORS SHOULD BE 36"(91) WIDE IF POSSIBLE

PROVIDE MINIMUM 1 ENTRY AT GRADE, AVOID RAMP TO ENTRY (SOME CODES DO NOT ALLOW EXTERIOR RAMPS)

HANDICAPPED ACCESSIBLE DOORS SHOULD BE AT BUILDING FIRE EXIT LOCATIONS

LOCATE ACCESSIBLE ENTRANCES TO PROVIDE ACCESS TO LOBBIES, ELEVATORS, PHONES AND VENDING AREAS

DETAIL 4.1   Accessible exterior entrance conditions

Entry

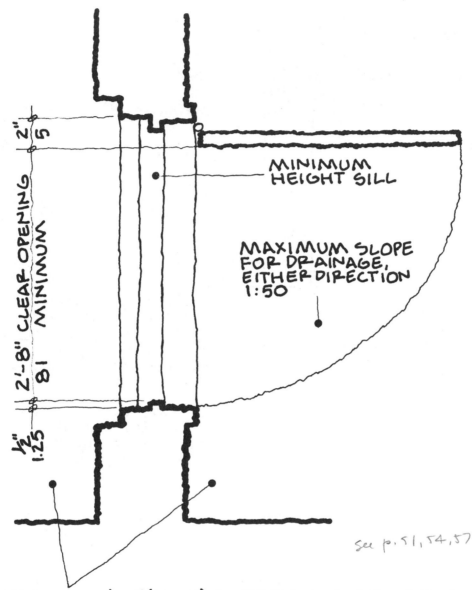

2"
5

2'-8" CLEAR OPENING
81 MINIMUM

½"
1.25

MINIMUM
HEIGHT SILL

MAXIMUM SLOPE
FOR DRAINAGE,
EITHER DIRECTION
1:50

see p. 51, 54, 57

MINIMUM 1'-0"(30.5) CLEARANCE AT LATCH
EDGE OF DOOR, BOTH SIDES

NOTE THAT A 2'-8"(81) DOOR DOES NOT GIVE THE
REQUIRED 2'-8" CLEAR OPENING

MINIMUM DOOR WIDTH = 2'-8"(81.25)+DOOR
THICKNESS + 1"(2.5)

DETAIL 4.2 Entry door

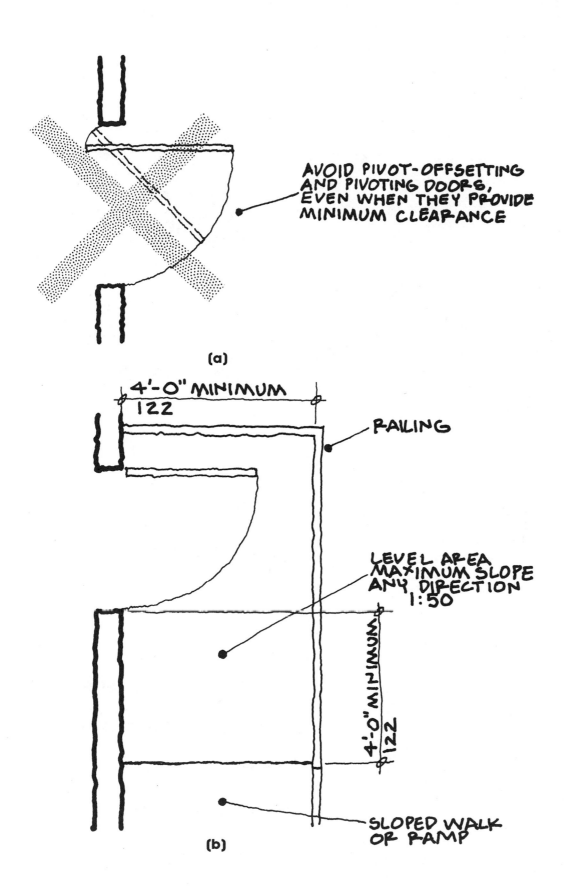

AVOID PIVOT-OFFSETTING
AND PIVOTING DOORS,
EVEN WHEN THEY PROVIDE
MINIMUM CLEARANCE

(a)

4'-0" MINIMUM
122

RAILING

LEVEL AREA
MAXIMUM SLOPE
ANY DIRECTION
1:50

4'-0" MINIMUM
122

SLOPED WALK
OR RAMP

(b)

DETAIL 4.3a   Offsetting entry door
DETAIL 4.3b   Entry door at ramp

Entry

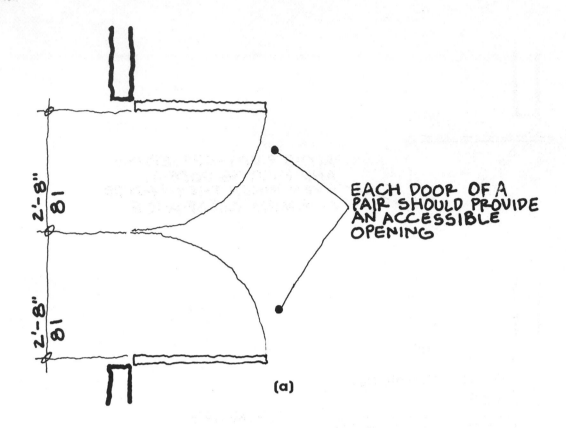

2'-8"
8'

2'-8"
8'

EACH DOOR OF A
PAIR SHOULD PROVIDE
AN ACCESSIBLE
OPENING

(a)

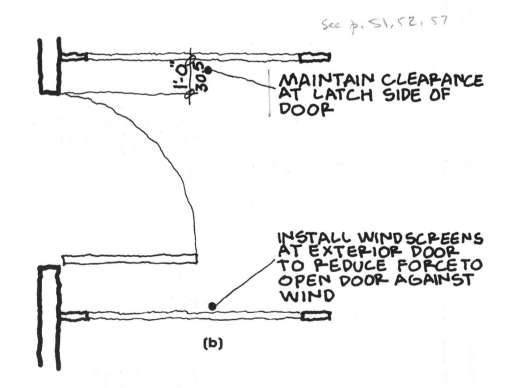

See p. 51, 52, 57

1'-0"
305

MAINTAIN CLEARANCE
AT LATCH SIDE OF
DOOR

INSTALL WINDSCREENS
AT EXTERIOR DOOR
TO REDUCE FORCE TO
OPEN DOOR AGAINST
WIND

(b)

DETAIL 4.4a   Double-entry doors
DETAIL 4.4b   Shielded-entry doors

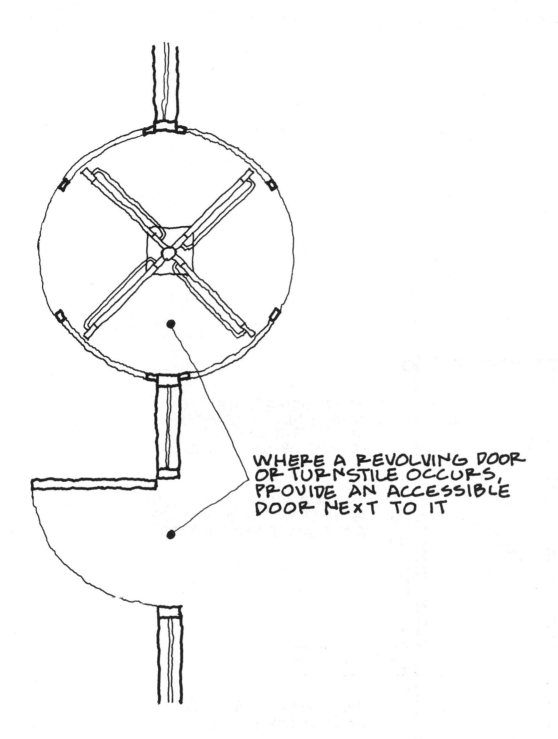

WHERE A REVOLVING DOOR
OR TURNSTILE OCCURS,
PROVIDE AN ACCESSIBLE
DOOR NEXT TO IT

DOOR SHOULD BE MANUALLY OPERABLE WHEN
POWER IS OFF

REVOLVING DOORS ARE DANGEROUS FOR
ELDERLY, BLIND AND UNSTABLE PERSONS

DETAIL 4.5   Revolving-entry doors

Entry

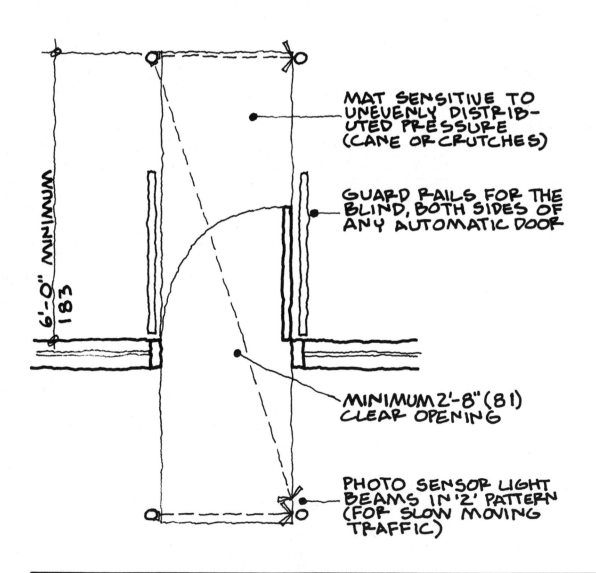

MAT SENSITIVE TO
UNEVENLY DISTRIB-
UTED PRESSURE
(CANE OR CRUTCHES)

GUARD RAILS FOR THE
BLIND, BOTH SIDES OF
ANY AUTOMATIC DOOR

6'-0" MINIMUM
183

MINIMUM 2'-8" (81)
CLEAR OPENING

PHOTO SENSOR LIGHT
BEAMS IN '2' PATTERN
(FOR SLOW MOVING
TRAFFIC)

DETAIL 4.6   Automatic door (swing or slide)

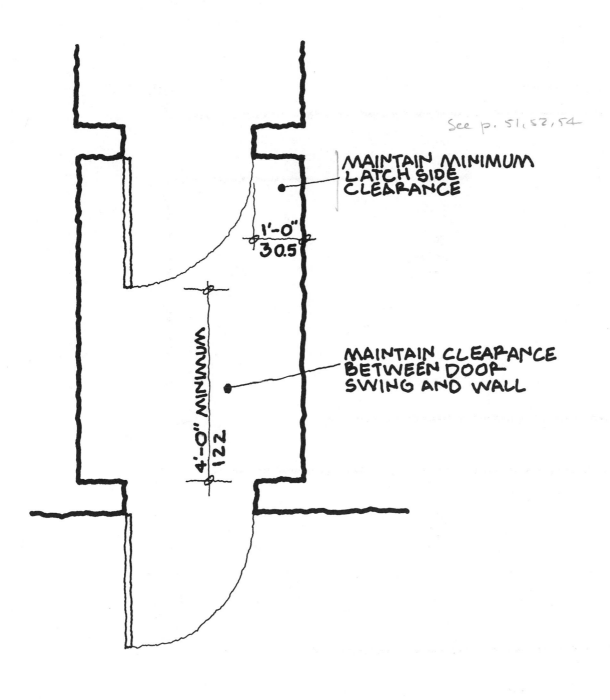

See p. 51,52,54

MAINTAIN MINIMUM
LATCH SIDE
CLEARANCE

1'-0"
30.5

4'-0" MINIMUM
122

MAINTAIN CLEARANCE
BETWEEN DOOR
SWING AND WALL

DETAIL 4.7 Minimum vestibule

Entry

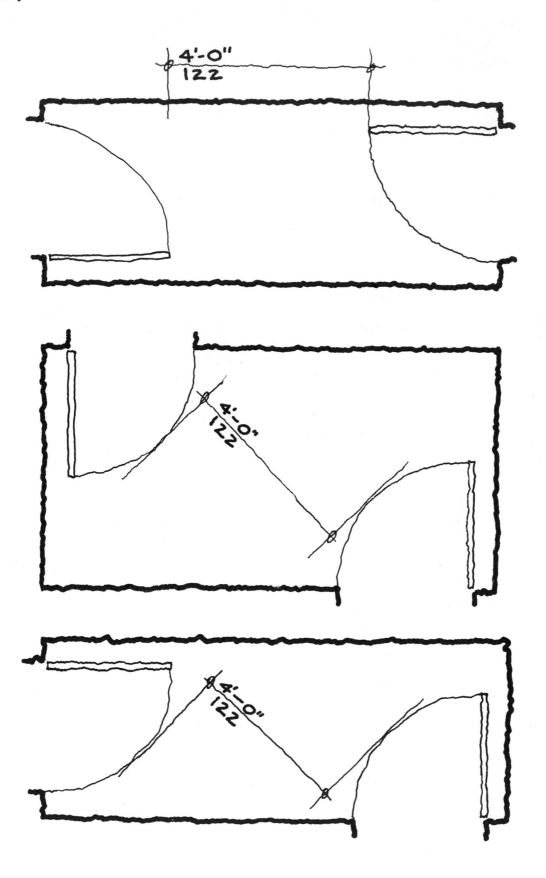

DETAIL 4.8   Alternate vestibules

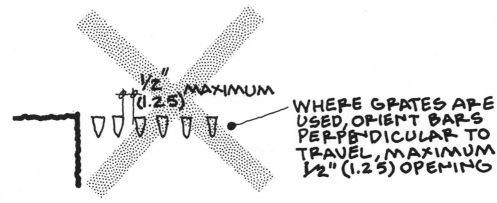

½" (1.25) MAXIMUM

WHERE GRATES ARE USED, ORIENT BARS PERPENDICULAR TO TRAVEL, MAXIMUM ½" (1.25) OPENING

AVOID ENTRY GRATES IF POSSIBLE
(a)

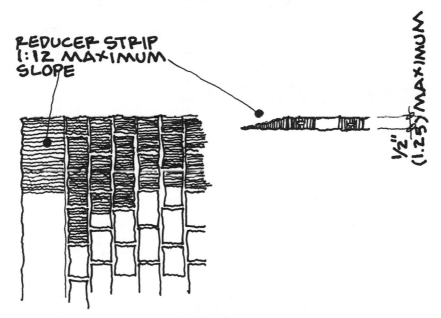

REDUCER STRIP 1:12 MAXIMUM SLOPE

½" (1.25) MAXIMUM

PREFER THIN HARD RUBBER OR PLASTIC SAND TRAP MAT (RECESSED, OR ANCHORED WITH REDUCER STRIP)
(b)

DETAIL 4.9a   Entry grate
DETAIL 4.9b   Entry mat

Entry

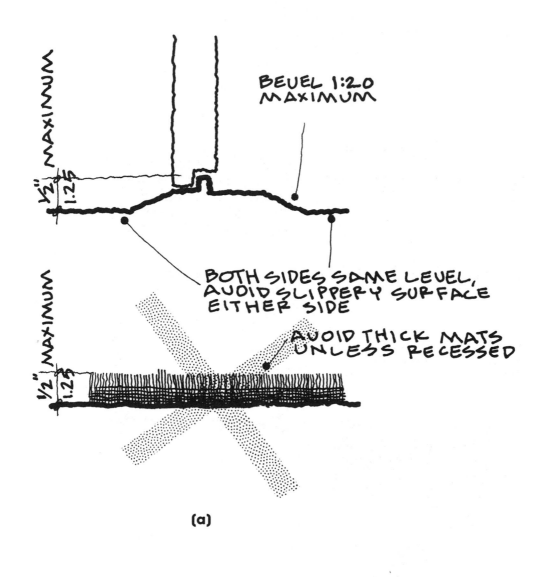

BEVEL 1:20
MAXIMUM

½" MAXIMUM

1.25

BOTH SIDES SAME LEVEL,
AVOID SLIPPERY SURFACE
EITHER SIDE

AVOID THICK MATS
UNLESS RECESSED

½" MAXIMUM

1.25

(a)

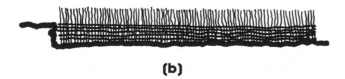

(b)

DETAIL 4.10a   Entry threshold
DETAIL 4.10b   Entry mats

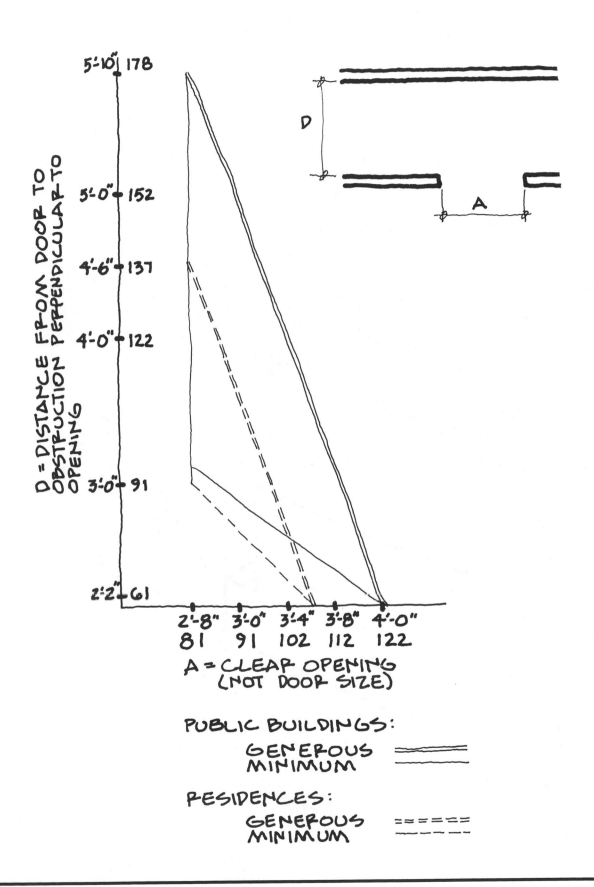

D = DISTANCE FROM DOOR TO OBSTRUCTION PERPENDICULAR TO OPENING

5'-10" 178
5'-0" 152
4'-6" 137
4'-0" 122
3'-0" 91
2'-2" 61

2'-8" 3'-0" 3'-4" 3'-8" 4'-0"
81   91   102   112   122

A = CLEAR OPENING
(NOT DOOR SIZE)

PUBLIC BUILDINGS:
GENEROUS
MINIMUM

RESIDENCES:
GENEROUS
MINIMUM

DETAIL 4.11 Door-to-obstruction clearance

Circulation

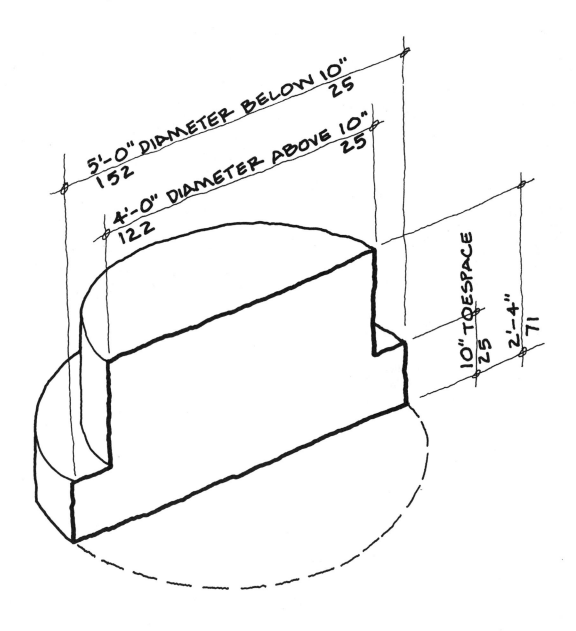

5'-0" DIAMETER BELOW 10" 25

152

4'-0" DIAMETER ABOVE 10" 25

122

10" TOESPACE 25

2'-4" 71

DETAIL 4.12   Wheelchair turning volume

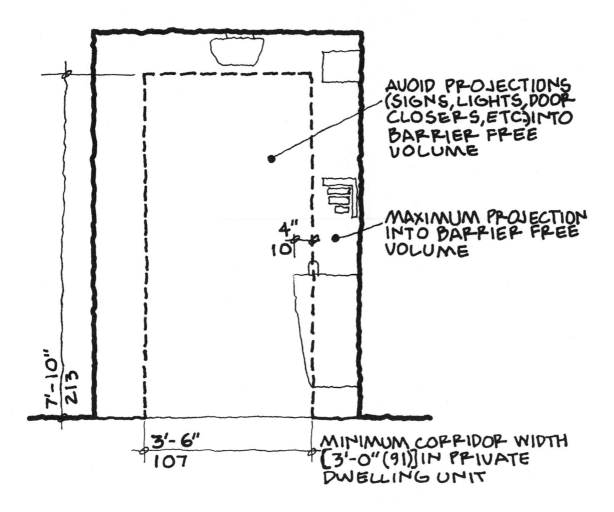

AVOID PROJECTIONS (SIGNS, LIGHTS, DOOR CLOSERS, ETC.) INTO BARRIER FREE VOLUME

MAXIMUM PROJECTION INTO BARRIER FREE VOLUME

4"
10

7'-10"
213

3'-6"
107

MINIMUM CORRIDOR WIDTH [3'-0" (91)] IN PRIVATE DWELLING UNIT

DETAIL 4.13   Barrier-free circulation volume

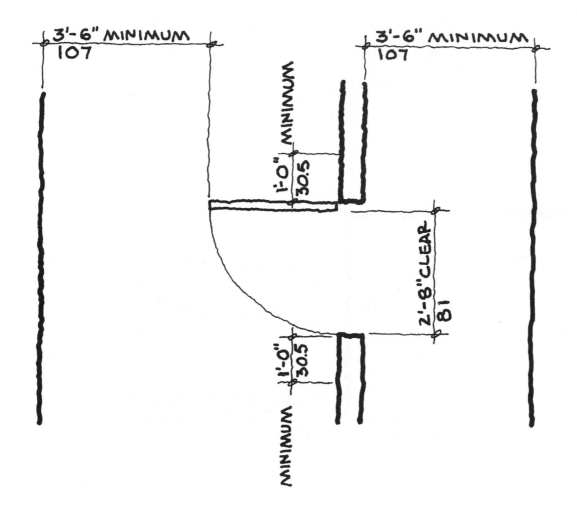

PROVIDE CLOSERS (PART OPEN DOORS ARE
HAZARDOUS TO THE BLIND)
NOTE THAT A 2'-8" (81) DOOR DOES NOT
GIVE THE REQUIRED 2'-8" (81) CLEAR
OPENING

MINIMUM DOOR WIDTH =
   2'-8" (81.25) + DOOR THICKNESS + 1" (2.5)
MAINTAIN 1'-0" (30.5) SIDE CLEARANCE
ON LATCH SIDE, EVEN WHERE SMALLER
DOOR (DOWN TO 2'-8" (81) MINIMUM
CLEARANCE) MUST BE USED

DETAIL 4.14 Typical interior door

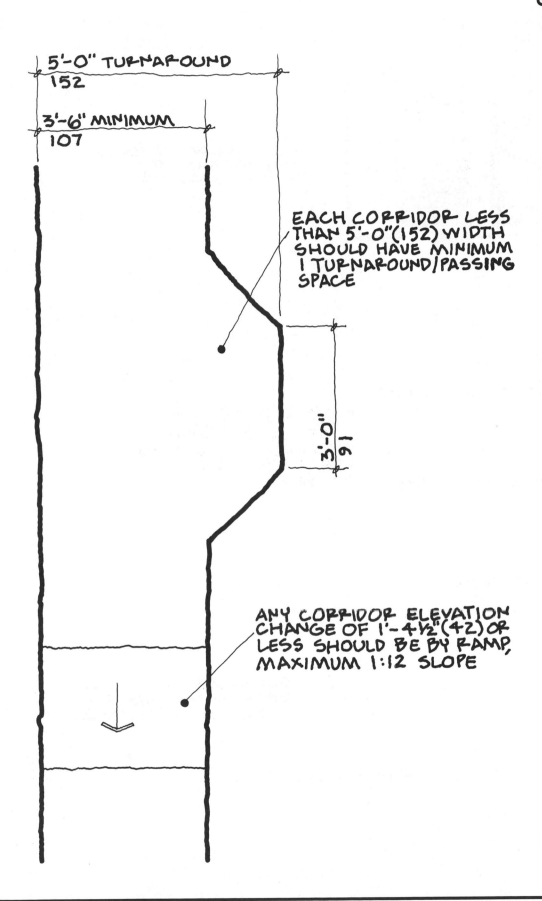

5'-0" TURNAROUND
152

3'-6" MINIMUM
107

EACH CORRIDOR LESS
THAN 5'-0"(152) WIDTH
SHOULD HAVE MINIMUM
1 TURNAROUND/PASSING
SPACE

3'-0"
91

ANY CORRIDOR ELEVATION
CHANGE OF 1'-4½"(42) OR
LESS SHOULD BE BY RAMP,
MAXIMUM 1:12 SLOPE

DETAIL 4.15 Interior corridor

Circulation

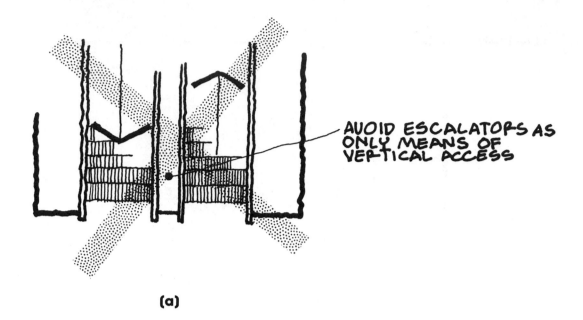

AVOID ESCALATORS AS ONLY MEANS OF VERTICAL ACCESS

(a)

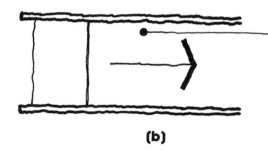

MOVING WALKS, ACCEPTABLE FOR WHEELCHAIRS, ARE HAZARDOUS FOR BLIND AND AMBULATORY DISABLED

(b)

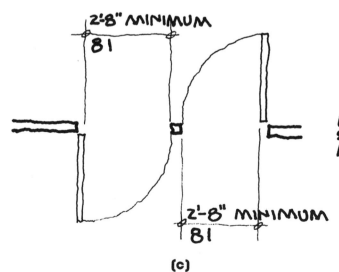

2'-8" MINIMUM
81

2'-8" MINIMUM
81

EACH DOOR OF A PAIR SHOULD PROVIDE FULL MINIMUM CLEARANCE

(c)

DETAIL 4.16a   **Escalator**
DETAIL 4.16b   **Moving walk**
DETAIL 4.16c   **Door pairs**

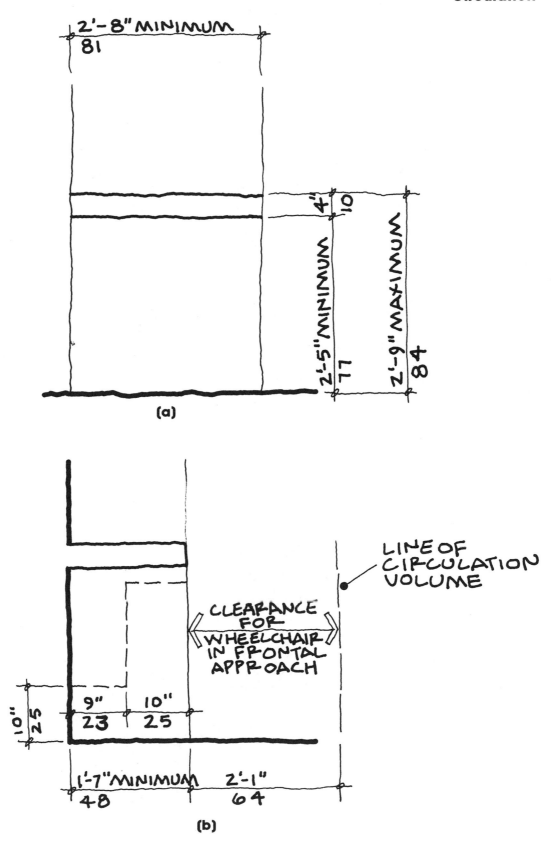

2'-8" MINIMUM
81

4"
10

2'-5" MINIMUM
77

2'-9" MAXIMUM
84

(a)

LINE OF
CIRCULATION
VOLUME

CLEARANCE
FOR
WHEELCHAIR
IN FRONTAL
APPROACH

9"
23

10"
25

10"
25

1'-7" MINIMUM
48

2'-1"
64

(b)

DETAIL 4.17a   Minimum accessible alcove: elevation
DETAIL 4.17b   Minimum accessible alcove: section

Circulation

ALCOVE FOR 'OUT OF CIRULATION PATH'
ACCESS TO: PHONE
            FOUNTAINS
            STAMP MACHINES
            CIGARETTE DISPENSER
            INSTANT CASH MACHINES
            T.V. TELLERS
            POST OFFICE BOXES
            APARTMENT MAIL BOXES
            BANK DEPOSITORIES
            SAFETY DEPOSIT BOXES

DETAIL 4.18 Alcove

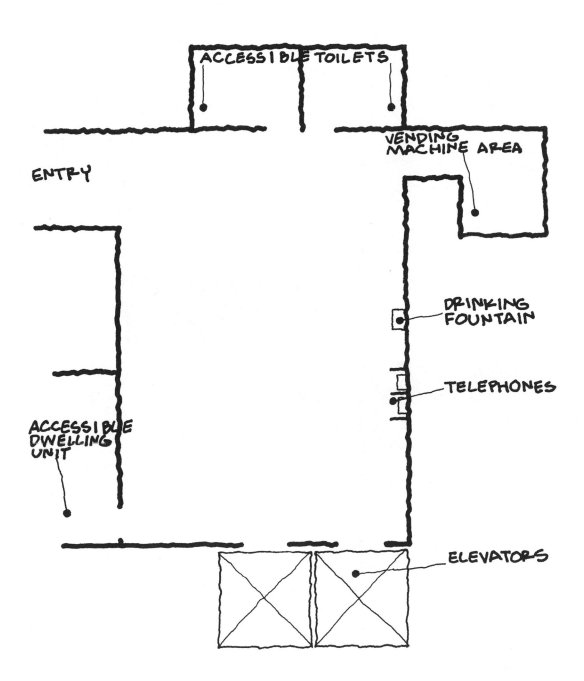

DETAIL 4.19   Minimum building access

Circulation

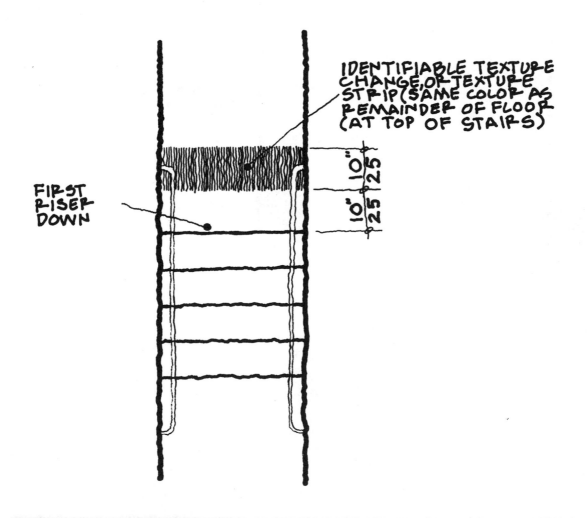

IDENTIFIABLE TEXTURE CHANGE, OR TEXTURE STRIP (SAME COLOR AS REMAINDER OF FLOOR) (AT TOP OF STAIRS)

FIRST RISER DOWN

10" 10"
25 25

10" 25

DETAIL 4.20 Corridor stair warming

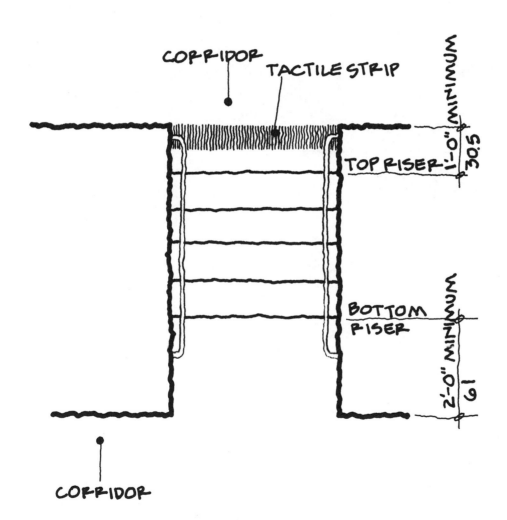

CORRIDOR TACTILE STRIP

1'-0" MINIMUM 30.5

TOP RISER

BOTTOM RISER

2'-0" MINIMUM 61

CORRIDOR

INCREASE MINIMUM SETBACK UP TO 2'-6"
(76) WHERE POSSIBLE

DETAIL 4.21   Perpendicular corridor stair warning

Circulation

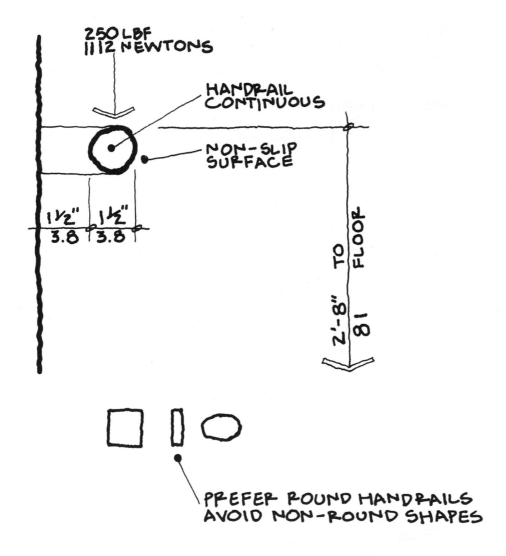

250 LBF
1112 NEWTONS

HANDRAIL
CONTINUOUS

NON-SLIP
SURFACE

1½" 3.8   1½" 3.8

2'-8" TO FLOOR
81

PREFER ROUND HANDRAILS
AVOID NON-ROUND SHAPES

DETAIL 4.22   Interior handrail

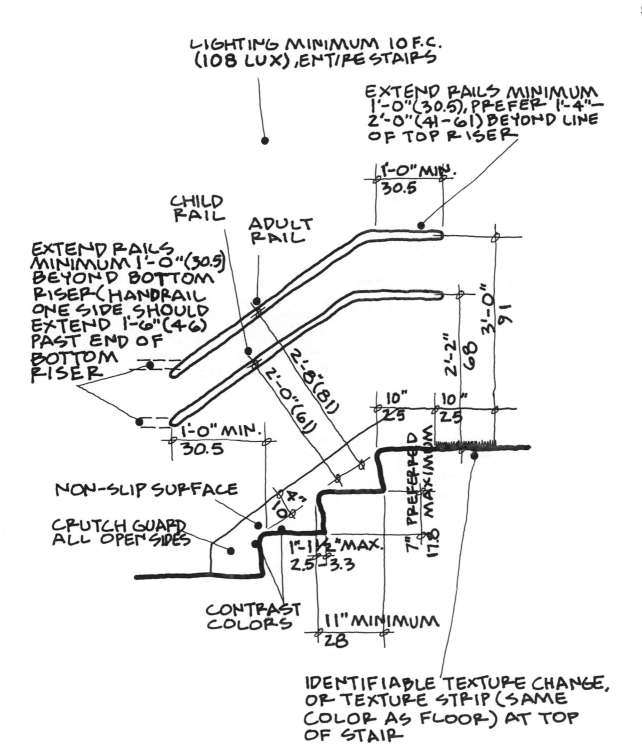

LIGHTING MINIMUM 10 F.C. (108 LUX), ENTIRE STAIRS

EXTEND RAILS MINIMUM 1'-0" (30.5), PREFER 1'-4" - 2'-0" (41-61) BEYOND LINE OF TOP RISER

1'-0" MIN. 30.5

CHILD RAIL

ADULT RAIL

EXTEND RAILS MINIMUM 1'-0" (30.5) BEYOND BOTTOM RISER (HANDRAIL ONE SIDE SHOULD EXTEND 1'-6" (46) PAST END OF BOTTOM RISER

3'-0" 91

2'-2" 68

2'-8" (81)

2'-0" (61)

10" 25

10" 25

1'-0" MIN. 30.5

NON-SLIP SURFACE

4 10

7" PREFERRED MAXIMUM 17.8

CRUTCH GUARD ALL OPEN SIDES

1"-1½" MAX. 2.5-3.3

CONTRAST COLORS

11" MINIMUM 28

IDENTIFIABLE TEXTURE CHANGE, OR TEXTURE STRIP (SAME COLOR AS FLOOR) AT TOP OF STAIR

PREFER MAXIMUM RISER HEIGHT OF 7" (17.8)
CONTRAST COLOR OF TREAD/RISER
AVOID STAIRS OF 1 OR 2 RISERS (PROVIDE RAMPS)
MORE THAN 1 RISER IS IMPASSABLE BY WHEELCHAIR

DETAIL 4.23 Typical stair

Stairs

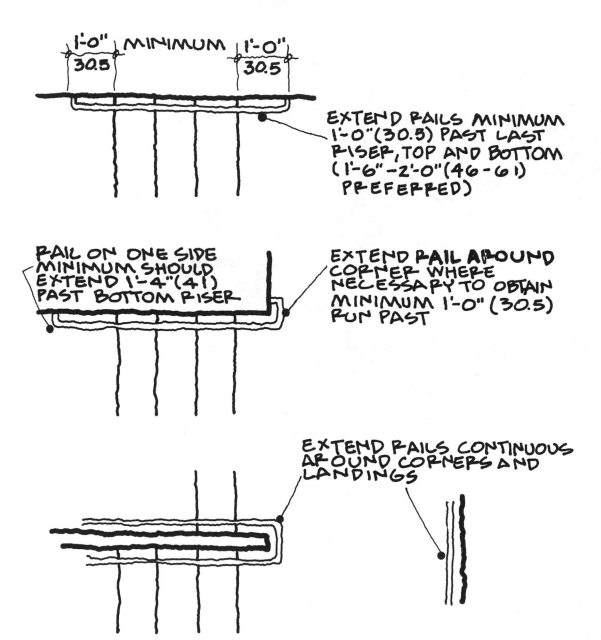

I'-0" | MINIMUM | I'-0"
30.5 | | 30.5

EXTEND RAILS MINIMUM
I'-0"(30.5) PAST LAST
RISER, TOP AND BOTTOM
(I'-6"-2'-0"(46-61)
PREFERRED)

RAIL ON ONE SIDE
MINIMUM SHOULD
EXTEND I'-4"(41)
PAST BOTTOM RISER

EXTEND RAIL AROUND
CORNER WHERE
NECESSARY TO OBTAIN
MINIMUM I'-0" (30.5)
RUN PAST

EXTEND RAILS CONTINUOUS
AROUND CORNERS AND
LANDINGS

DETAIL 4.24   Stair handrails

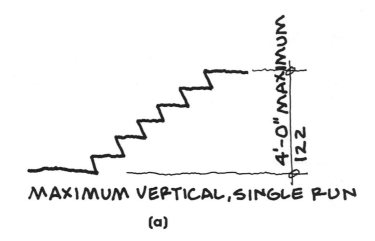

MAXIMUM VERTICAL, SINGLE RUN

(a)

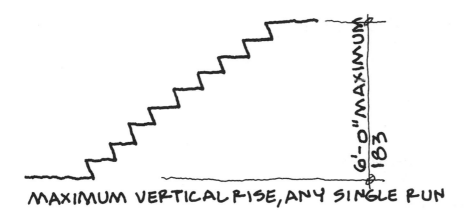

MAXIMUM VERTICAL RISE, ANY SINGLE RUN

PROVIDE PLATFORM IN CENTER OF SINGLE
RUN STAIR WHERE VERTICAL RISE
EXCEEDS MAXIMUM

(b)

DETAIL 4.25a   Exterior stair
DETAIL 4.25b   Interior stair

Stairs

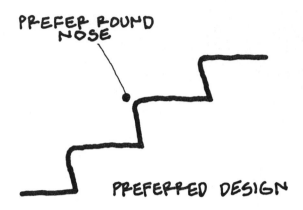

PREFER ROUND NOSE

PREFERRED DESIGN

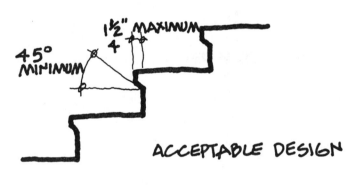

1½" MAXIMUM
4

45° MINIMUM

ACCEPTABLE DESIGN

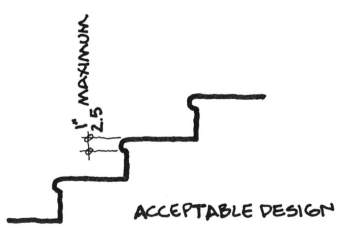

1" MAXIMUM
2.5

ACCEPTABLE DESIGN

DETAIL 4.26   Stair riser profiles

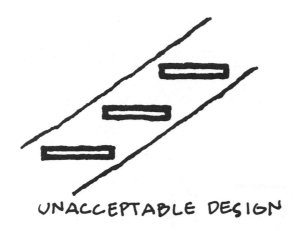

UNACCEPTABLE DESIGN

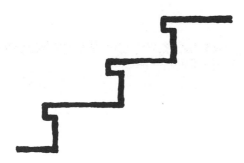

UNACCEPTABLE DESIGN

AVOID STAIR DESIGNS WHICH 'TRAP' THE TOES OF THOSE WEARING LEG BRACES

USE OPEN RISER STAIRS ONLY WHERE ALTERNATE ACCESSIBLE STAIRS ARE AVAILABLE

DETAIL 4.27   Stair riser profiles

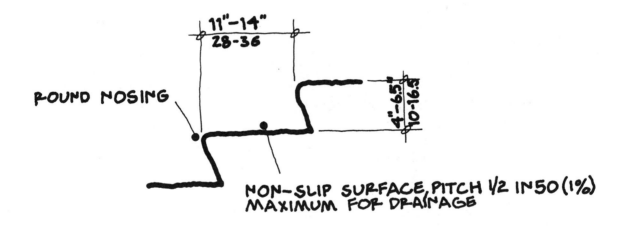

11"-14"
28-36

ROUND NOSING

4"-6.5"
10-16.5

NON-SLIP SURFACE, PITCH 1/2 IN 50 (1%)
MAXIMUM FOR DRAINAGE

ACCEPTABLE

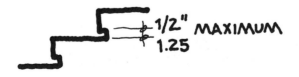

1/2" MAXIMUM
1.25

ACCEPTABLE

DETAIL 4.28 Exterior stair riser profiles

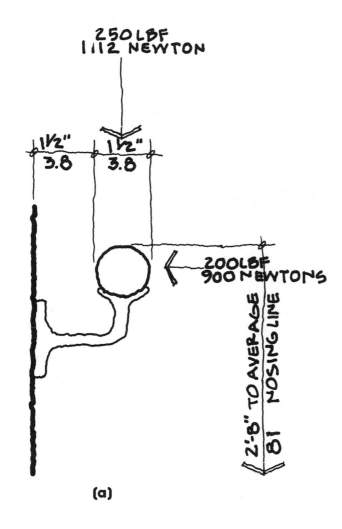

250 LBF
1112 NEWTON

1½"
3.8

1½"
3.8

200 LBF
900 NEWTONS

2'-8" TO AVERAGE
NOSING LINE
81

(a)

LOW WALL ALONE IS
INSUFFICIENT, PROVIDE
HANDRAIL IN ADDITION

(b)

DETAIL 4.29a   Handrail forces and clearances
DETAIL 4.29b   Handrail at low wall

Stairs

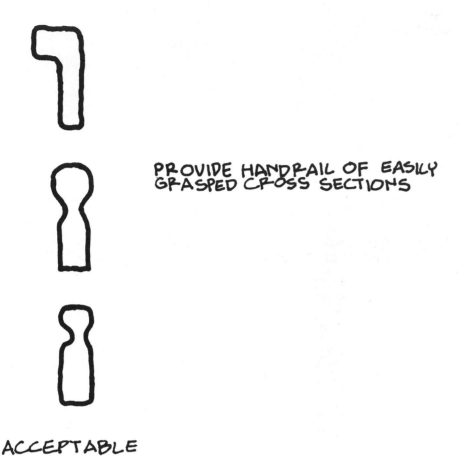

PROVIDE HANDRAIL OF EASILY
GRASPED CROSS SECTIONS

ACCEPTABLE

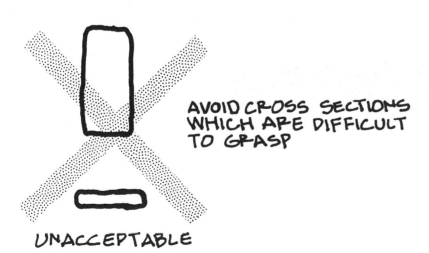

AVOID CROSS SECTIONS
WHICH ARE DIFFICULT
TO GRASP

UNACCEPTABLE

DETAIL 4.30   Handrail shapes

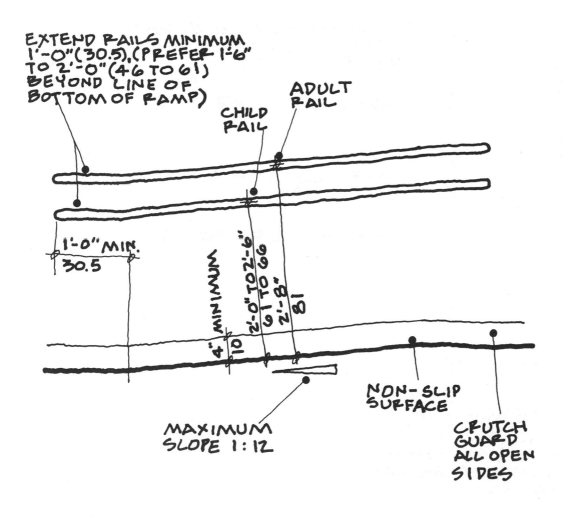

EXTEND RAILS MINIMUM
1'-0" (30.5), (PREFER 1'-6"
TO 2'-0" (46 TO 61)
BEYOND LINE OF
BOTTOM OF RAMP)

ADULT RAIL

CHILD RAIL

1'-0" MIN.
30.5

4" MINIMUM
10

2'-0" TO 2'-6"
61 TO 66

2'-8"
81

MAXIMUM
SLOPE 1:12

NON-SLIP
SURFACE

CRUTCH
GUARD
ALL OPEN
SIDES

DETAIL 4.31   Ramp section

Ramps

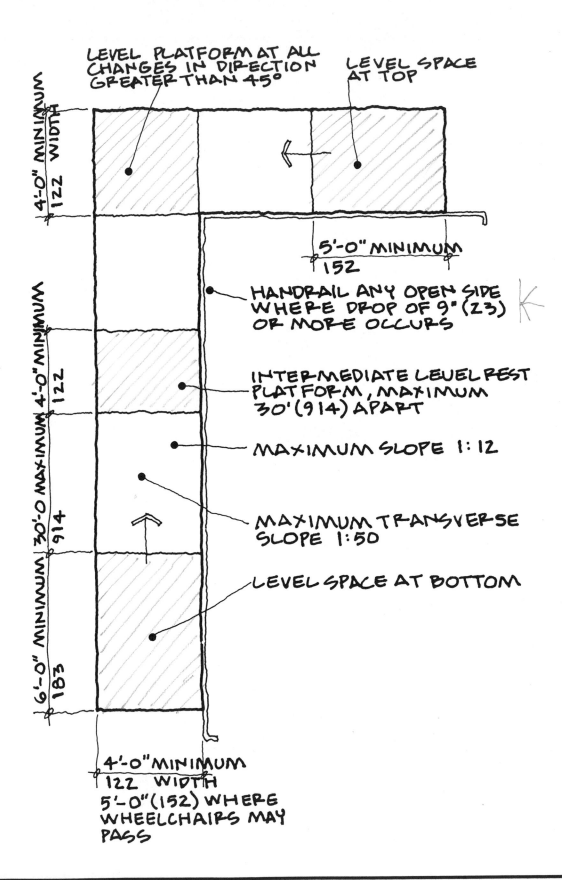

LEVEL PLATFORM AT ALL CHANGES IN DIRECTION GREATER THAN 45°

LEVEL SPACE AT TOP

4'-0" MINIMUM 122 WIDTH

5'-0" MINIMUM 152

HANDRAIL ANY OPEN SIDE WHERE DROP OF 9" (23) OR MORE OCCURS

INTERMEDIATE LEVEL REST PLATFORM, MAXIMUM 30' (914) APART

MAXIMUM SLOPE 1:12

MAXIMUM TRANSVERSE SLOPE 1:50

LEVEL SPACE AT BOTTOM

4'-0" MINIMUM 30'-0 MAXIMUM 4'-0" MINIMUM 122

6'-0" MINIMUM 183

914

4'-0" MINIMUM 122 WIDTH
5'-0" (152) WHERE WHEELCHAIRS MAY PASS

DETAIL 4.32 Typical ramp

AVOID ANY TYPE CARPET ON RAMPS

ESPECIALLY AVOID INDOOR/OUTDOOR (PLASTIC FIBRE) CARPET

PROVIDE NON-SLIP SURFACE (CARBORUNDUM, BROOMED CONCRETE, ETC.)

AVOID EXTERIOR RAMPS WHERE SNOW OR ICE OCCUR, WHERE WINTER TEMPERATURE FALLS BELOW 32°F (0°C)

SOME LOCAL JURISDICTIONS PERMIT 1:10 AND 1:8 SLOPES ON PRIVATE, SECONDARY OR NON-EXIT RAMPS

DETAIL 4.33   Ramps

RAMP SLOPE	MAXIMUM RISE OF A SINGLE RUN	MAXIMUM LENGTH OF A SINGLE RUN	MAXIMUM TOTAL (AGGREGATE) LENGTH OF RUN
1:8	3"(7.5)	2'(61)	2'(61)
1:10	9"(23)	8'(244)	8'(244)
1:12	2'-6"(76)	30'(914)	60'(18.3M)
1:16	2'-6"(76)	40'(12.2M)	160'(49M)
1:20	2'-6"(76)	50'(15.2M)	—

DETAIL 4.34   Ramp criteria

Elevators

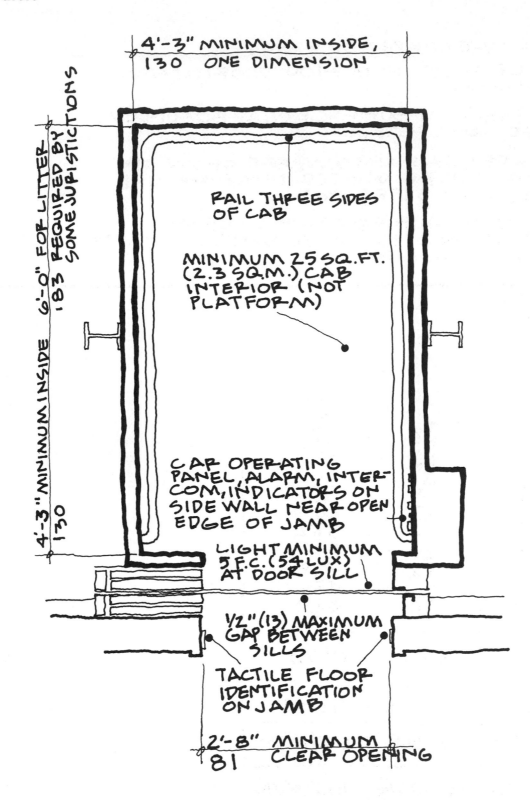

4'-3" MINIMUM INSIDE, 130 ONE DIMENSION

6'-0" FOR LITTER 183 REQUIRED BY SOME JURISDICTIONS

4'-3" MINIMUM INSIDE 130

RAIL THREE SIDES OF CAB

MINIMUM 25 SQ. FT. (2.3 SQ. M.) CAB INTERIOR (NOT PLATFORM)

CAR OPERATING PANEL, ALARM, INTERCOM, INDICATORS ON SIDE WALL NEAR OPEN EDGE OF JAMB

LIGHT MINIMUM 5 F.C. (54 LUX) AT DOOR SILL

½" (13) MAXIMUM GAP BETWEEN SILLS

TACTILE FLOOR IDENTIFICATION ON JAMB

2'-8" MINIMUM CLEAR OPENING 81

VARIABLE SPEED MOTORS WITH LESS INITIAL ACCELERATION ARE BETTER FOR THE ELDERLY AND AMBULATORY HANDICAPPED

DETAIL 4.35 Elevator plan

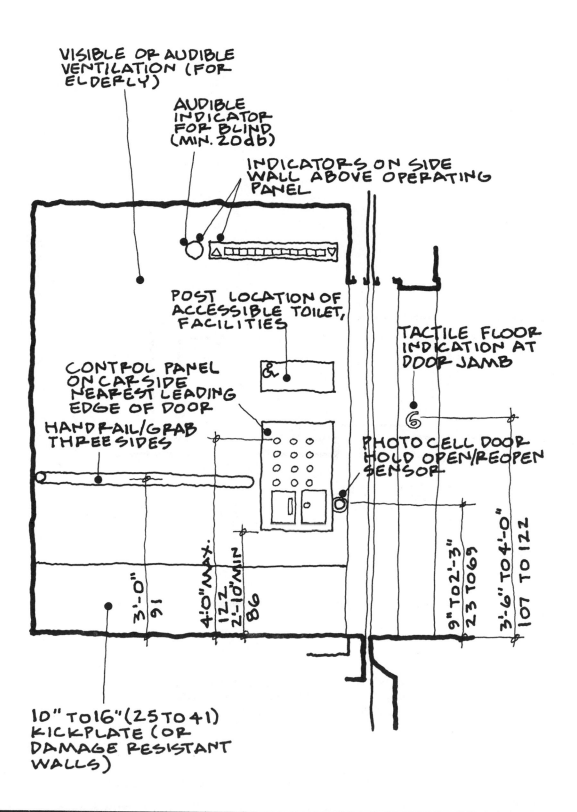

VISIBLE OR AUDIBLE
VENTILATION (FOR
ELDERLY)

AUDIBLE
INDICATOR
FOR BLIND
(MIN. 20db)

INDICATORS ON SIDE
WALL ABOVE OPERATING
PANEL

POST LOCATION OF
ACCESSIBLE TOILET,
FACILITIES

TACTILE FLOOR
INDICATION AT
DOOR JAMB

CONTROL PANEL
ON CAR SIDE
NEAREST LEADING
EDGE OF DOOR

HANDRAIL/GRAB
THREE SIDES

PHOTO CELL DOOR
HOLD OPEN/REOPEN
SENSOR

3'-0"
91

4'-0" MAX.
122
2'-10" MIN
86

9" TO 2'-3"
23 TO 69

3'-6" TO 4'-0"
107 TO 122

10" TO 16" (25 TO 41)
KICKPLATE (OR
DAMAGE RESISTANT
WALLS)

DETAIL 4.36   Elevator section

Elevators

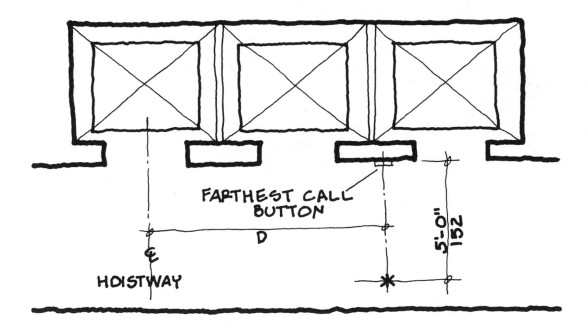

$$T = \frac{D}{1.5 \, FT/SEC}$$

$$T = \frac{D}{455 \, MM/SEC}$$

WHERE T IS TIME FROM ELEVATOR ARRIVAL SIGNAL TO FIRST CLOSING OF DOOR

DETAIL 4.37   Minimum door-open time

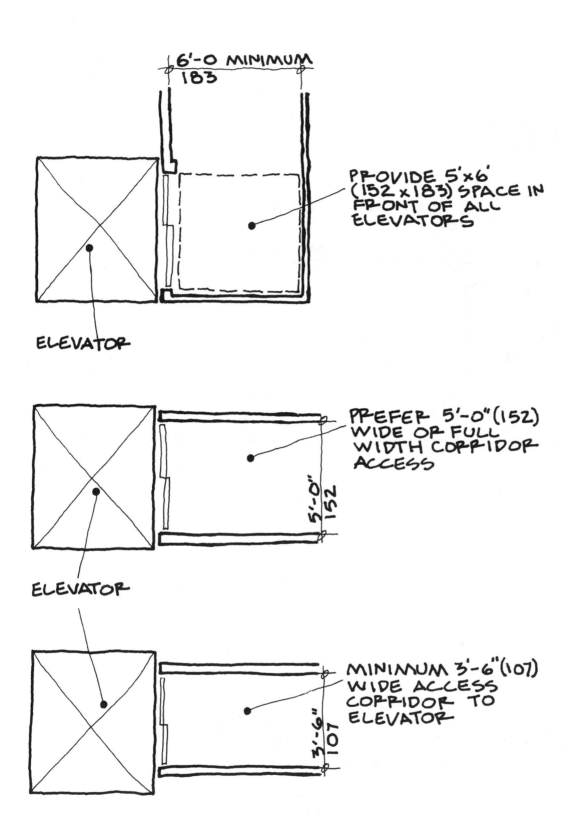

6'-0 MINIMUM
183

PROVIDE 5'x6'
(152 x 183) SPACE IN
FRONT OF ALL
ELEVATORS

ELEVATOR

PREFER 5'-0"(152)
WIDE OR FULL
WIDTH CORRIDOR
ACCESS

5'-0"
152

ELEVATOR

MINIMUM 3'-6"(107)
WIDE ACCESS
CORRIDOR TO
ELEVATOR

3'-6"
107

DETAIL 4.38 Elevator approach corridors

Elevators

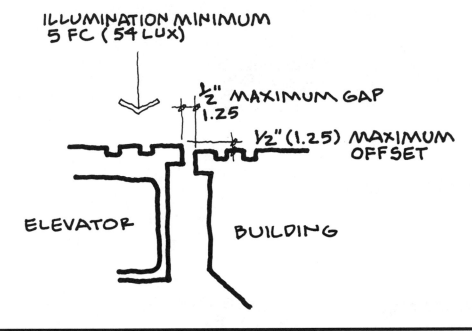

ILLUMINATION MINIMUM
5 FC (54 LUX)

½" MAXIMUM GAP
1.25

½" (1.25) MAXIMUM
OFFSET

ELEVATOR

BUILDING

DETAIL 4.39 Elevator sill

MINIMUM FULL OPEN TIME 3 SEC., PREFER 5-6 SEC.
FOR AMBULANT, 7 SEC. FOR WHEELCHAIR

MINIMUM CLOSING TIME 3 SEC.

MAXIMUM CLOSING SPEED 80 FPM (24.4 M/SEC.)
FOR AMBULATORY HANDICAPPED, 40 FPM (12.2
M/SEC.) FOR ELDERLY

DETAIL 4.40 Elevator doors

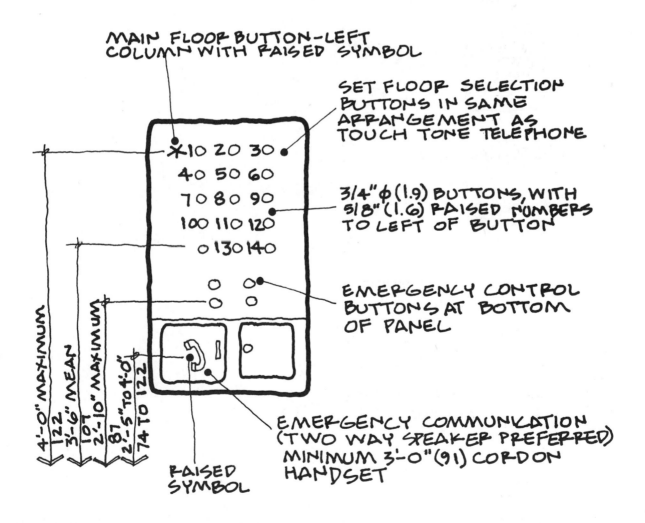

MAIN FLOOR BUTTON-LEFT COLUMN WITH RAISED SYMBOL

SET FLOOR SELECTION BUTTONS IN SAME ARRANGEMENT AS TOUCH TONE TELEPHONE

3/4"ϕ(1.9) BUTTONS, WITH 5/8"(1.6) RAISED NUMBERS TO LEFT OF BUTTON

EMERGENCY CONTROL BUTTONS AT BOTTOM OF PANEL

EMERGENCY COMMUNICATION (TWO WAY SPEAKER PREFERRED) MINIMUM 3'-0"(91) CORD ON HANDSET

RAISED SYMBOL

4'-0" MAXIMUM 122
3'-6" MEAN 107
2'-10" MAXIMUM 87
2'-5" TO 4'-0" 74 TO 122

DETAIL 4.41 Elevator control panel

Elevators

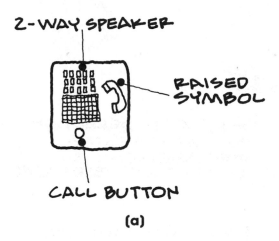

2-WAY SPEAKER

RAISED SYMBOL

CALL BUTTON

(a)

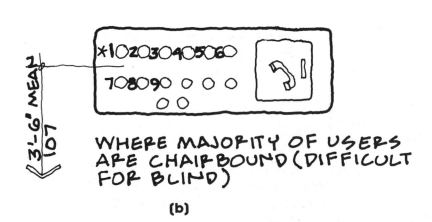

3'-6" MEAN
107

WHERE MAJORITY OF USERS
ARE CHAIRBOUND (DIFFICULT
FOR BLIND)

(b)

DETAIL 4.42a   Elevator communication panel
DETAIL 4.42b   Elevator wheelchair control panel

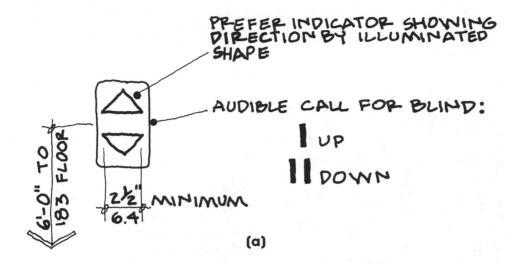

PREFER INDICATOR SHOWING DIRECTION BY ILLUMINATED SHAPE

AUDIBLE CALL FOR BLIND:

I UP

II DOWN

6'-0" TO 183 FLOOR

2½" / 6.4 MINIMUM

(a)

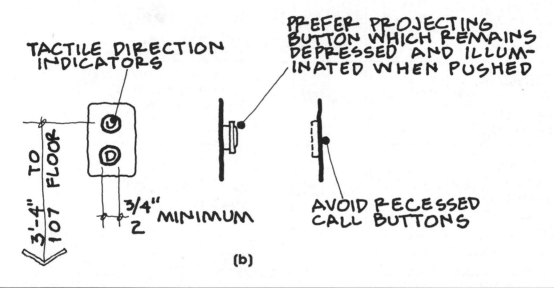

TACTILE DIRECTION INDICATORS

PREFER PROJECTING BUTTON WHICH REMAINS DEPRESSED AND ILLUMINATED WHEN PUSHED

3'-4" TO 107 FLOOR

3/4" / 2 MINIMUM

AVOID RECESSED CALL BUTTONS

(b)

DETAIL 4.43a **Hall indicator**
DETAIL 4.43b **Call buttons**

 OPEN DOOR

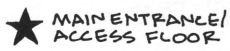 CLOSE DOOR

 ALARM OR EMERGENCY CALL

⊗ EMERGENCY STOP

★ MAIN ENTRANCE/ ACCESS FLOOR

DETAIL 4.44 **Elevator standard symbols**

Toilets

	MINIMUM NUMBER OF FIXTURES			NUMBER OF FIXTURES			
	W.C.	LAV.	BATH	W.C.	LAV.	BATH	UNITS/ REMARKS
RESIDENTIAL[A] (WITH PRIVATE FACILITIES)	1	1	1	1/3 4%	1/3 4%	1/3 4%	PER RESIDENT PER D.U. OR SLEEPING ROOM
RESIDENTIAL[A,D] (WITH COMMON OR CENTRAL FACILITIES)	2[B]	2[B]	2[B]	1/2 2%	1/2 2%	1/4 2%	PER RESIDENT PER D.U. OR SLEEPING ROOM
INSTITUTIONAL/ COMMERCIAL[E] (WITH PRIVATE TOILET ROOMS)	2[B]	2[B]	—	10%	10%	—	% OF TOILET FACILITIES
INSTITUTIONAL/ COMMERCIAL[E] (WITH COMMON OR CENTRAL FACILITIES)	2[B,C]	2[B,C]	—	10%	10%	—	% OF TOILET FACILITIES

A. RESIDENTIAL D.U. OR INSTITUTIONS FOR THE HANDICAPPED

B. ONE FOR EACH SEX

C. MINIMUM ONE IN EACH BANK OF FIXTURES

D. MAXIMUM 3 MINUTE (ONE WAY) TRIP FROM ANY LOCATION

E. MAXIMUM 5 MINUTE (ONE WAY) TRIP FROM ANY LOCATION

WHERE TOILETS ARE SIZED FOR LATERAL TRANSFER, PROVIDE 1/2 FOR RIGHT HAND, 1/2 FOR LEFT HAND

WHERE ELEVATOR SERVICE IS AVAILABLE, ACCESSIBLE TOILET SHOULD NOT BE MORE THAN 2 FLOORS AWAY

DETAIL 4.45   Toilet planning criteria

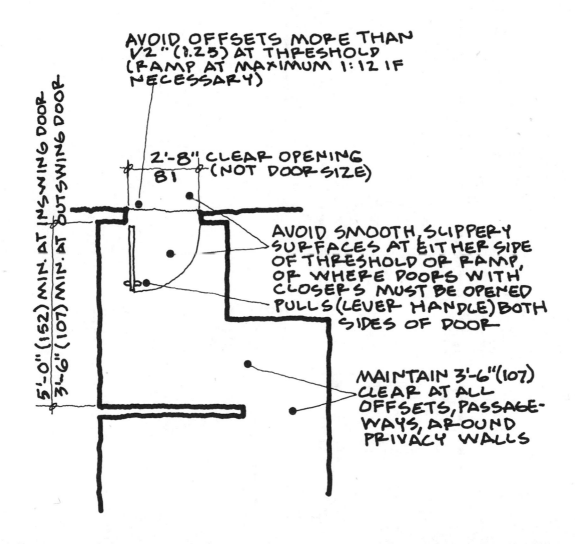

AVOID OFFSETS MORE THAN
1/2" (1.25) AT THRESHOLD
(RAMP AT MAXIMUM 1:12 IF
NECESSARY)

2'-8" CLEAR OPENING
(NOT DOOR SIZE)

B1

AVOID SMOOTH, SLIPPERY
SURFACES AT EITHER SIDE
OF THRESHOLD OR RAMP,
OR WHERE DOORS WITH
CLOSERS MUST BE OPENED

PULLS (LEVER HANDLE) BOTH
SIDES OF DOOR

5'-0" (152) MIN. AT INSWING DOOR
3'-6" (107) MIN. AT OUTSWING DOOR

MAINTAIN 3'-6" (107)
CLEAR AT ALL
OFFSETS, PASSAGE-
WAYS, AROUND
PRIVACY WALLS

DETAIL 4.46   Toilet access

Toilets

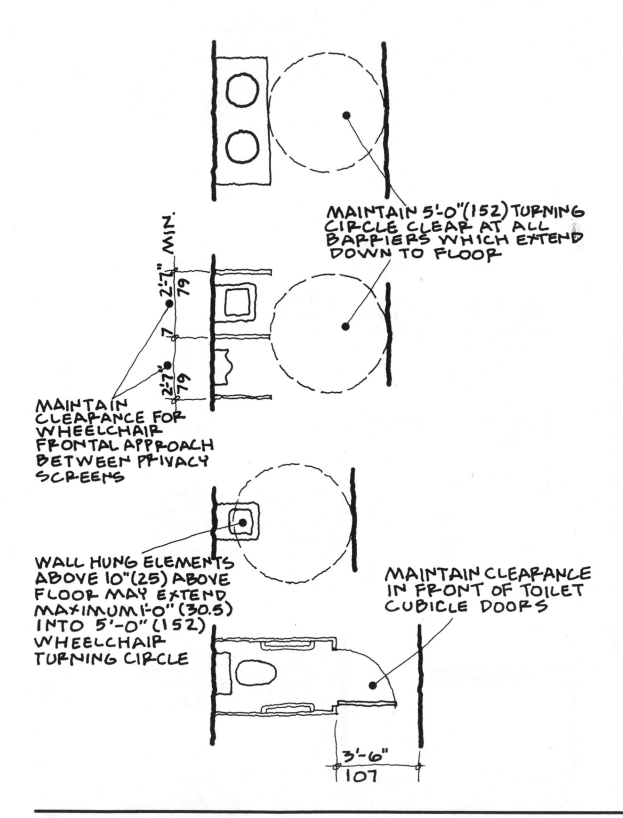

MAINTAIN 5'-0"(152) TURNING CIRCLE CLEAR AT ALL BARRIERS WHICH EXTEND DOWN TO FLOOR

2'-7" MIN.

79

7

2'-7"

79

MAINTAIN CLEARANCE FOR WHEELCHAIR FRONTAL APPROACH BETWEEN PRIVACY SCREENS

WALL HUNG ELEMENTS ABOVE 10"(25) ABOVE FLOOR MAY EXTEND MAXIMUM 1'-0" (30.5) INTO 5'-0" (152) WHEELCHAIR TURNING CIRCLE

MAINTAIN CLEARANCE IN FRONT OF TOILET CUBICLE DOORS

3'-6"
107

DETAIL 4.47   Toilet clearances

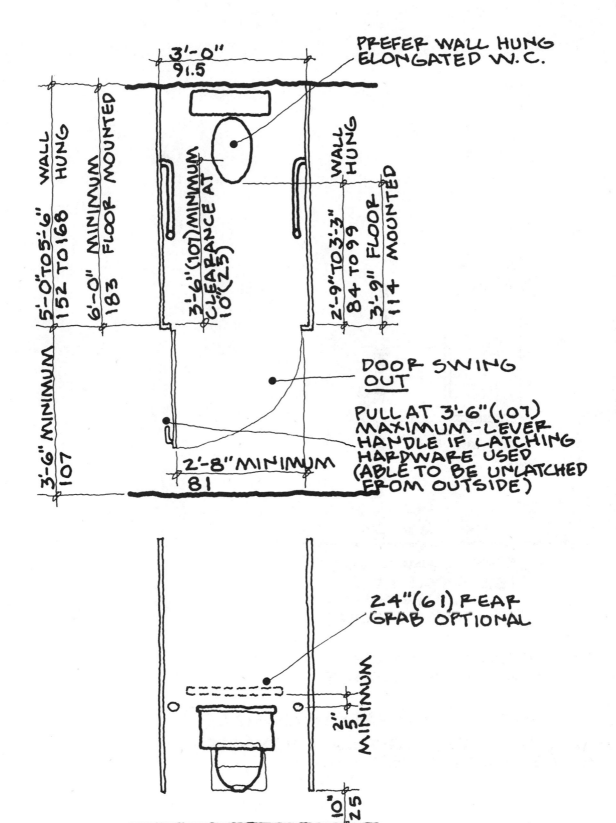

PREFER WALL HUNG ELONGATED W.C.

3'-0" 91.5

5'-0" TO 5'-6" WALL HUNG 152 TO 168

6'-0" MINIMUM FLOOR MOUNTED 183

3'-6" (107) MINIMUM CLEARANCE AT 10" (25)

2'-9" TO 3'-3" WALL HUNG 84 TO 99

3'-9" FLOOR MOUNTED 114

3'-6" MINIMUM 107

DOOR SWING OUT

PULL AT 3'-6" (107) MAXIMUM-LEVER HANDLE IF LATCHING HARDWARE USED (ABLE TO BE UNLATCHED FROM OUTSIDE)

2'-8" MINIMUM 81

24" (61) REAR GRAB OPTIONAL

2" 5 MINIMUM

10" 25

NOTE: 3'-0" (91.5) WIDTH NOT PERMITTED UNDER ANSI 117.1

DETAIL 4.48   Minimum toilet

Toilets

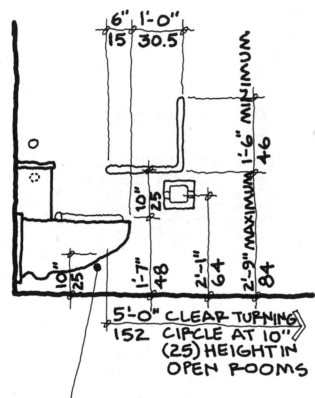

6"   1'-0"
15   30.5

1'-6" MINIMUM
46

10"
25

10"
25

1'-7"
48

2'-1"
64

2'-9" MAXIMUM
84

10"
25

5'-0" CLEAR TURNING
152 CIRCLE AT 10"
(25) HEIGHT IN
OPEN ROOMS

PREFER DEEPLY RECESSED FRONT
WALL HUNG WATER CLOSET

PROVIDE LATERAL TRANSFER IF POSSIBLE
FRONTAL TRANSFER DIFFICULT/IMPOSSIBLE
FOR SOME HANDICAPPED

DETAIL 4.49   Typical toilet stall

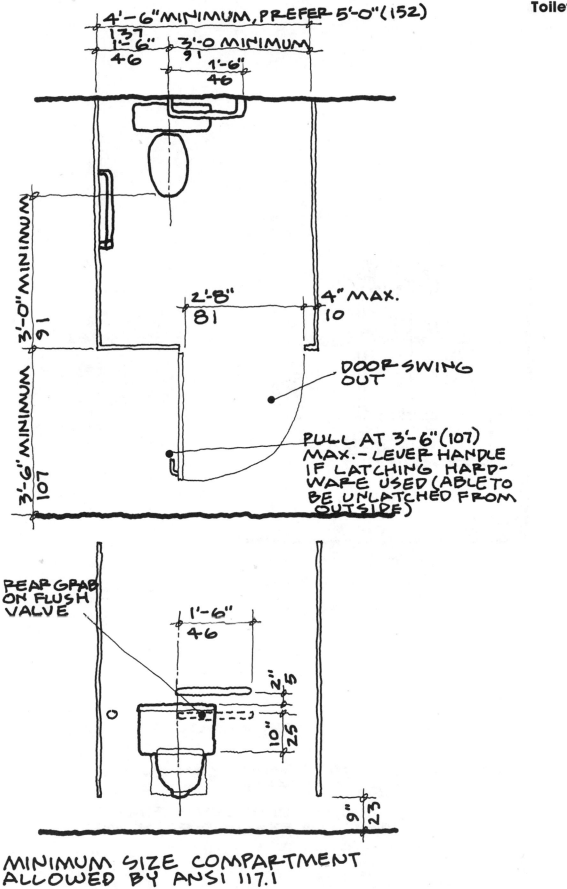

4'-6" MINIMUM, PREFER 5'-0" (152)
137
1'-6" 3'-0 MINIMUM
46   91
1'-6"
46

3'-0" MINIMUM
91

3'-6" MINIMUM
107

2'-8"
81

4" MAX.
10

DOOR SWING OUT

PULL AT 3'-6" (107) MAX. — LEVER HANDLE IF LATCHING HARDWARE USED (ABLE TO BE UNLATCHED FROM OUTSIDE)

REAR GRAB ON FLUSH VALVE

1'-6"
46

2"
5

10"
25

9"
23

MINIMUM SIZE COMPARTMENT ALLOWED BY ANSI 117.1

DETAIL 4.50   Side and lateral transfer compartment

Toilets

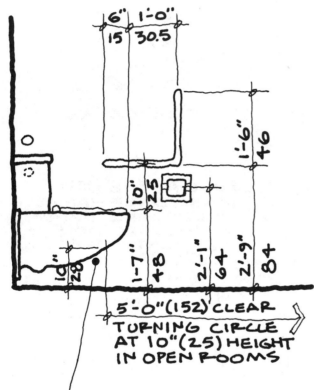

6" 1'-0"
15 30.5

1'-6"
46

10"
25

1'-7"
48

2'-1"
64

2'-9"
84

10"
28

5'-0"(152) CLEAR
TURNING CIRCLE
AT 10"(25) HEIGHT
IN OPEN ROOMS

PREFER DEEPLY RECESSED
FRONT, WALL HUNG WATER CLOSET

THIS TYPE MUCH PREFERRED OVER FRONT
TRANSFER

MANY HANDICAPPED PERSONS CAN MAKE
ONLY LATERAL TRANSFER

WHERE POSSIBLE, PROVIDE BOTH RIGHT
AND LEFT HAND TOILETS FOR EACH SEX

DETAIL 4.51 Side and lateral transfer compartment

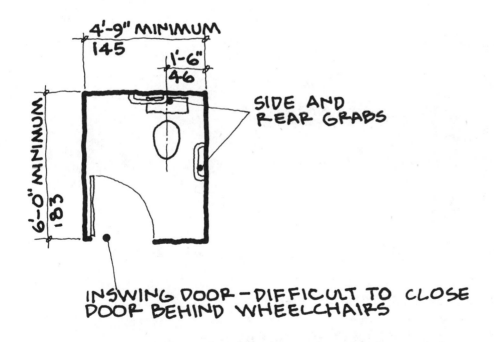

4'-9" MINIMUM
145

1'-6"
46

6'-0" MINIMUM
183

SIDE AND
REAR GRABS

INSWING DOOR — DIFFICULT TO CLOSE
DOOR BEHIND WHEELCHAIRS

→ DOOR MUST BE LOCATED DIAGONALLY
FROM FIXTURE

DETAIL 4.52   Inswing door toilet compartment

Toilets

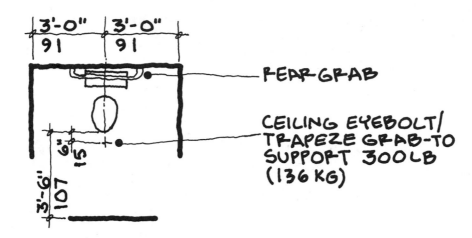

3'-0" 91   3'-0" 91

— REAR GRAB

CEILING EYEBOLT/
TRAPEZE GRAB-TO
SUPPORT 300 LB
(136 KG)

6" 15

3'-6" 107

PROVIDE ONE FOR EACH SEX IN INSTITUTIONS

(a)

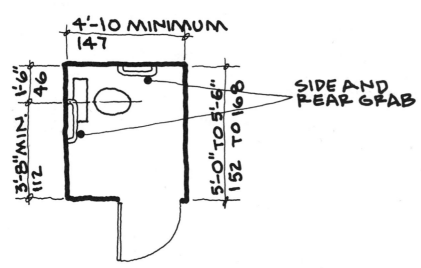

4'-10 MINIMUM 147

1'-6" 46

3'-8" MIN. 112

5'-0" TO 5'-6" 152 TO 168

SIDE AND
REAR GRAB

ALLOWS PREFERRED LATERAL TRANSFER

→ **ALL COMPARTMENTS SHOULD BE CEILING HUNG, LARGER WHERE EPILEPTICS ARE PRESENT**

(b)

DETAIL 4.53a   Dual-approach watercloset
DETAIL 4.53b   Side-located watercloset

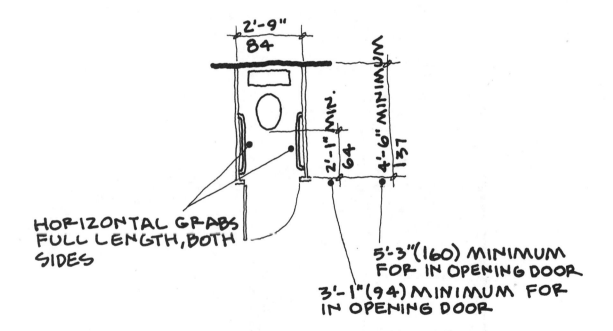

HORIZONTAL GRABS
FULL LENGTH, BOTH
SIDES

5'-3"(160) MINIMUM
FOR IN OPENING DOOR

3'-1"(94) MINIMUM FOR
IN OPENING DOOR

MAY BE USED BY WHEELCHAIR USERS WHO ARE
ABLE TO STAND/MOVE 1-2 STEPS

PROVIDE 1 STALL, THUS, IN ADDITION TO FULL
WHEELCHAIR ACCESSIBLE STALL

(b)

DETAIL 4.54   Ambulant watercloset stall

Toilets

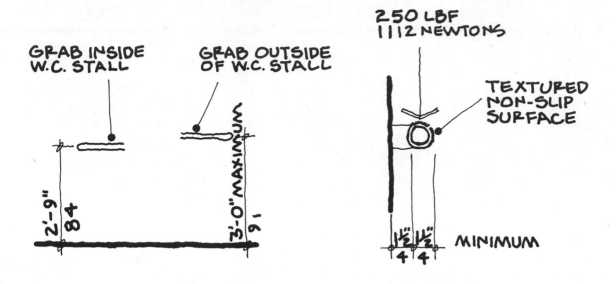

DETAIL 4.55   Toilet grab bar heights

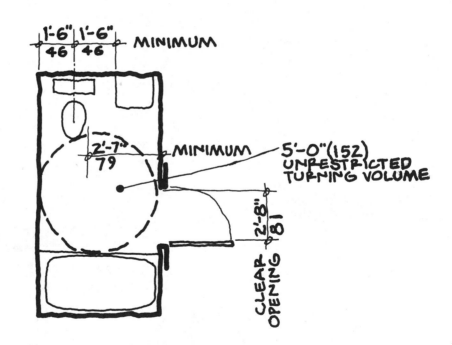

PROVIDE GRABS AS FOR COMMERCIAL TOILET STALLS

LOCATE TUB IN SEPARATE COMPARTMENT IF POSSIBLE

LAVATORY NEAR W.C. FACILITATES WASHING WITHOUT NEED TO GET INTO WHEELCHAIR FIRST

LOCATE STOP VALUES IN ACCESSIBLE LOCATION IN PRIVATE RESIDENCES

DETAIL 4.56   Private toilet room

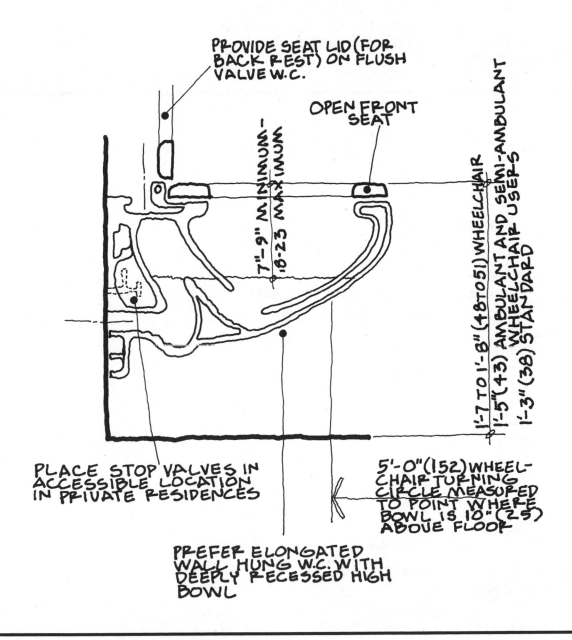

PROVIDE SEAT LID (FOR BACK REST) ON FLUSH VALVE W.C.

OPEN FRONT SEAT

1'-7 TO 1'-8" (48 TO 51) WHEELCHAIR

1'-5" (43) AMBULANT AND SEMI-AMBULANT WHEELCHAIR USERS

1'-3" (38) STANDARD

7"-9" MINIMUM — 18-23 MAXIMUM

PLACE STOP VALVES IN ACCESSIBLE LOCATION IN PRIVATE RESIDENCES

PREFER ELONGATED WALL HUNG W.C. WITH DEEPLY RECESSED HIGH BOWL

5'-0" (152) WHEEL-CHAIR TURNING CIRCLE MEASURED TO POINT WHERE BOWL IS 10" (25) ABOVE FLOOR

DETAIL 4.57 Typical watercloset

Toilets

LEVER HANDLE CONTROLS-
THERMOSTATIC TEMPERATURE
CONTROL

PROVIDE W.C./BIDET COMBINATION IN
RESIDENTIAL INSTITUTIONS WHERE
RESIDENTS HAVE RESTRICTED HAND
OR ARM MOVEMENT ABILITY FOR
SELF CLEANSING

DETAIL 4.58 Bidet

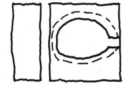

PROVIDE WIDE 'BENCH' SEAT WHERE
POSSIBLE TO PROVIDE GRASPING
SURFACE

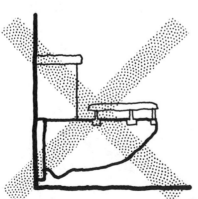

AVOID HIGH, UNSTABLE APPEARING
SEAT EXTENSION

DETAIL 4.59 Watercloset seats

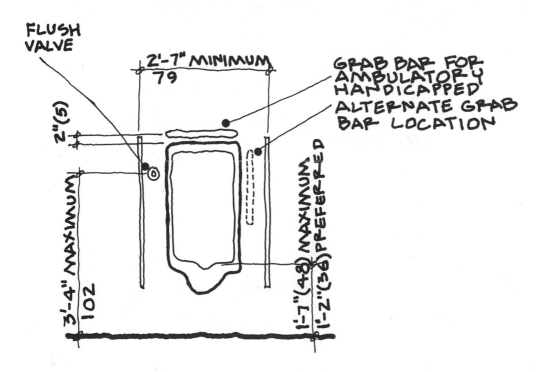

FLUSH VALVE

2'-7" MINIMUM
79

2"(5)

3'-4" MAXIMUM
102

GRAB BAR FOR AMBULATORY HANDICAPPED ALTERNATE GRAB BAR LOCATION

1'-7"(48) MAXIMUM
1'-2"(36) PREFERRED

URINALS ARE DIFFICULT FOR THE BLIND, AND ARE LITTLE USED BY THOSE IN WHEEL CHAIR

DETAIL 4.60   Typical urinal

Toilets

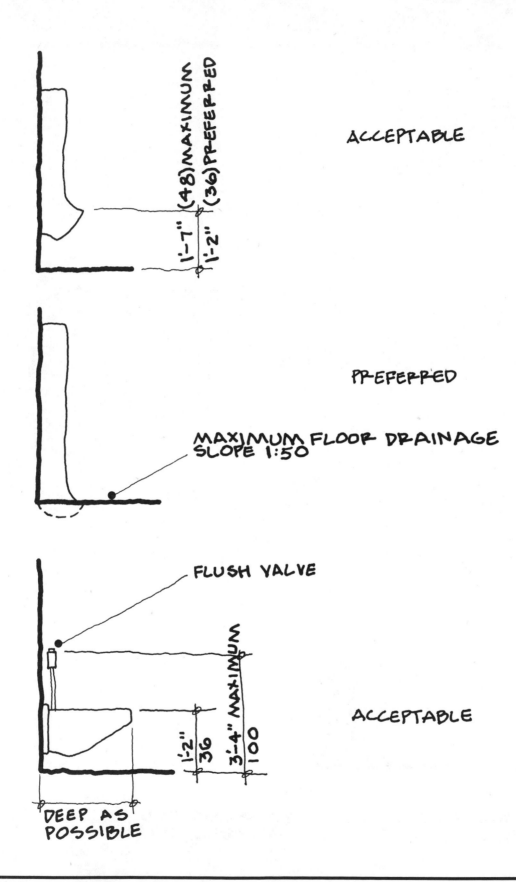

ACCEPTABLE

1'-7" (48)MAXIMUM
1'-2" (36)PREFERRED

PREFERRED

MAXIMUM FLOOR DRAINAGE
SLOPE 1:50

FLUSH VALVE

1'-2" 36
3'-4" MAXIMUM 100

ACCEPTABLE

DEEP AS POSSIBLE

DETAIL 4.61   Urinals

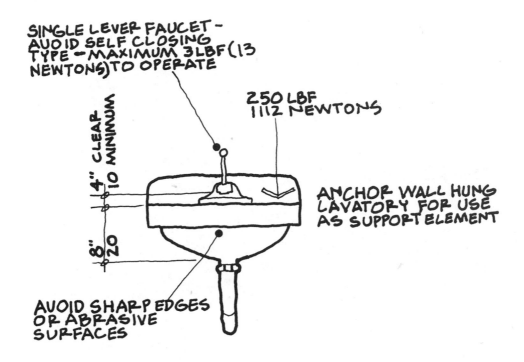

SINGLE LEVER FAUCET —
AVOID SELF CLOSING
TYPE — MAXIMUM 3 LBF (13
NEWTONS) TO OPERATE

250 LBF
1112 NEWTONS

4" CLEAR
10 MINIMUM

8"
20

ANCHOR WALL HUNG
LAVATORY FOR USE
AS SUPPORT ELEMENT

AVOID SHARP EDGES
OR ABRASIVE
SURFACES

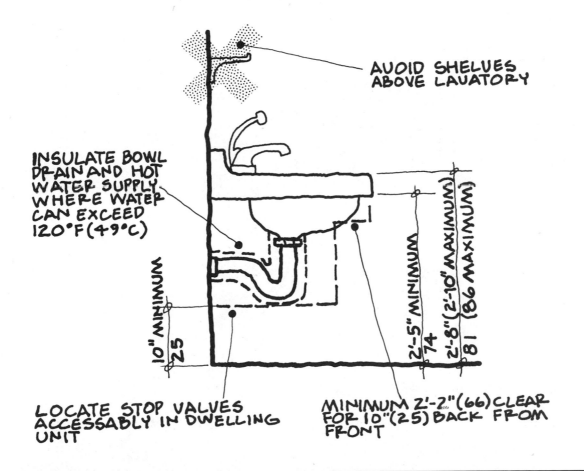

AVOID SHELVES
ABOVE LAVATORY

INSULATE BOWL
DRAIN AND HOT
WATER SUPPLY
WHERE WATER
CAN EXCEED
120°F (49°C)

10" MINIMUM
25

2'-5" MINIMUM
74

2'-8" (2'-10" MAXIMUM)
81 (86 MAXIMUM)

LOCATE STOP VALVES
ACCESSABLY IN DWELLING
UNIT

MINIMUM 2'-2" (66) CLEAR
FOR 10" (25) BACK FROM
FRONT

DETAIL 4.62 Typical lavatory

Toilets

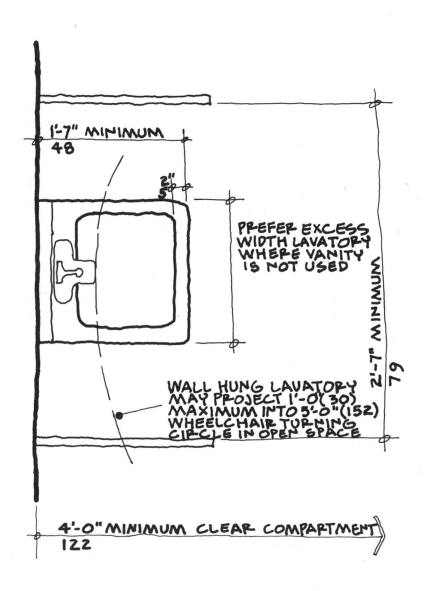

1'-7" MINIMUM
48

2" 5

PREFER EXCESS
WIDTH LAVATORY
WHERE VANITY
IS NOT USED

2'-7" MINIMUM
79

WALL HUNG LAVATORY
MAY PROJECT 1'-0 (30)
MAXIMUM INTO 5'-0"(152)
WHEELCHAIR TURNING
CIRCLE IN OPEN SPACE

4'-0" MINIMUM CLEAR COMPARTMENT
122

DETAIL 4.63   Typical lavatory

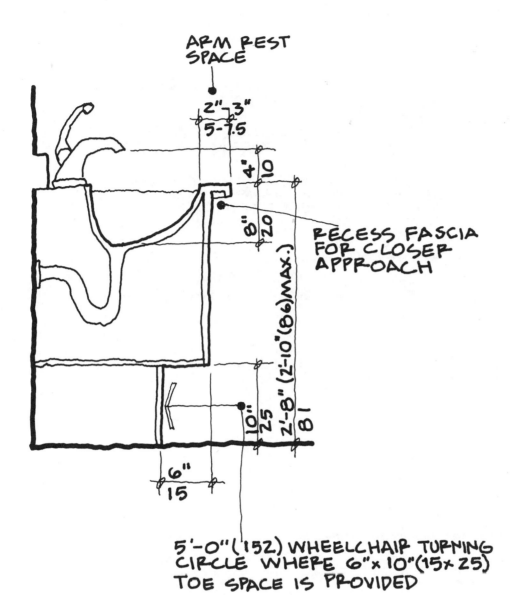

ARM REST SPACE

2"-3"
5-7.5

4" 10

RECESS FASCIA FOR CLOSER APPROACH

8" 20

2'-10"(86)MAX.

10" 25

2'-8" 81

6"
15

5'-0" (152) WHEELCHAIR TURNING CIRCLE WHERE 6"x 10"(15x25) TOE SPACE IS PROVIDED

FAUCETS SHOULD BE SINGLE LEVER TYPE ONLY (MAXIMUM-3LBF (13 NEWTONS) TO OPERATE)

AVOID SELF-CLOSING FAUCETS

AVOID FAUCETS, VALVES WHICH REQUIRE GRASPING OR COMPLEX ARM OR HAND MOVEMENTS

FAUCETS, AT LEAST IN RESIDENTIAL INSTITUTIONS, SHOULD BE THERMOSTATIC-ALLY GUARDED

DETAIL 4.64 Typical lavatory

Toilets

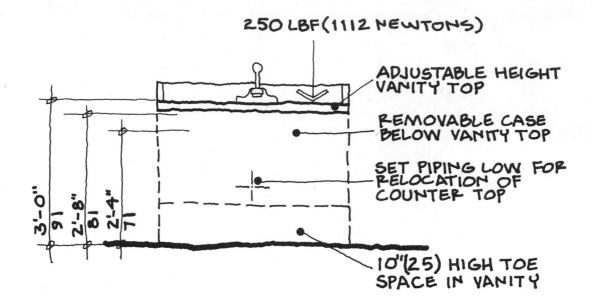

250 LBF (1112 NEWTONS)

ADJUSTABLE HEIGHT VANITY TOP

REMOVABLE CASE BELOW VANITY TOP

SET PIPING LOW FOR RELOCATION OF COUNTER TOP

3'-0" (9)
2'-8" (8)
2'-4" (7)

10"(25) HIGH TOE SPACE IN VANITY

ADJUSTABLE HEIGHT TOP, REMOVABLE CASE BELOW PROVIDES CONVERTABILITY FOR RESIDENTIAL UNIT

DETAIL 4.65   Typical lavatory

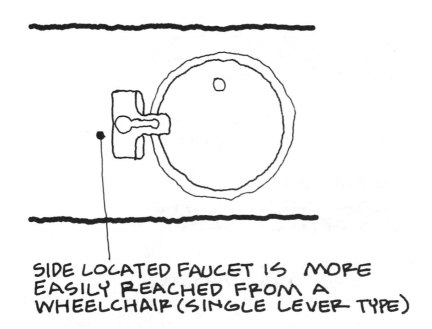

SIDE LOCATED FAUCET IS MORE EASILY REACHED FROM A WHEELCHAIR (SINGLE LEVER TYPE)

DETAIL 4.66   Lavatory faucet location

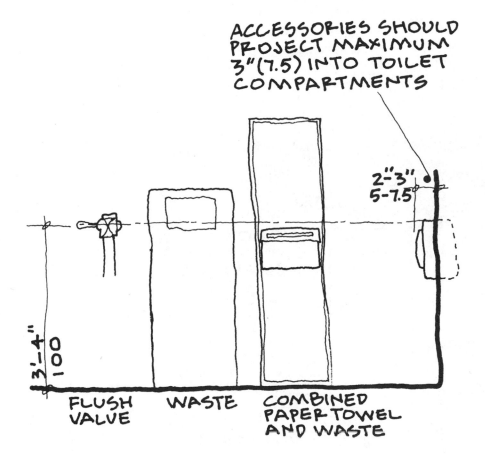

ACCESSORIES SHOULD
PROJECT MAXIMUM
3"(7.5) INTO TOILET
COMPARTMENTS

2"-3"
5-7.5

3'-4"
100

FLUSH
VALVE   WASTE   COMBINED
                           PAPER TOWEL
                           AND WASTE

WORKING MECHANISM OF ANY ACCESSORY
SHOULD BE LOCATED MAXIMUM OF 3'-4"(102)
ABOVE FLOOR

REACHING OR OPERATED PORTION OF ANY
ACCESSORY SHOULD BE LOCATED
MINIMUM 2'-0" (61) ABOVE FLOOR

AVOID FIXTURE MOUNTED GRABS WHICH
MAY LOOSEN

USE TOWEL BARS WHICH ARE OBVIOUSLY
NOT GRABS, MOUNT HIGHER THAN GRABS

DETAIL 4.67   Accessory heights

Toilets

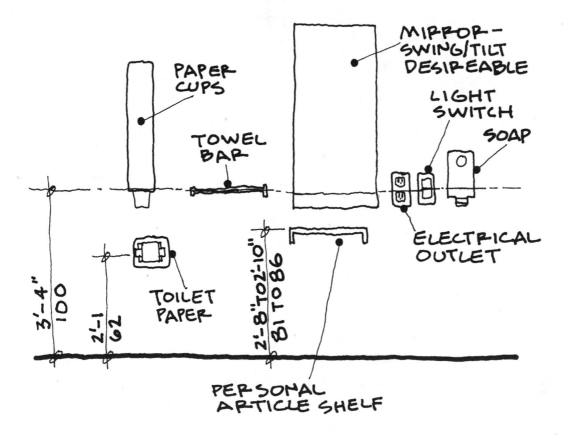

DETAIL 4.68   Accessory heights

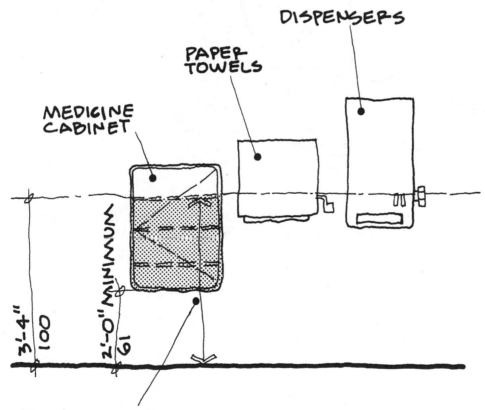

DISPENSERS

PAPER
TOWELS

MEDICINE
CABINET

2'-0" MINIMUM
61

3'-4"
100

5'-0" FOR AMBULANT
4'-3" FOR WHEELCHAIR
75% OF STORAGE VOLUME
WITHIN 4'-0" (122) OF FLOOR

DETAIL 4.69   Accessory heights

Bath

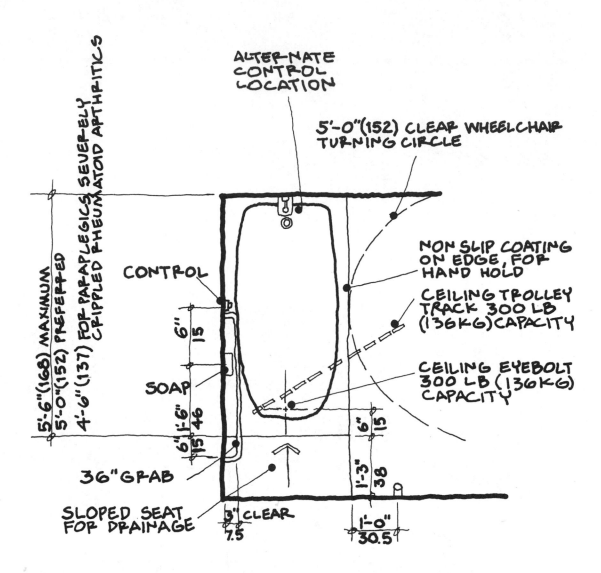

ALTERNATE CONTROL LOCATION

5'-0"(152) CLEAR WHEELCHAIR TURNING CIRCLE

NON SLIP COATING ON EDGE, FOR HAND HOLD

CEILING TROLLEY TRACK 300 LB (136KG) CAPACITY

CEILING EYEBOLT 300 LB (136KG) CAPACITY

5'-6"(168) MAXIMUM
5'-0"(152) PREFERRED
4'-6"(137) FOR PARAPLEGICS SEVERELY CRIPPLED RHEUMATOID ARTHRITICS

CONTROL

6"
15

SOAP

6" 1'-6"
15 46

6"
15

36"GRAB

6"
15

1'-3"
38

SLOPED SEAT FOR DRAINAGE

3" CLEAR
7.5

1'-0"
30.5

PROVIDE TUB SEAT 15"(38) BY FULL WIDTH, MAXIMUM 17"-20"(43-51) ABOVE BOTTOM OF TUB

ALL WATER CONTROLS SINGLE LEVER, THERMOSTATICALLY GUARDED

HAND HELD SHOWER SHOULD HAVE SHUT OFF; MIX VALVE IN HANDLE IS DESIRABLE

AVOID DOUBLE HANDLE MIX VALVES

ALL MIX VALVES SHOULD BE OPERATED BY GROSS HAND MOVEMENTS ONLY

AVOID SHOWER DOORS ON TUB

ALL GRABS SHOULD HAVE NON-SLIP SURFACES

PROVIDE LEVER TYPE DRAIN PLUG CONTROL

AVOID COLD (TILE/ENAMELED CAST IRON) SURFACES

DO NOT USE DIAGONAL GRABS (EXTREMELY DANGEROUS)

DETAIL 4.70   Wheelchair tub with seat

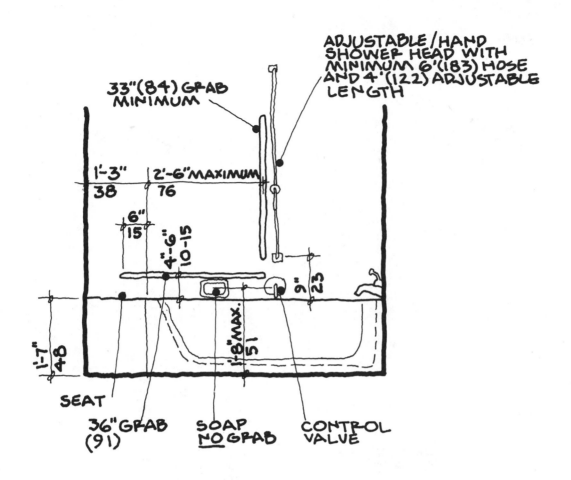

ADJUSTABLE/HAND
SHOWER HEAD WITH
MINIMUM 6'(183) HOSE
AND 4'(122) ADJUSTABLE
LENGTH

33"(84) GRAB
MINIMUM

1'-3"
38

2'-6" MAXIMUM
76

6"
15

4'-6"
10-15

9"
23

1'-7"
48

1'-8" MAX.
51

SEAT

36" GRAB
(91)

SOAP
NO GRAB

CONTROL
VALUE

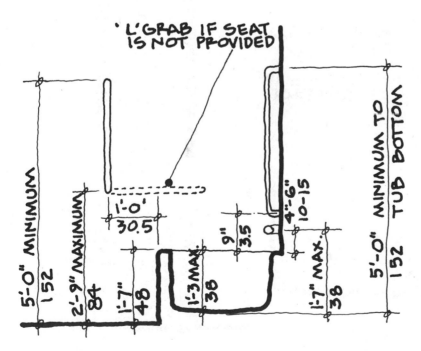

'L' GRAB IF SEAT
IS NOT PROVIDED

5'-0" MINIMUM
152

2'-9" MAXIMUM
84

1'-7"
48

1'-3" MAX.
38

9"
3.5

1'-0'
30.5

4'-6"
10-15

1'-7" MAX.
38

5'-0" MINIMUM TO
152 TUB BOTTOM

DETAIL 4.71 Wheelchair tub with seat

Bath

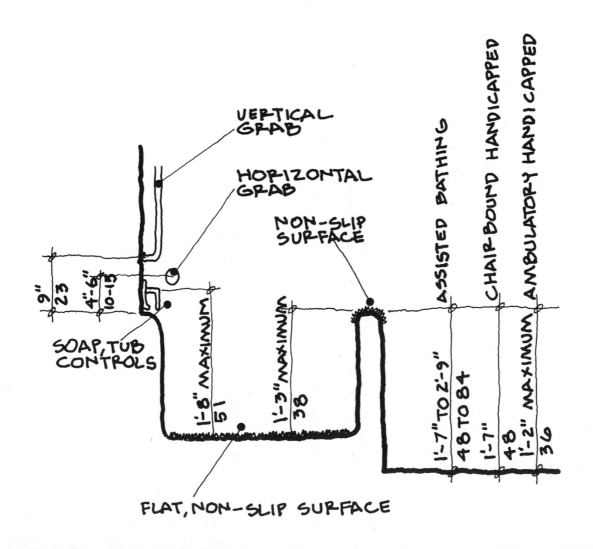

DETAIL 4.72 Accessible bathtub

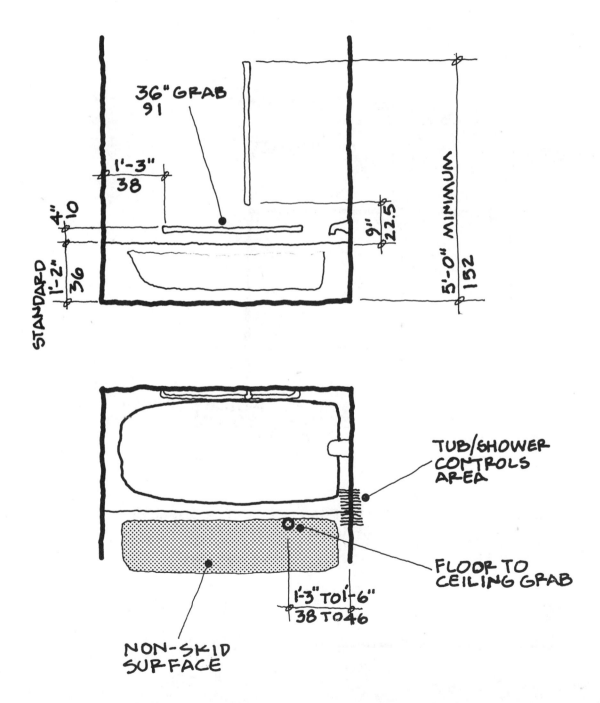

36" GRAB
91

1'-3"
38

4"
10

STANDARD
1'-2"
36

9"
22.5

5'-0" MINIMUM
152

TUB/SHOWER
CONTROLS
AREA

FLOOR TO
CEILING GRAB

1'-3" TO 1'-6"
38 TO 46

NON-SKID
SURFACE

DETAIL 4.73 Ambulatory tub

Bath

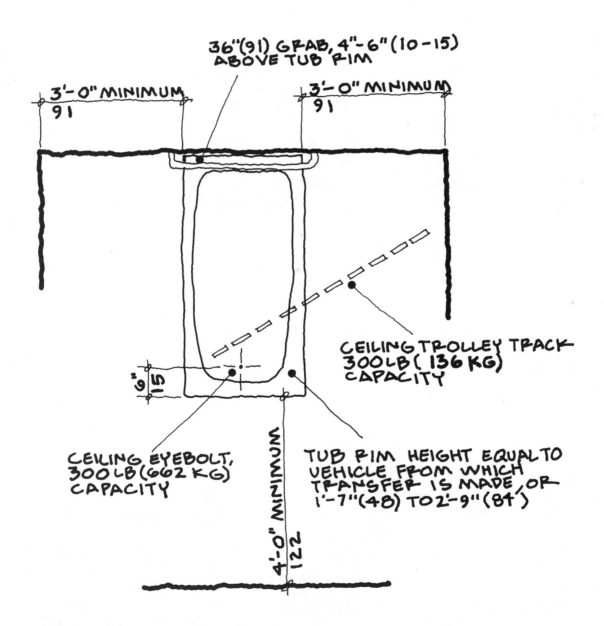

36"(91) GRAB, 4"-6"(10-15) ABOVE TUB RIM

3'-0" MINIMUM 91

3'-0" MINIMUM 91

CEILING TROLLEY TRACK 300 LB (136 KG) CAPACITY

6" 15

CEILING EYEBOLT, 300 LB (662 KG) CAPACITY

4'-0" MINIMUM 122

TUB RIM HEIGHT EQUAL TO VEHICLE FROM WHICH TRANSFER IS MADE, OR 1'-7"(48) TO 2'-9"(84)

DETAIL 4.74   Assisted tub

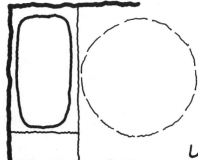

LEFT LATERAL APPROACH

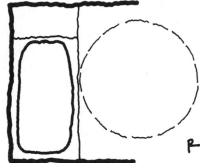

RIGHT LATERAL APPROACH

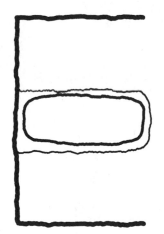

ASSISTED BATHING

IN RESIDENTIAL FACILITIES FOR THE
HANDICAPPED, PROVIDE 3 (DIFFERENT)
TYPE TUBS

DETAIL 4.75 Bathtub approaches

Shower

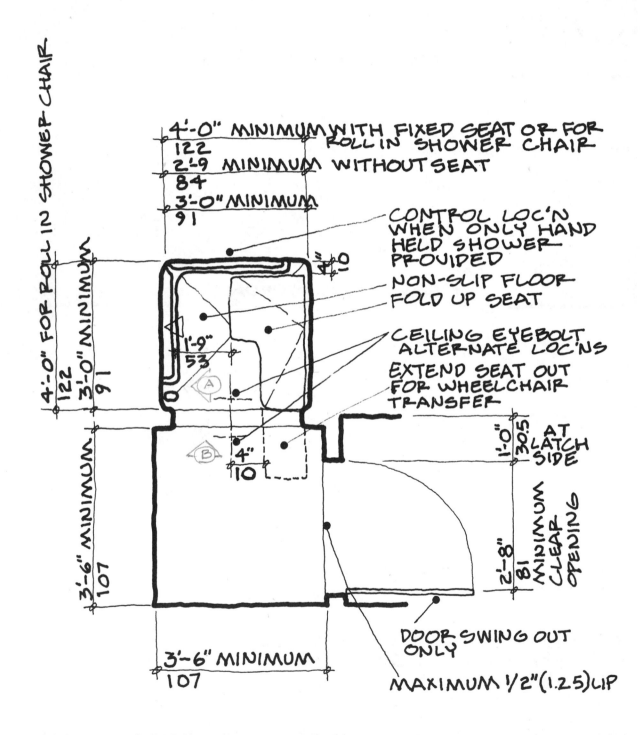

4'-0" FOR ROLL IN SHOWER CHAIR

4'-0" MINIMUM WITH FIXED SEAT OR FOR ROLL IN SHOWER CHAIR
122

2'-9 MINIMUM WITHOUT SEAT
84

3'-0" MINIMUM
91

4'-0" FOR ROLL IN SHOWER CHAIR

3'-0" MINIMUM
91

4'-0"
122

3'-0"
91

CONTROL LOC'N WHEN ONLY HAND HELD SHOWER PROVIDED

NON-SLIP FLOOR
FOLD UP SEAT

CEILING EYEBOLT ALTERNATE LOC'NS

EXTEND SEAT OUT FOR WHEELCHAIR TRANSFER

1'-9"
53

A

B

4"
10

3'-6" MINIMUM
107

1'-0"
305

AT LATCH SIDE

2'-8"
81

MINIMUM CLEAR OPENING

3'-6" MINIMUM
107

DOOR SWING OUT ONLY

MAXIMUM 1/2"(1.25)LIP

DETAIL 4.76   Wheelchair shower

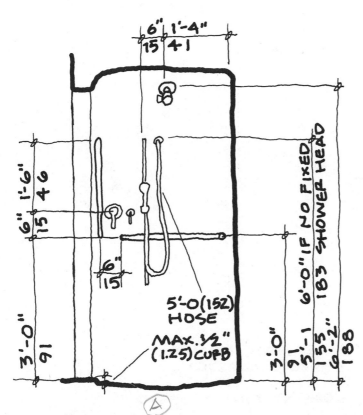

SECOND MIX VALVE LOCATION ON SIDE WALL
AND ACCESSIBLE FROM SEAT WITH LIMITED
ARM REACH

ALL WATER SUPPLY — SHOWER HEAD AND
HOSE MUST BE THERMOSTATICALLY
GUARDED

PROVIDE SINGLE LEVER MIXING VALVE ONLY

HAND HELD SHOWER SHOULD HAVE SHUT OFF;
IF ONLY HAND SHOWER IS PROVIDED, IT
SHOULD HAVE MIX VALVE IN HANDLE

AVOID SLATTED BOARD SEAT

SEAT SHOULD BE SELF DRAINING

DETAIL 4.77   Wheelchair shower

Shower

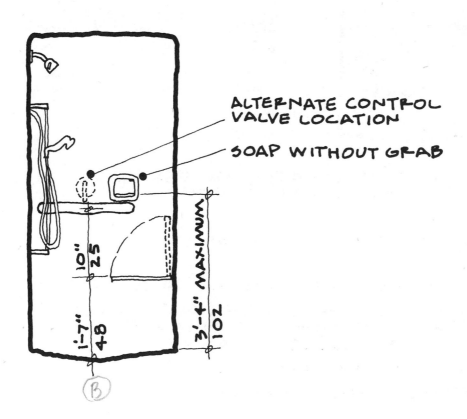

ALTERNATE CONTROL
VALVE LOCATION

SOAP WITHOUT GRAB

10" 25

1'-7" 48

3'-4" MAXIMUM 102

B

DETAIL 4.78   Wheelchair shower

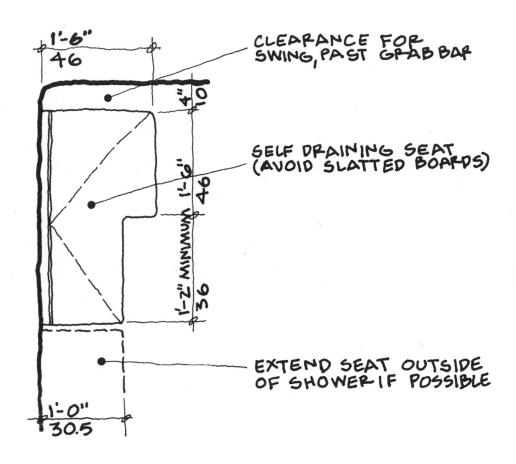

CLEARANCE FOR
SWING, PAST GRAB BAR

1'-6"
46

4" / 10

SELF DRAINING SEAT
(AVOID SLATTED BOARDS)

1'-6"
46

1'-2" MINIMUM
36

EXTEND SEAT OUTSIDE
OF SHOWER IF POSSIBLE

1'-0"
30.5

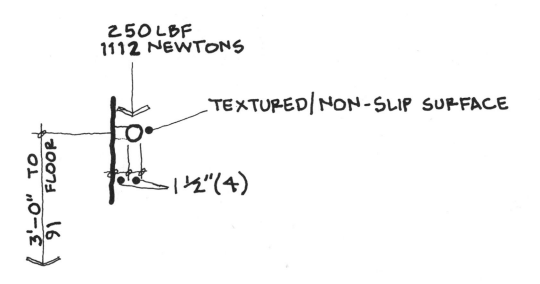

250 LBF
1112 NEWTONS

TEXTURED/NON-SLIP SURFACE

3'-0" TO FLOOR
91

1½"(4)

DETAIL 4.79   Shower seat

Kitchen

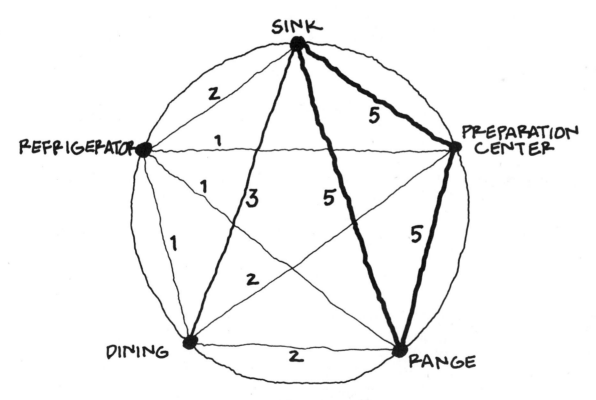

STRONG RELATIONSHIP: 5
WEAK RELATIONSHIP: 1

DETAIL 4.80   Dining/preparation relationships

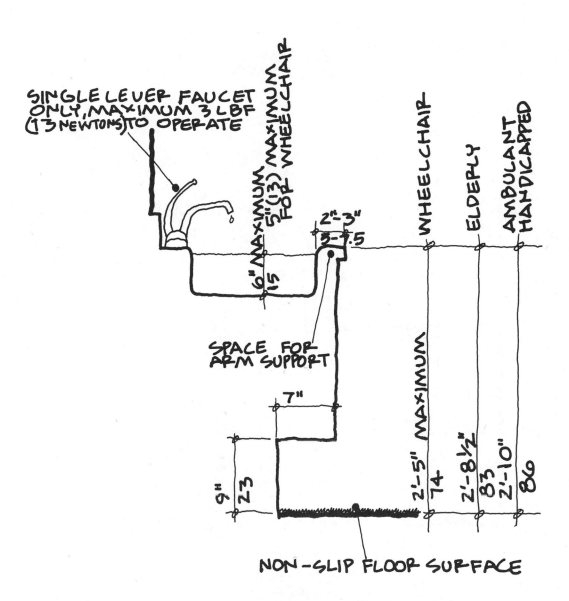

SINGLE LEVER FAUCET ONLY, MAXIMUM 3 LBF (13 NEWTONS) TO OPERATE

5" (13) MAXIMUM MAXIMUM FOR WHEELCHAIR

6" 15

2"-3"
5-7.5

SPACE FOR ARM SUPPORT

7"

9" 23

WHEELCHAIR

ELDERLY

AMBULANT HANDICAPPED

2'-5" MAXIMUM 74

2'-8½" 83

2'-10" 86

NON-SLIP FLOOR SURFACE

BELT ATTACHED TO CABINET FRONT AIDS PARAPLEGICS TO STAND AND WORK AT SINK (MEDICALLY DESIREABLE)

AVOID SELF CLOSING TAPS

SCREW TYPE TAPS MUST HAVE EASILY GRASPED HANDLES (PREFER SINGLE LEVER TYPE VALVES)

DETAIL 4.81 Kitchen sink

Kitchen

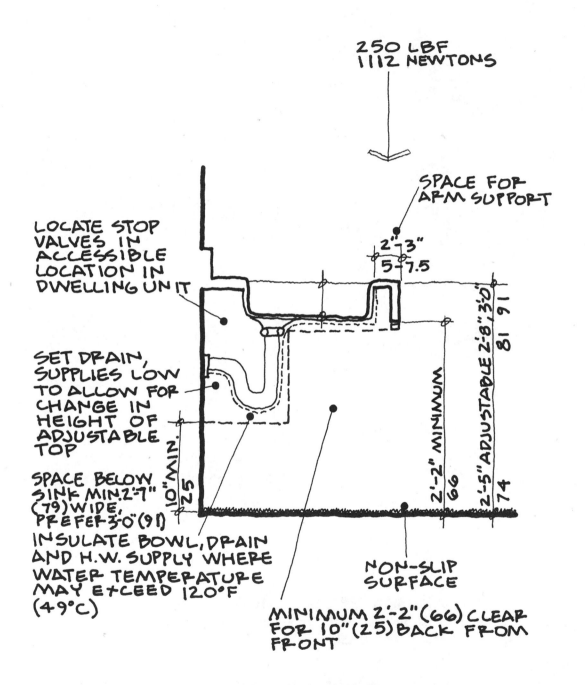

250 LBF
1112 NEWTONS

SPACE FOR
ARM SUPPORT

2"-3"
5-7.5

LOCATE STOP
VALVES IN
ACCESSIBLE
LOCATION IN
DWELLING UNIT

81 91
ADJUSTABLE 2'-8",3'-0"

2'-2" MINIMUM
66

SET DRAIN,
SUPPLIES LOW
TO ALLOW FOR
CHANGE IN
HEIGHT OF
ADJUSTABLE
TOP

2'-5" ADJUSTABLE
74

10" MIN.
25

SPACE BELOW
SINK MIN 2'-7"
(79) WIDE,
PREFER 3'-0" (91)

NON-SLIP
SURFACE

INSULATE BOWL, DRAIN
AND H.W. SUPPLY WHERE
WATER TEMPERATURE
MAY EXCEED 120°F
(49°C)

MINIMUM 2'-2" (66) CLEAR
FOR 10" (25) BACK FROM
FRONT

BELT ATTACHED TO CABINET FRONT
AIDS PARAPLEGICS TO STAND AND
WORK AT SINK (MEDICALLY DESIREABLE)

DETAIL 4.82 Kitchen sink

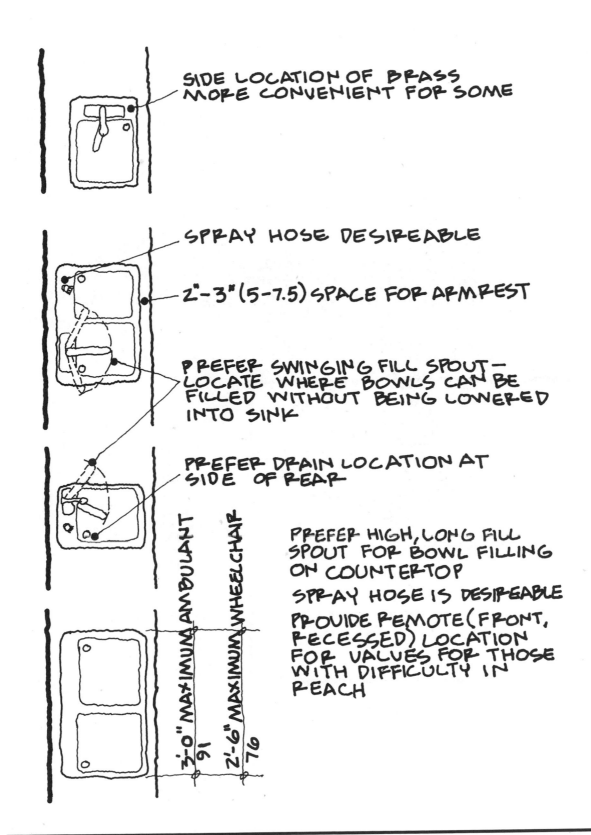

SIDE LOCATION OF BRASS
MORE CONVENIENT FOR SOME

SPRAY HOSE DESIREABLE

2"-3" (5-7.5) SPACE FOR ARMREST

PREFER SWINGING FILL SPOUT —
LOCATE WHERE BOWLS CAN BE
FILLED WITHOUT BEING LOWERED
INTO SINK

PREFER DRAIN LOCATION AT
SIDE OF REAR

PREFER HIGH, LONG FILL
SPOUT FOR BOWL FILLING
ON COUNTERTOP

SPRAY HOSE IS DESIREABLE

PROVIDE REMOTE (FRONT,
RECESSED) LOCATION
FOR VALVES FOR THOSE
WITH DIFFICULTY IN
REACH

3'-0" MAXIMUM AMBULANT
91

2'-6" MAXIMUM WHEELCHAIR
76

DETAIL 4.83   Kitchen sink conditions

Kitchen

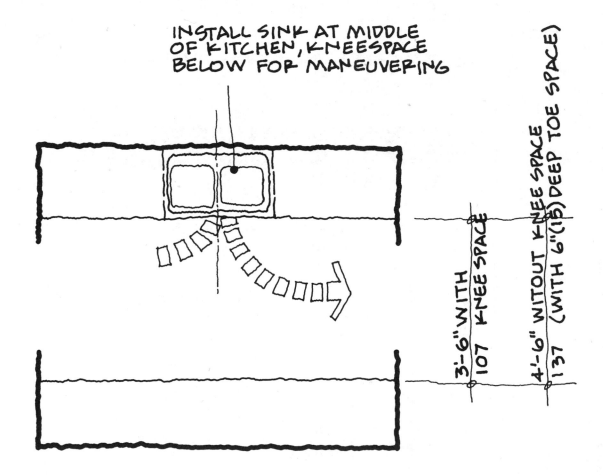

INSTALL SINK AT MIDDLE
OF KITCHEN, KNEESPACE
BELOW FOR MANEUVERING

3'-6" WITH
107 KNEE SPACE

4'-6" WITOUT KNEE SPACE
137 (WITH 6"(15) DEEP TOE SPACE)

DETAIL 4.84   Sink location

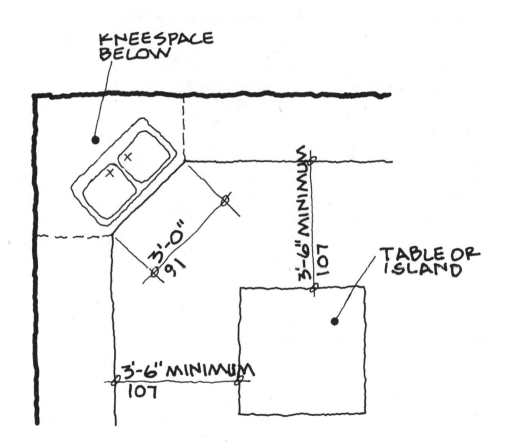

KNEESPACE
BELOW

3'-0"
91

3'-6" MINIMUM
107

TABLE OR
ISLAND

3'-6" MINIMUM
107

KITCHEN SIZED FOR TABLE, AVOIDS NEED
TO CARRY FOOD TO OTHER LOCATIONS

DETAIL 4.85   Kitchen table

Kitchen

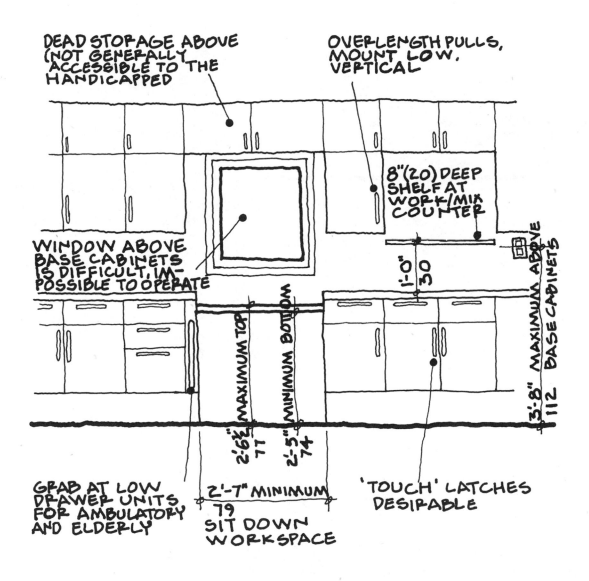

DEAD STORAGE ABOVE (NOT GENERALLY ACCESSIBLE TO THE HANDICAPPED

OVERLENGTH PULLS, MOUNT LOW, VERTICAL

8" (20) DEEP SHELF AT WORK/MIX COUNTER

WINDOW ABOVE BASE CABINETS IS DIFFICULT, IMPOSSIBLE TO OPERATE

1'-0" 30

2'-6½" 77 MAXIMUM TOP

2'-5" 74 MINIMUM BOTTOM

3'-8" 112 MAXIMUM ABOVE BASE CABINETS

GRAB AT LOW DRAWER UNITS FOR AMBULATORY AND ELDERLY

2'-7" MINIMUM 79 SIT DOWN WORKSPACE

'TOUCH' LATCHES DESIRABLE

DETAIL 4.86 Kitchen cabinets

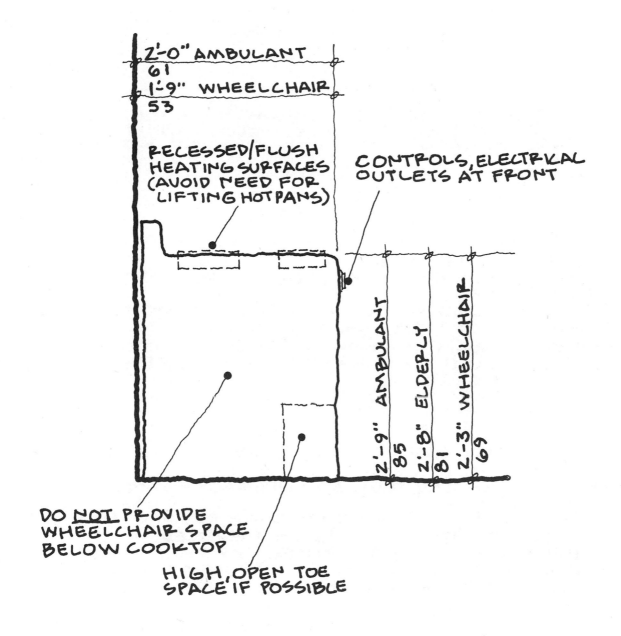

2'-0" AMBULANT
61
1'-9" WHEELCHAIR
53

RECESSED/FLUSH
HEATING SURFACES
(AVOID NEED FOR
LIFTING HOT PANS)

CONTROLS, ELECTRICAL
OUTLETS AT FRONT

2'-9" AMBULANT
85

2'-8" ELDERLY
81

2'-3" WHEELCHAIR
69

DO NOT PROVIDE
WHEELCHAIR SPACE
BELOW COOKTOP

HIGH, OPEN TOE
SPACE IF POSSIBLE

DETAIL 4.87   Range/cooktop

Kitchen

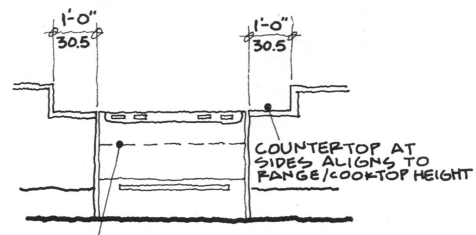

ALTERNATE: ADJUSTIBLE HEIGHT 'DROP IN' COOKTOP (BLANK PANEL BELOW TO AVOID WHEELCHAIR KNEESPACE: ADJUSTIBLE TO 2'-4", 2'-8", 3'-0" (71.5, 81, 91) HEIGHTS

COUNTERTOP AT SIDES ALIGNS TO RANGE/COOKTOP HEIGHT

(a)

GAS:

CAN BE HEARD BY BLIND
HEAT CEASES QUICKLY - FOOD CAN BE LEFT ON RANGE WHEN DONE
PROVIDE AUTOMATIC SHUTOFF CONTROL FOR FLAME/PILOT LIGHT NON FUNCTION
GENERAL USE; RESIDENCES FOR THE BLIND RANGE SHOULD HAVE EASILY SEEN CONTROLS:

ELECTRIC:

MORE EASILY SHUTOFF BY THOSE WITH HAND DISORDERS
MANY ELDERLY AND DISABLED PERSONS CANNOT SMELL GAS
RESIDUAL HEAT IN ELECTRIC COILS IS DANGEROUS FOR THE BLIND AND SENSORY DISABLED
PREFER FOR THE RESIDENCES FOR THE ELDERLY, THOSE WITH OLEFACTORY DISORDERS, THOSE WITH HAND DISORDERS

(b)

DETAIL 4.88a   Range/cooktop
DETAIL 4.88b   Range/cooktop selection

IN LINE COOKING ELEMENTS

'UP FRONT' CONTROLS

'UP FRONT' CONTROLS

PREFER ELEMENT ARRANGEMENT TO AVOID REACH OVER OTHER COOKING ELEMENTS

WHERE IN LINE COOKING IS NOT AVAILABLE, PROVIDE FULLY STAGGERED ELEMENTS, AVOID REACH OVER OTHER COOKING ELEMENTS

LOCATE CONTROLS TO AVOID REACHING OVER HEATING ELEMENTS

DETAIL 4.89   Range/cooktops

Kitchen

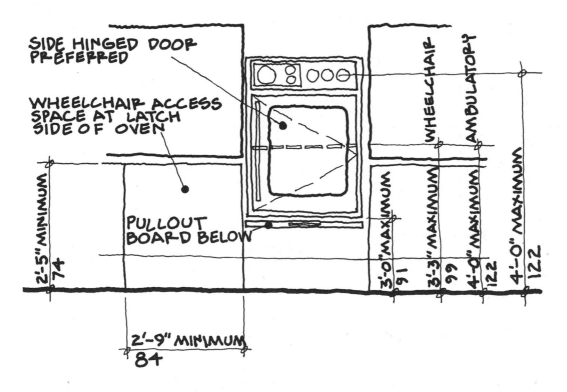

SIDE HINGED DOOR PREFERRED

WHEELCHAIR ACCESS SPACE AT LATCH SIDE OF OVEN

PULLOUT BOARD BELOW

2'-5" MINIMUM
74

2'-9" MINIMUM
84

3'-0" MAXIMUM
91

3'-3" MAXIMUM
99

WHEELCHAIR

4'-0" MAXIMUM
122

AMBULATORY

4'-0" MAXIMUM
122

OVEN SHELVES: NON TIP
NON PULL OUT

OVENS WITHOUT SIDE WHEELCHAIR SPACE FOR ACCESS SHOULD BE SELF CLEANING

OVENS SHOULD HAVE INTERIOR LIGHT

DETAIL 4.90   Oven

MINIMUM 50% OF FREEZER VOLUME SHOULD BE BELOW 4'-6" (137) FOR SIDE WHEELCHAIR APPROACH, 4'-0" (122) FOR FRONT (PERPENDICULAR APPROACH)

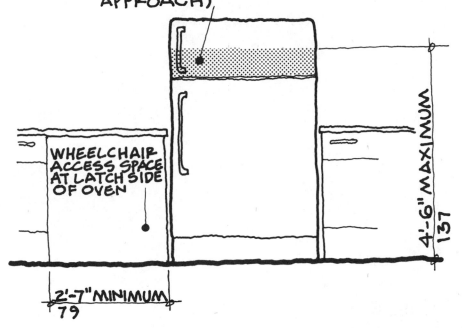

WHEELCHAIR ACCESS SPACE AT LATCH SIDE OF OVEN

4'-6" MAXIMUM
137

2'-7" MINIMUM
79

FREEZER SHOULD BE SELF DEFROSTING TYPE

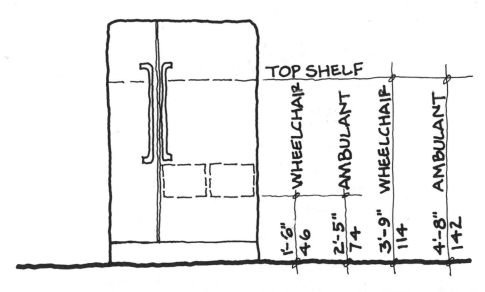

TOP SHELF

WHEELCHAIR

AMBULANT

WHEELCHAIR

AMBULANT

1'-6"
46

2'-5"
74

3'-9"
114

4'-8"
142

WHEELCHAIR ACCESS SPACE DOES NOT APPLY

DETAIL 4.91   Refrigerator/freezer

Kitchen

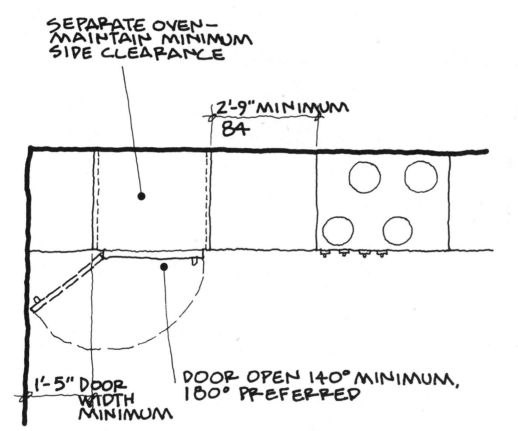

SEPARATE OVEN—
MAINTAIN MINIMUM
SIDE CLEARANCE

2'-9" MINIMUM
84

1'-5" DOOR
WIDTH
MINIMUM

DOOR OPEN 140° MINIMUM,
180° PREFERRED

CLEAR WHEELCHAIR ACCESS MORE
IMPORTANT TO SEPARATE RANGE/COOKTOP
THAN TO OVEN

DETAIL 4.92 Range/oven access

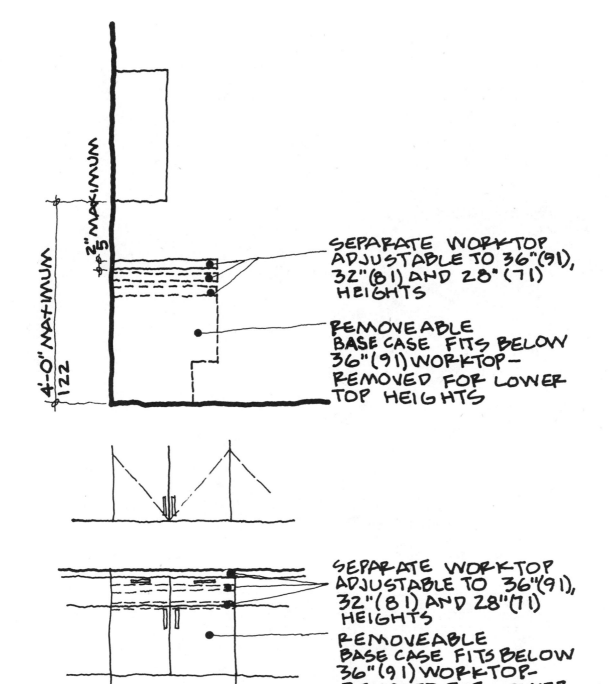

SEPARATE WORKTOP
ADJUSTABLE TO 36"(91),
32"(81) AND 28"(71)
HEIGHTS

REMOVEABLE
BASE CASE FITS BELOW
36"(91) WORKTOP-
REMOVED FOR LOWER
TOP HEIGHTS

SEPARATE WORKTOP
ADJUSTABLE TO 36"(91),
32"(81) AND 28"(71)
HEIGHTS

REMOVEABLE
BASE CASE FITS BELOW
36"(91) WORKTOP-
REMOVED FOR LOWER
TOP HEIGHTS

2" MAXIMUM / 5

4'-0" MAXIMUM / 122

2'-7" MINIMUM / 79

DETAIL 4.93   Kitchen work area

Kitchen

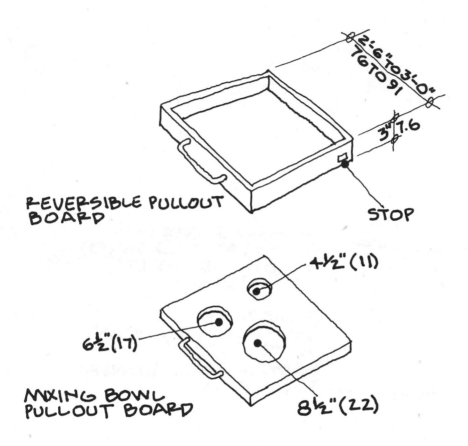

REVERSIBLE PULLOUT BOARD

2'-6" TO 3'-0"
76 TO 91

3" 7.6

STOP

4½" (11)

6½" (17)

MIXING BOWL PULLOUT BOARD

8½" (22)

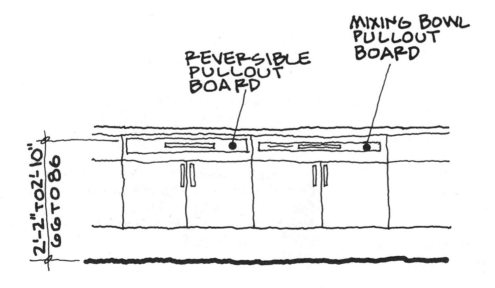

REVERSIBLE PULLOUT BOARD

MIXING BOWL PULLOUT BOARD

2'-2" TO 2'-10"
66 TO 86

DETAIL 4.94   Preparation center

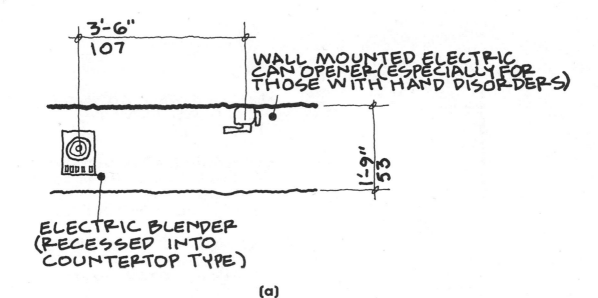

3'-6"
107

WALL MOUNTED ELECTRIC
CAN OPENER (ESPECIALLY FOR
THOSE WITH HAND DISORDERS)

1'-9"
53

ELECTRIC BLENDER
(RECESSED INTO
COUNTERTOP TYPE)

(a)

PREFER FRONT LOADING
PULLOUT OR SWING
DOWN DOOR, ALL SHELVES
ACCESSIBLE

(b)

DETAIL 4.95a　Electric utensils
DETAIL 4.95b　Dishwasher

Kitchen

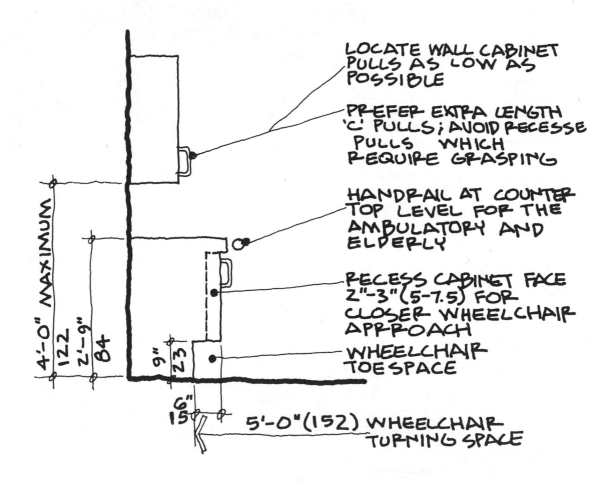

LOCATE WALL CABINET PULLS AS LOW AS POSSIBLE

PREFER EXTRA LENGTH 'C' PULLS; AVOID RECESSE PULLS WHICH REQUIRE GRASPING

HANDRAIL AT COUNTER TOP LEVEL FOR THE AMBULATORY AND ELDERLY

RECESS CABINET FACE 2"-3" (5-7.5) FOR CLOSER WHEELCHAIR APPROACH

WHEELCHAIR TOE SPACE

4'-0" MAXIMUM 122

2'-9" 84

9" 23

6" 15

5'-0" (152) WHEELCHAIR TURNING SPACE

DETAIL 4.96   Typical cabinets

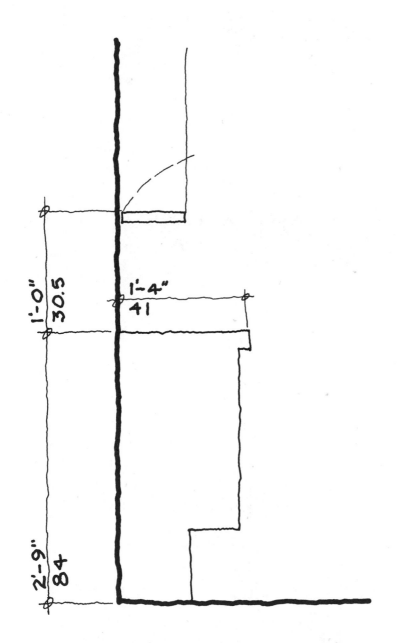

AVOID HIGH DEEP SHELVES (DANGEROUS)
PROVIDE 8"(20) DEEP AUXILARY SHELF
ABOVE COUNTERTOP WHERE POSSIBLE

DETAIL 4.97 "Ideal" wheelchair cabinets

Kitchen

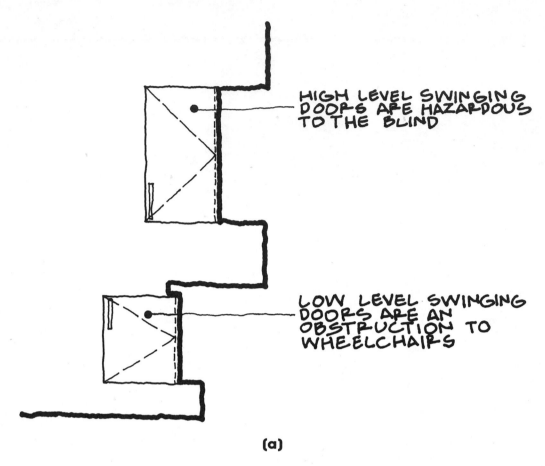

HIGH LEVEL SWINGING
DOORS ARE HAZARDOUS
TO THE BLIND

LOW LEVEL SWINGING
DOORS ARE AN
OBSTRUCTION TO
WHEELCHAIRS

(a)

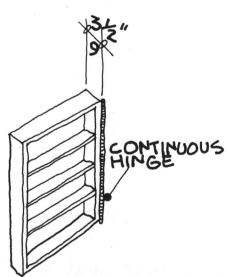

3½"

CONTINUOUS
HINGE

PROVIDE 'LAZY SUSAN'
IN CORNER CABINETS

PROVIDE SHALLOW
STORAGE ON BASE
CABINET DOORS

(b)

DETAIL 4.98a   Cabinet door types
DETAIL 4.98b   In-cabinet storage

LONGEST POSSIBLE CONTINUOUS COUNTERTOP
ALLOW PANS, ETC. TO BE SLID AS MUCH AS
POSSIBLE

DETAIL 4.99   Countertops

Kitchen

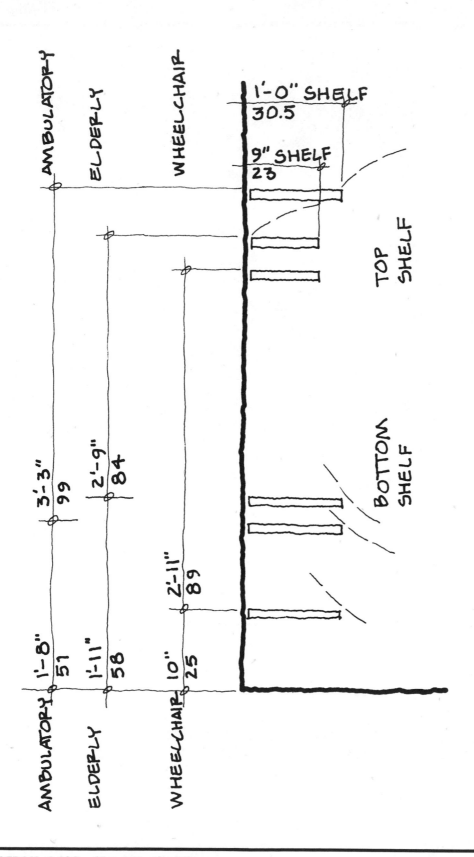

DETAIL 4.100 Storage shelving

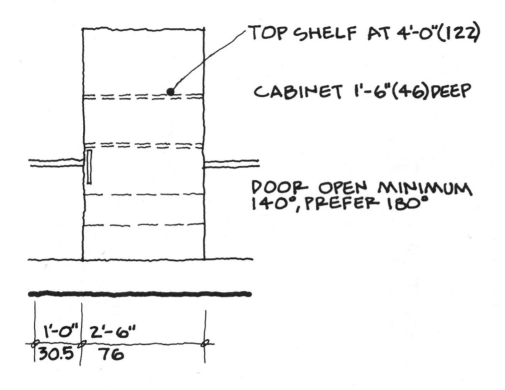

TOP SHELF AT 4'-0"(122)

CABINET 1'-6"(46)DEEP

DOOR OPEN MINIMUM
140°, PREFER 180°

1'-0" | 2'-6"
30.5 | 76

DETAIL 4.101 Storage cabinets

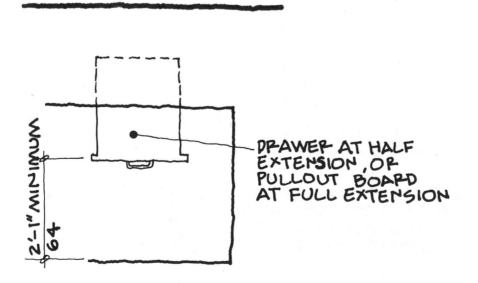

DRAWER AT HALF
EXTENSION, OR
PULLOUT BOARD
AT FULL EXTENSION

2'-1" MINIMUM
64

DETAIL 4.102 Drawer clearance

Kitchen

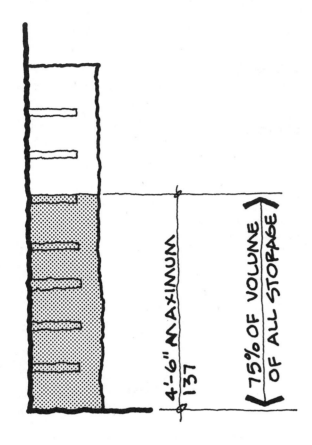

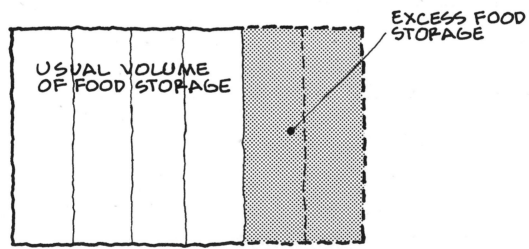

USUAL VOLUME OF FOOD STORAGE

EXCESS FOOD STORAGE

4'-6" MAXIMUM
137

75% OF VOLUME OF ALL STORAGE

PROVIDE EXCESS FOOD STORAGE IN RESIDENCES, APARTMENTS FOR THE HANDICAPPED. (THE HANDICAPPED DEPEND ON DELIVERIES OR DIFFICULT, INFREQUENT SHOPPING TRIPS)

DETAIL 4.103 Kitchen storage volume

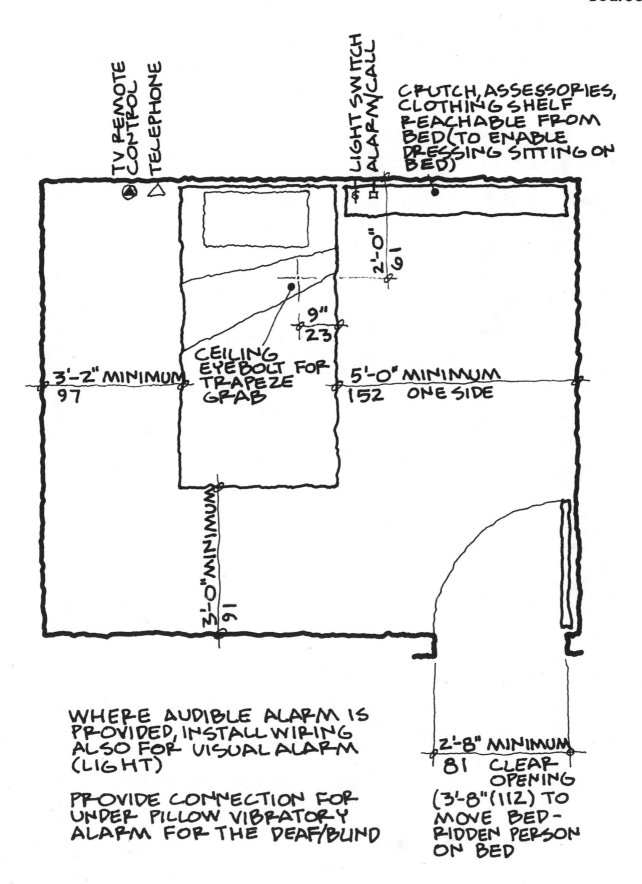

TV REMOTE CONTROL

TELEPHONE

LIGHT SWITCH

ALARM/CALL

CRUTCH, ASSESSORIES, CLOTHING SHELF REACHABLE FROM BED (TO ENABLE DRESSING SITTING ON BED)

2'-0"
61

9"
23

CEILING EYEBOLT FOR TRAPEZE GRAB

3'-2" MINIMUM
97

5'-0" MINIMUM
152   ONE SIDE

3'-0" MINIMUM
91

2'-8" MINIMUM
81   CLEAR OPENING (3'-8" (112) TO MOVE BED-RIDDEN PERSON ON BED

WHERE AUDIBLE ALARM IS PROVIDED, INSTALL WIRING ALSO FOR VISUAL ALARM (LIGHT)

PROVIDE CONNECTION FOR UNDER PILLOW VIBRATORY ALARM FOR THE DEAF/BLIND

DETAIL 4.104 Accessible bedroom

Bedroom

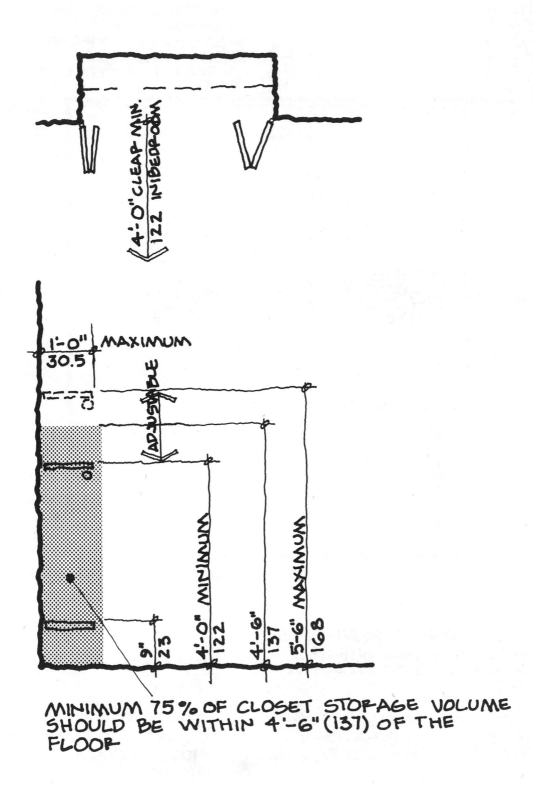

4'-0" CLEAR MIN.
122 IN BEDROOM

1'-0" MAXIMUM
30.5

12

ADJUSTABLE

9" 23

4'-0" MINIMUM 122

4'-6" 137

5'-6" MAXIMUM 168

MINIMUM 75% OF CLOSET STORAGE VOLUME SHOULD BE WITHIN 4'-6" (137) OF THE FLOOR

DETAIL 4.105   Closets

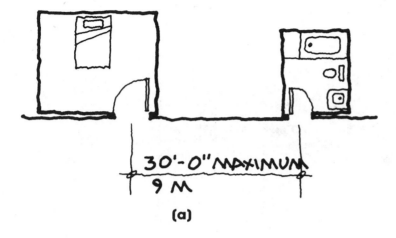

30'-0" MAXIMUM
9 M

(a)

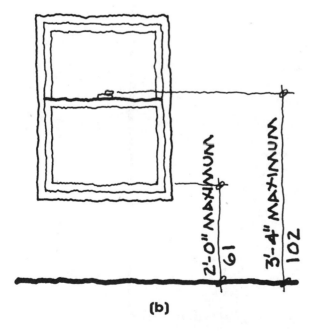

2'-0" MAXIMUM
61

3'-4" MAXIMUM
102

(b)

DETAIL 4.106a   Toilet distance
DETAIL 4.106b   Bedroom window

Dining

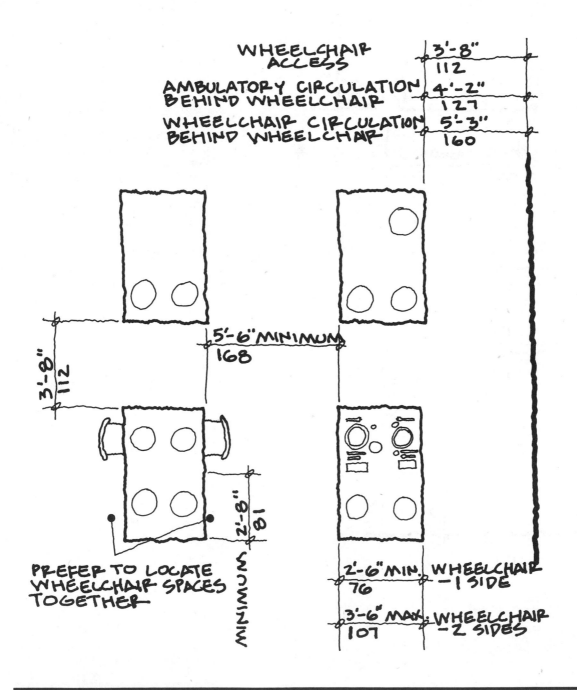

WHEELCHAIR ACCESS — 3'-8" / 112

AMBULATORY CIRCULATION BEHIND WHEELCHAIR — 4'-2" / 127

WHEELCHAIR CIRCULATION BEHIND WHEELCHAIR — 5'-3" / 160

5'-6" MINIMUM / 168

3'-8" / 112

2'-8" / 81 MINIMUM

PREFER TO LOCATE WHEELCHAIR SPACES TOGETHER

2'-6" MIN. / 76 — WHEELCHAIR — 1 SIDE

3'-6" MAX. / 107 — WHEELCHAIR — 2 SIDES

DETAIL 4.107   Dining table

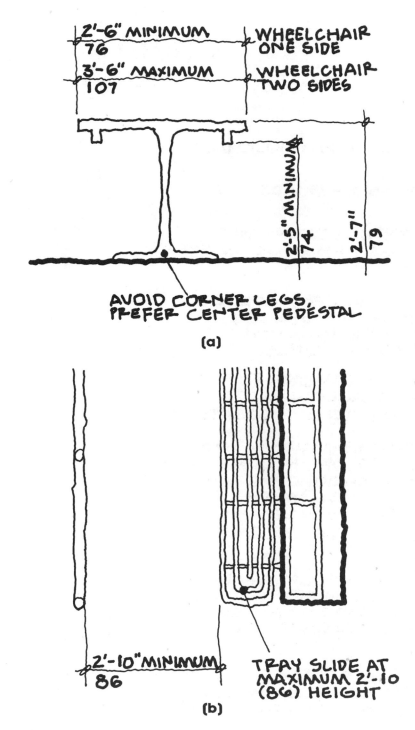

2'-6" MINIMUM
76
3'-6" MAXIMUM
107

WHEELCHAIR ONE SIDE
WHEELCHAIR TWO SIDES

2'-5" MINIMUM
74

2'-7"
79

AVOID CORNER LEGS, PREFER CENTER PEDESTAL

(a)

2'-10" MINIMUM
86

TRAY SLIDE AT MAXIMUM 2'-10 (86) HEIGHT

(b)

DETAIL 4.108a   Dining table
DETAIL 4.108b   Serving line

Assembly

PROVIDE 1% OF SEATING IN WHEELCHAIR SPACES

PROVIDE 1% OF SEATING AS AMBULATORY SEATING

PROVIDE 2% OF EACH TYPE SEATING IN FACILITIES WITH MORE THAN 5000 SQ.FT. (464 SQ.M.) OF SPACE

PROVIDE MINIMUM 8 HANDICAPPED SPACES IN EACH PUBLIC ASSEMBLY SPACE; LOCATE SEATING IN AREAS WITH REPRESENTATIVE SIGHT LINES

PROVIDE WHEELCHAIR LOCATIONS FOR 2 CHAIRS TOGETHER TO ALLOW HANDICAPPED PERSONS TO SIT TOGETHER

PROVIDE 1% OF SEATS, MINIMUM 2, TO BE EQUIPPED WITH LOOP, RF, OR FM LISTENING SYSTEMS. SUCH SEATS SHOULD BE WITHIN 50' (15 M) VIEWING DISTANCE WITH COMPLETE VIEWS. SUCH SPACES SHOULD NOT BE COMBINED WITH WHEELCHAIR SPACES

DISTRIBUTE WHEELCHAIR, AMBULATORY HAND-CAPPED, AND HEARING AIDED SEATING THROUGH-OUT ENTIRE ASSEMBLY AREA - AVOID SEGREGATION, PROVIDE CHOICE OF LOCATION

PROVIDE DEMOUNTABLE SEATS FOR NON-HANDICAPPED USE TO UTILIZE WHEELCHAIR SPACES WHERE SPACE IS AT A PREMIUM

DETAIL 4.109   Assembly seating

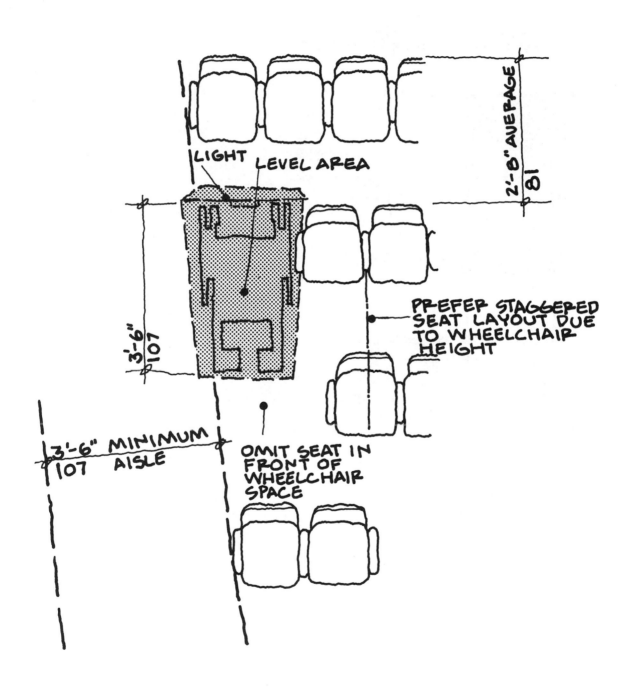

LIGHT LEVEL AREA

2'-8" AVERAGE
81

PREFER STAGGERED
SEAT LAYOUT DUE
TO WHEELCHAIR
HEIGHT

3'-6"
107

3'-6" MINIMUM
107 AISLE

OMIT SEAT IN
FRONT OF
WHEELCHAIR
SPACE

DETAIL 4.110   Wheelchair in seating area

Assembly

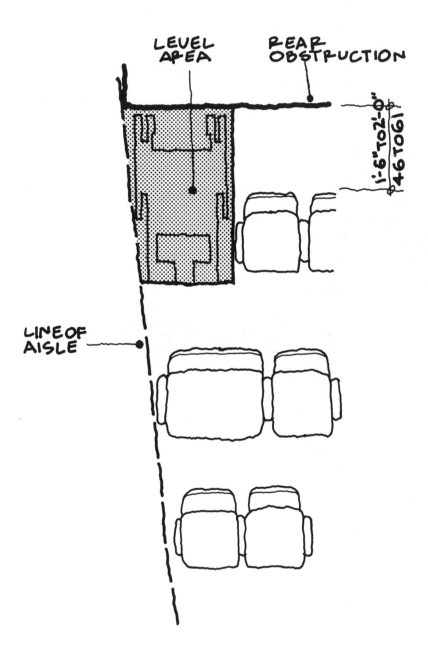

LEVEL AREA

REAR OBSTRUCTION

LINE OF AISLE

1'-6" to 2'-0"
46 to 61

DETAIL 4.111   Wheelchair at rear

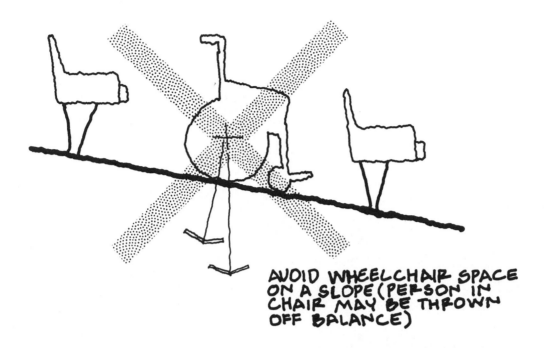

AVOID WHEELCHAIR SPACE ON A SLOPE (PERSON IN CHAIR MAY BE THROWN OFF BALANCE)

DETAIL 4.112

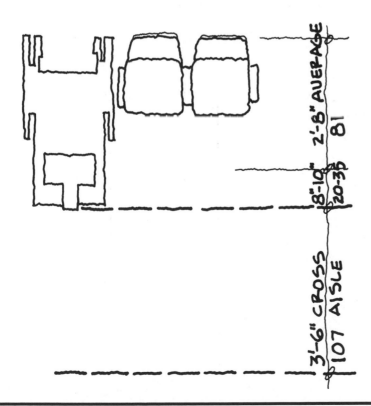

2'-8" AVERAGE
81

8"-10"
20-35

3'-6" CROSS
107 AISLE

DETAIL 4.113   Wheelchair space at cross aisle

Assembly

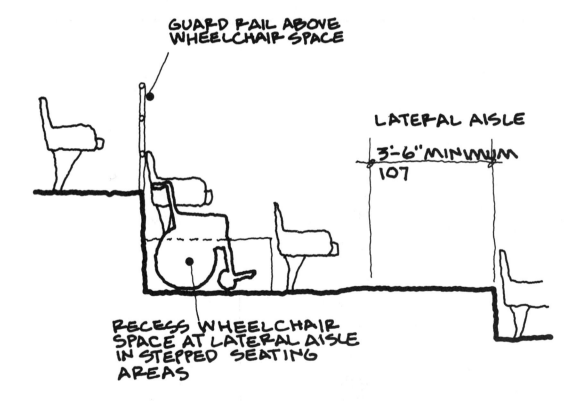

GUARD RAIL ABOVE
WHEELCHAIR SPACE

LATERAL AISLE

3'-6" MINIMUM
107

RECESS WHEELCHAIR
SPACE AT LATERAL AISLE
IN STEPPED SEATING
AREAS

ALL HANDICAPPED SEATING SPACES SHOULD
BE ACCESSIBLE WITHOUT STEPS

DETAIL 4.114   Wheelchair space at cross aisle

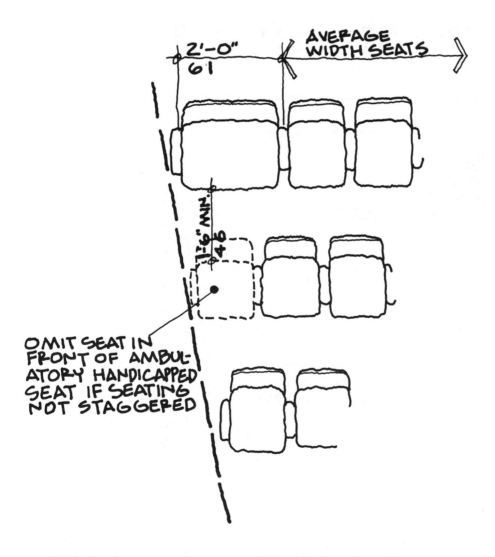

2'-0"
61

AVERAGE WIDTH SEATS

1'-6" MIN.
46

OMIT SEAT IN FRONT OF AMBULATORY HANDICAPPED SEAT IF SEATING NOT STAGGERED

DETAIL 4.115 Ambulant seating

Swimming Pool

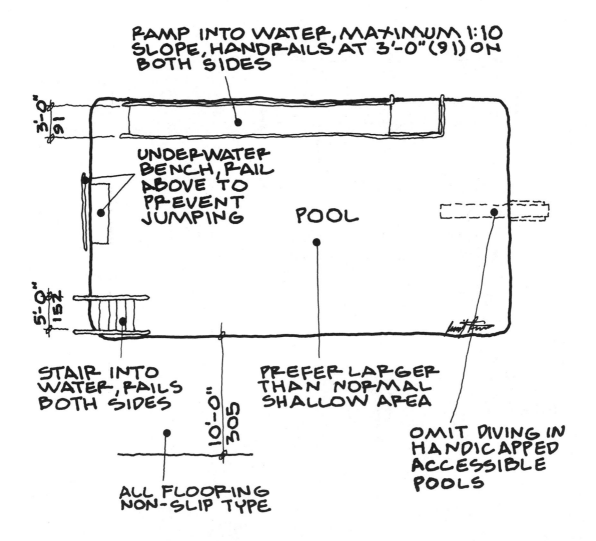

RAMP INTO WATER, MAXIMUM 1:10
SLOPE, HANDRAILS AT 3'-0" (91) ON
BOTH SIDES

3'-0" 91

UNDERWATER
BENCH, RAIL
ABOVE TO
PREVENT
JUMPING

POOL

5'-0" 152

STAIR INTO
WATER, RAILS
BOTH SIDES

10'-0" 305

PREFER LARGER
THAN NORMAL
SHALLOW AREA

OMIT DIVING IN
HANDICAPPED
ACCESSIBLE
POOLS

ALL FLOORING
NON-SLIP TYPE

DETAIL 4.116   Accessible indoor pool

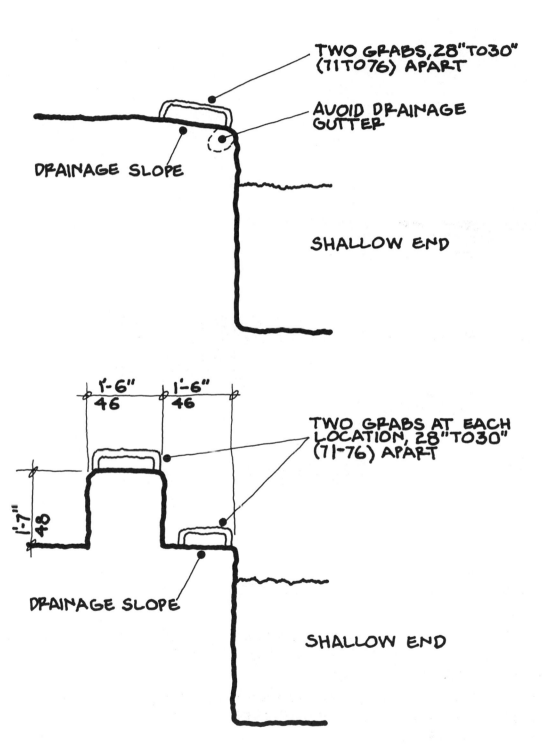

TWO GRABS, 28"TO30"
(71TO76) APART

AVOID DRAINAGE
GUTTER

DRAINAGE SLOPE

SHALLOW END

1'-6"
46

1'-6"
46

TWO GRABS AT EACH
LOCATION, 28"TO30"
(71-76) APART

1'-7"
48

DRAINAGE SLOPE

SHALLOW END

DETAIL 4.117   Pool access locations

Laundry

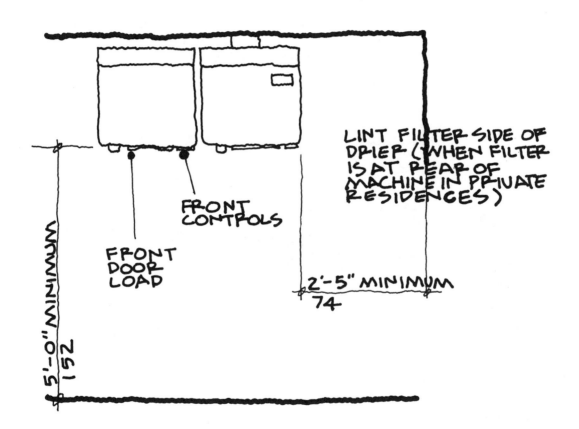

LINT FILTER SIDE OF DRIER (WHEN FILTER IS AT REAR OF MACHINE IN PRIVATE RESIDENCES)

FRONT CONTROLS

FRONT DOOR LOAD

5'-0" MINIMUM 152

2'-5" MINIMUM 74

MINIMUM 1 WASHER, 1 DRIER IN EACH GROUP TO BE WHEELCHAIR ACCESSIBLE (FRONT CONTROLS, FRONT LOAD

PREFER FRONT LOADING WASHER/DRIER COMBINATION FOR WHEELCHAIR USE WHERE POSSIBLE

DETAIL 4.118   Washer/drier criteria

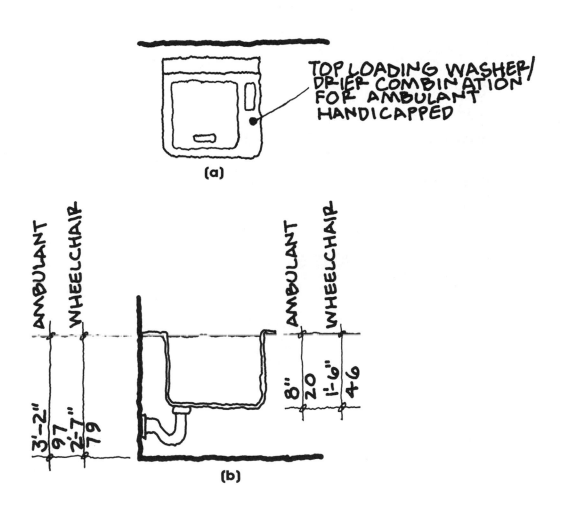

(a)

TOP LOADING WASHER/
DRIER COMBINATION
FOR AMBULANT
HANDICAPPED

AMBULANT

WHEELCHAIR

AMBULANT

WHEELCHAIR

3'-2"
97

2'-7"
79

8"
20

1'-6"
46

(b)

DETAIL 4.119a   Washer/drier combination
DETAIL 4.119b   Laundry sink

Laundry

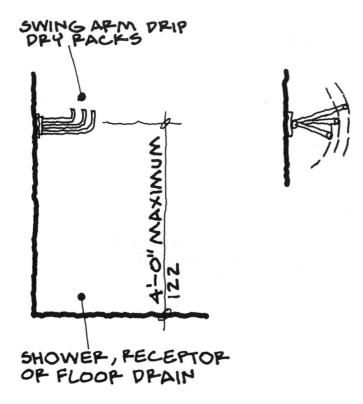

SWING ARM DRIP
DRY RACKS

4'-0" MAXIMUM
122

SHOWER, RECEPTOR
OR FLOOR DRAIN

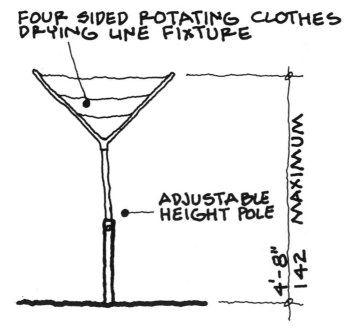

FOUR SIDED ROTATING CLOTHES
DRYING LINE FIXTURE

ADJUSTABLE
HEIGHT POLE

4'-8" MAXIMUM
142

DETAIL 4.120   Drying racks

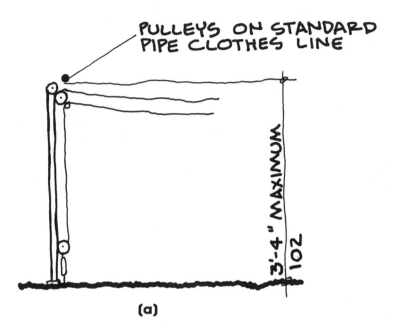

PULLEYS ON STANDARD
PIPE CLOTHES LINE

3'-4" MAXIMUM
102

(a)

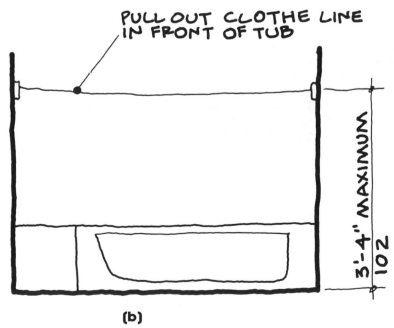

PULL OUT CLOTHE LINE
IN FRONT OF TUB

3'-4" MAXIMUM
102

(b)

DETAIL 4.121a Accessible clothesline
DETAIL 4.121b Laundry drying

Sewing and Ironing

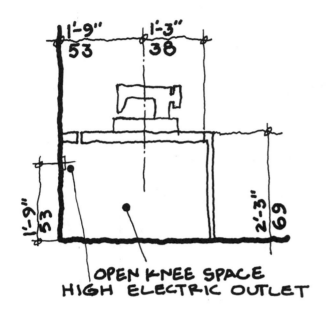

OPEN KNEE SPACE
HIGH ELECTRIC OUTLET

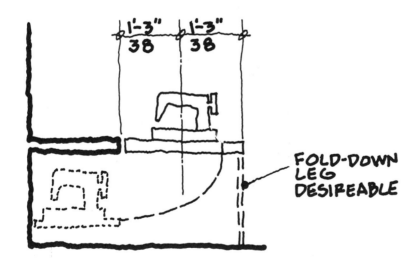

FOLD-DOWN
LEG
DESIREABLE

DETAIL 4.122   Sewing machine

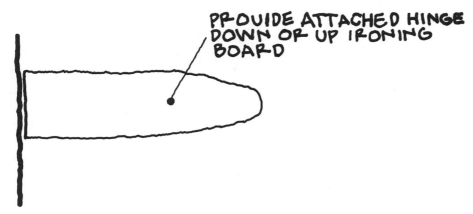

PROVIDE ATTACHED HINGE DOWN OR UP IRONING BOARD

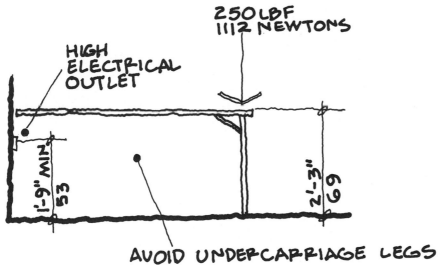

250 LBF
1112 NEWTONS

HIGH ELECTRICAL OUTLET

1'-9" MIN 53

2'-3" 69

AVOID UNDERCARRIAGE LEGS

AVOID PORTABLE IRONING BOARDS (UNSTABLE, DIFFICULT TO SET UP)

DETAIL 4.123 Ironing boards

Part Five
Building Elements

DOORS AND HARDWARE

Doors for use by the person with limited mobility would ideally be the lightest, smallest size usable. For a swinging door this would be a hollow-core door approximately 34 1/4' wide (53). Wider and heavier doors, having more inertia, are more difficult to open. A 4' wide (122) solid-core door is the maximum which should be used in a handicapped-accessible location. A door of such size and weight, if used with any frequency by those with difficulties of mobility, should be hung on ball-bearing butts.

Bifolding doors are probably the most easily operated by the person with difficulty in movement since they fold out of the person's way when operated. Open bifold doors, however, may pose a barrier to easy movement of handicapped persons. Wide folding and sliding doors are more difficult to use because of the need for a person, fixed in one location, to stretch to operate the door to its full width. Pocket sliding doors can pose special problems for those with limited hand manipulative ability if they are fully recessed. A pocket sliding door should be arranged to have either a nonrecessed pull on its leading edge or to have enough of the door side remain exposed to allow mounting a nonrecessed pull on the side when fully open. Totally recessed doors with recessed pulls are very difficult for those with hand and finger disabilities. Very heavy sliding doors should have a system of grabs nearby to provide the person in a wheelchair with a handhold to steady himself or herself while operating the door. The primary criterion for the selection of hardware must be its ability to be grasped and operated by those with limited ability to manipulate their hands. Generally this means that all hardware must be surface-mounted rather than recessed. Cabinet and lightweight door pulls should be in the form of "C" pulls at least 4″ (10) long or longer, with preferably up to 1½″ (3.75) clearances. Such pulls will allow a person to slip his or her hand behind the pull without the need to grasp it. Typical small knobs which require grasping should be avoided.

Door latch and locksets should use lever handles, again in order to avoid the need for grasping. Lever handles, since they are able to be operated without being taken hold of, are ideal for handicapped locations. Fountains, accessories, phones, and the operating controls of all equipment must be located so that a wheelchair can be either positioned under the element or brought alongside. For the operating elements which can be approached only head-on without kneespace below them, controls should be no higher than 3′-4″ (100), while those which a wheelchair can approach alongside may be located up to 4′-0″ (122) above the floor. Electrical switches and other controls must be located within the above limits; outlets should be relatively high off the floor. Higher mounting for electrical outlets is more convenient for those in crutches and walkers and for the elderly, who may be prone to dizziness. In institutions for the blind, spring-loaded outlet covers enable a person to feel the location of an outlet without danger of electrical shock.

Wall finishes should be relatively damage-resistant in areas with heavy wheelchair traffic, while at the same time avoiding an "institutional" appearance. The designer should consider the probability of damage at each location throughout a building, and prefer to guard the most vulnerable locations most heavily. The designer should recall the desirability of a relatively "live," sound-reflective environment for the blind, and of relatively "dead," quiet surroundings for the hearing-impaired. Floor coverings should generally be more hard or dense for wheelchair users and those with impediments of movement. Very soft, deep, or movable floor coverings should be avoided.

Uniform locations for tactile warnings and signage for the blind is highly desirable. The current recommendation for knurled or roughened door hardware at access points to areas dangerous for the blind exists in many codes. The designer should give careful and individual consideration to markings and warnings for the blind, since these warnings can be a matter of extreme consequence.

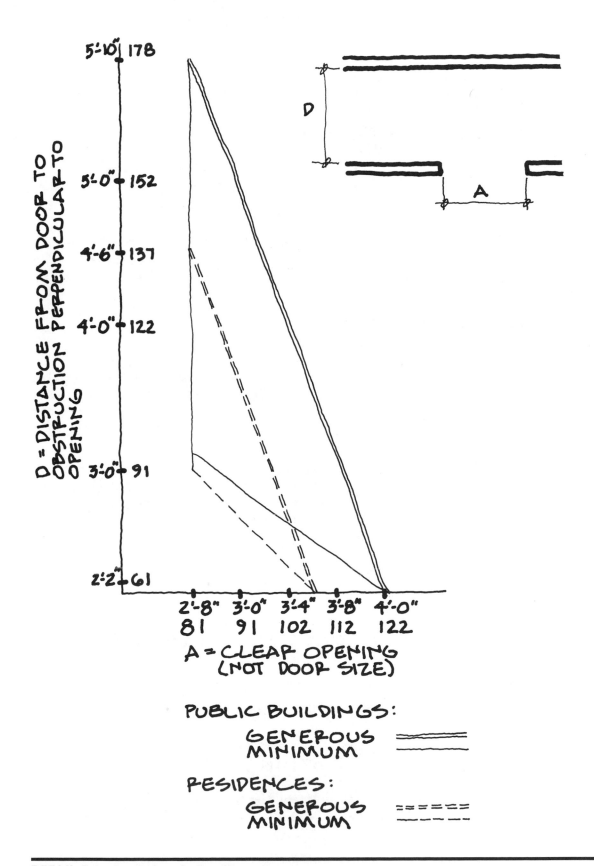

DETAIL 5.1   Door-to-obstruction clearance

Doors

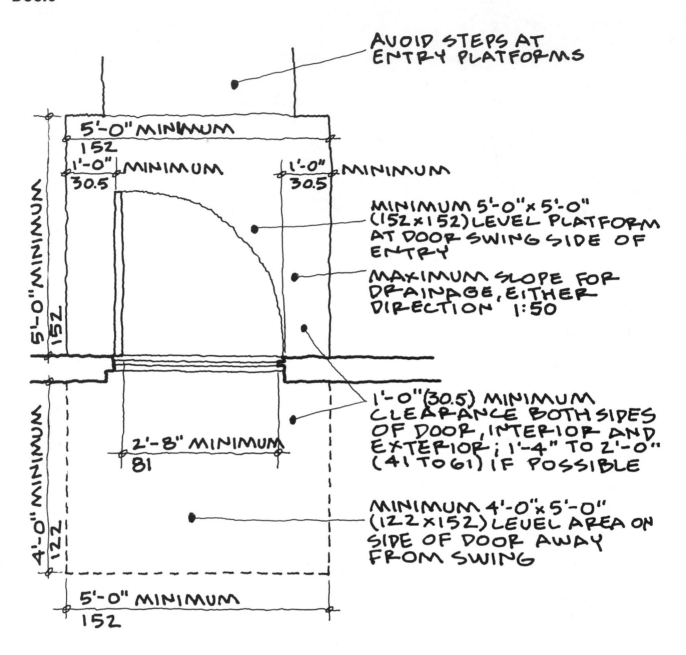

AVOID STEPS AT ENTRY PLATFORMS

5'-0" MINIMUM
152

1'-0" MINIMUM
30.5

1'-0" MINIMUM
30.5

5'-0" MINIMUM
152

MINIMUM 5'-0" x 5'-0" (152 x 152) LEVEL PLATFORM AT DOOR SWING SIDE OF ENTRY

MAXIMUM SLOPE FOR DRAINAGE, EITHER DIRECTION 1:50

4'-0" MINIMUM
122

2'-8" MINIMUM
81

1'-0" (30.5) MINIMUM CLEARANCE BOTH SIDES OF DOOR, INTERIOR AND EXTERIOR; 1'-4" TO 2'-0" (41 TO 61) IF POSSIBLE

MINIMUM 4'-0" x 5'-0" (122 x 152) LEVEL AREA ON SIDE OF DOOR AWAY FROM SWING

5'-0" MINIMUM
152

ENTRY/EXIT DOORS SHOULD BE 36" (91) WIDE IF POSSIBLE

PROVIDE MINIMUM 1 ENTRY AT GRADE, AVOID RAMP TO ENTRY (SOME CODES DO NOT ALLOW EXTERIOR RAMPS)

HANDICAPPED ACCESSIBLE DOORS SHOULD BE AT BUILDING FIRE EXIT LOCATIONS

LOCATE ACCESSIBLE ENTRANCES TO PROVIDE ACCESS TO LOBBIES, ELEVATORS, PHONES AND VENDING AREAS

DETAIL 5.2 Accessible exterior entrance conditions

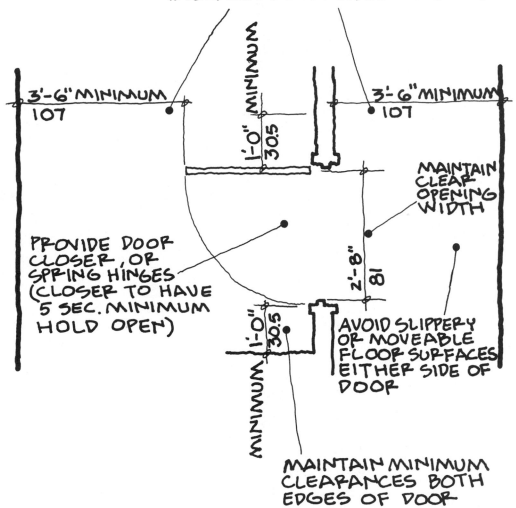

MAINTAIN MINIMUM CLEAR
PASSAGES BOTH SIDES OF DOOR

1'-0" MINIMUM
30.5

3'-6" MINIMUM
107

3'-6" MINIMUM
107

MAINTAIN CLEAR OPENING WIDTH

PROVIDE DOOR CLOSER, OR SPRING HINGES (CLOSER TO HAVE 5 SEC. MINIMUM HOLD OPEN)

2'-8"
81

1'-0" MINIMUM
30.5

AVOID SLIPPERY OR MOVEABLE FLOOR SURFACES EITHER SIDE OF DOOR

MAINTAIN MINIMUM CLEARANCES BOTH EDGES OF DOOR

PROVIDE CLOSERS (PARTIALLY OPEN DOORS ARE HAZARDOUS TO THE BLIND)

NOTE THAT A 2'-8" (81) DOOR DOES NOT GIVE THE REQUIRED 2'-8" (81) CLEAR OPENING

MINIMUM DOOR WIDTH = 2'-8" (81) + DOOR THICKNESS + 1" (2.5)

MAINTAIN 1'-0" (30.5) SIDE CLEARANCE ON LATCH SIDE, EVEN WHERE SMALLER DOOR (DOWN TO 2'-8" (81) MINIMUM CLEARANCE) MUST BE USED

DETAIL 5.3   Interior doors

Doors

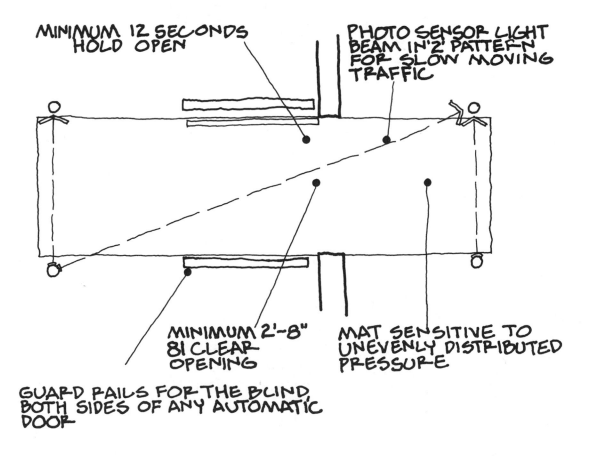

MINIMUM 12 SECONDS
HOLD OPEN

PHOTO SENSOR LIGHT
BEAM IN 'Z' PATTERN
FOR SLOW MOVING
TRAFFIC

MINIMUM 2'-8"
81 CLEAR
OPENING

MAT SENSITIVE TO
UNEVENLY DISTRIBUTED
PRESSURE

GUARD RAILS FOR THE BLIND
BOTH SIDES OF ANY AUTOMATIC
DOOR

DETAIL 5.4 Automatic doors

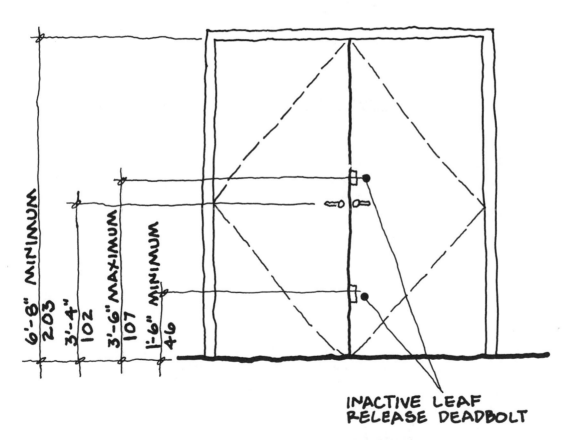

6'-8" MINIMUM
203

3'-4"
102

3'-6" MAXIMUM
107

1'-6" MINIMUM
46

INACTIVE LEAF
RELEASE DEADBOLT

EACH LEAF OF DOOR PAIR SHOULD
MEET ACCESSIBILITY STANDARDS

see next page

DETAIL 5.5   Door pairs

Doors

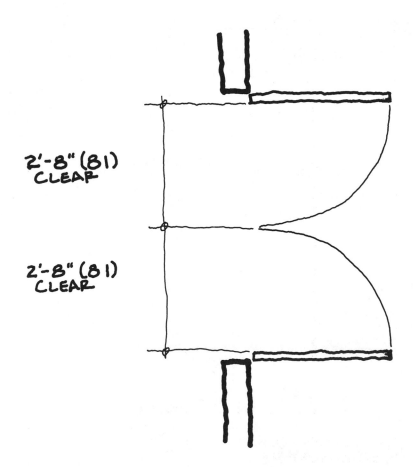

2'-8" (81)
CLEAR

2'-8" (81)
CLEAR

DETAIL 5.6   Door pairs

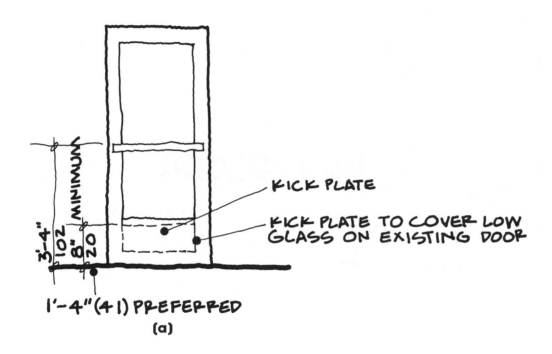

KICK PLATE

KICK PLATE TO COVER LOW
GLASS ON EXISTING DOOR

3'-4" 102 8" 20 MINIMUM

1'-4" (41) PREFERRED

(a)

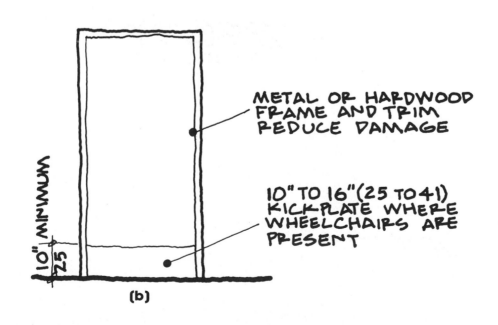

METAL OR HARDWOOD
FRAME AND TRIM
REDUCE DAMAGE

10" TO 16" (25 TO 41)
KICKPLATE WHERE
WHEELCHAIRS ARE
PRESENT

10" 25 MINIMUM

(b)

DETAIL 5.7a   **Glazed door**
DETAIL 5.7b   **Door protection**

Doors

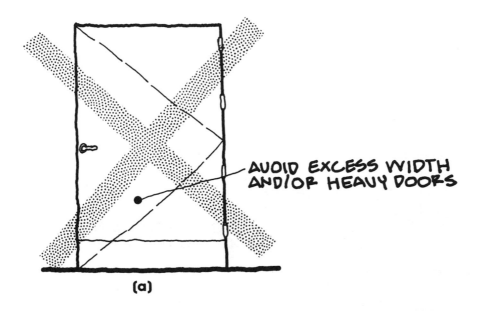

AVOID EXCESS WIDTH AND/OR HEAVY DOORS

(a)

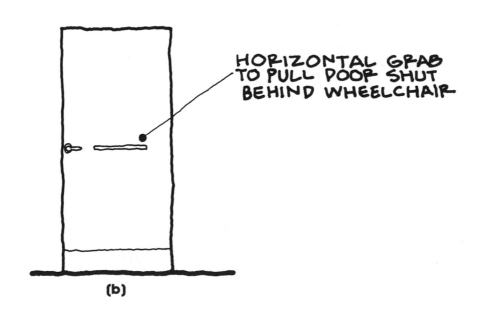

HORIZONTAL GRAB TO PULL DOOR SHUT BEHIND WHEELCHAIR

(b)

DETAIL 5.8a   Excess-width doors
DETAIL 5.8b   Door grabs

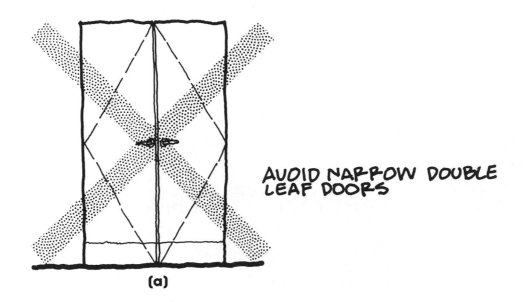

AVOID NARROW DOUBLE
LEAF DOORS

(a)

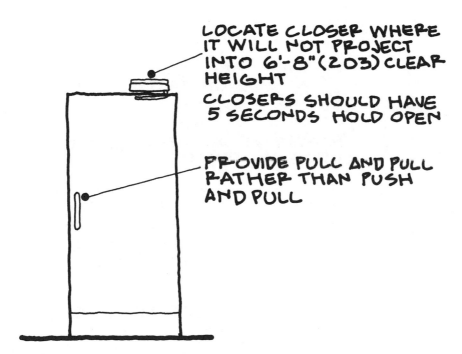

LOCATE CLOSER WHERE
IT WILL NOT PROJECT
INTO 6'-8" (203) CLEAR
HEIGHT

CLOSERS SHOULD HAVE
5 SECONDS HOLD OPEN

PROVIDE PULL AND PULL
RATHER THAN PUSH
AND PULL

PREFER AUTOMATIC FIRE RELEASE HOLD
OPEN INSTEAD OF CLOSER WHERE EVER
POSSIBLE

(b)

DETAIL 5.9a   Narrow double doors
DETAIL 5.9b   Door hold open/close

Doors

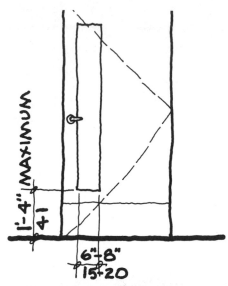

VISION PANELS DESIREABLE IN ALL AREAS WHERE BLIND OR HANDICAPPED PERSONS ARE PRESENT

LOCATE IN ALL DOUBLE ACTING DOORS, DOORS WHERE MINIMUM 1'-0" (30) LATCH CLEARANCE IS NOT AVAILABLE

(a)

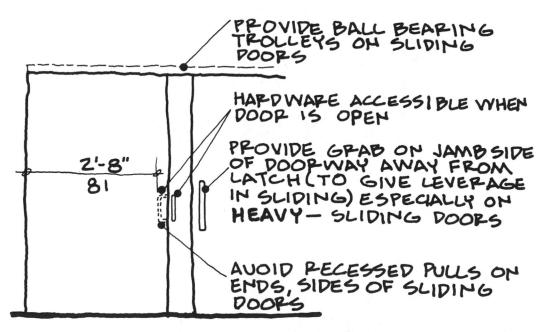

PROVIDE BALL BEARING TROLLEYS ON SLIDING DOORS

HARDWARE ACCESSIBLE WHEN DOOR IS OPEN

PROVIDE GRAB ON JAMB SIDE OF DOORWAY AWAY FROM LATCH (TO GIVE LEVERAGE IN SLIDING) ESPECIALLY ON HEAVY — SLIDING DOORS

AVOID RECESSED PULLS ON ENDS, SIDES OF SLIDING DOORS

AVOID SLIDING DOORS IF POSSIBLE

(b)

DETAIL 5.10a   Vision panel
DETAIL 5.10b   Sliding door

5LBF
22 NEWTONS

(a)

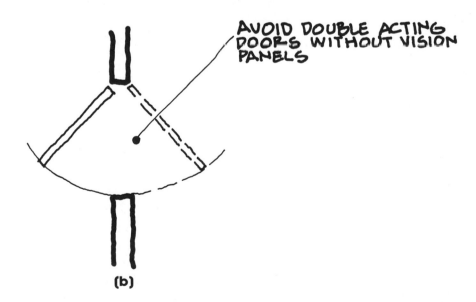

AVOID DOUBLE ACTING
DOORS WITHOUT VISION
PANELS

(b)

DETAIL 5.11a   Folding door force
DETAIL 5.11b   Double-acting door

Doors

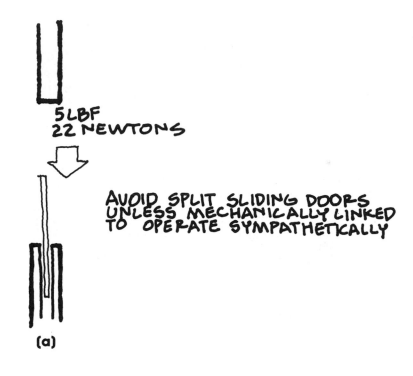

5 LBF
22 NEWTONS

AVOID SPLIT SLIDING DOORS
UNLESS MECHANICALLY LINKED
TO OPERATE SYMPATHETICALLY

(a)

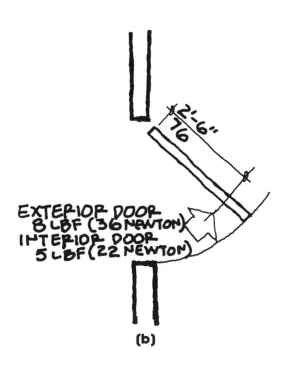

EXTERIOR DOOR
8 LBF (36 NEWTON)
INTERIOR DOOR
5 LBF (22 NEWTON)

(b)

DETAIL 5.12a   Sliding-door force
DETAIL 5.12b   Swinging-door force

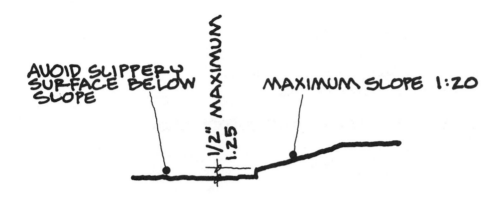

AVOID SLIPPERY SURFACE BELOW SLOPE

1/2" MAXIMUM 1.25

MAXIMUM SLOPE 1:20

CONTRAST COLOR OF RAISED THRESHOLDS COVER PLATES TO FLOOR

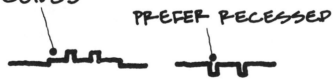

AVOID RAISED DOOR TRACKS OR GUIDES

PREFER RECESSED

WEATHER-STRIPPING OR THRESHOLD HIGHER THAN 1/2" SHOULD BE COMPRESSIBLE

1/2" 1.25

DETAIL 5.13 Thresholds

Hardware

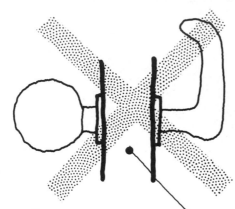

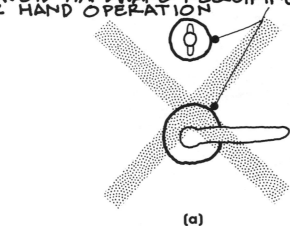

AVOID KNOB/LEVER COMBINATIONS (LEVER SPRING TOO STRONG FOR KNOB

AVOID HARDWARE REQUIRING SIMULTANEOUS 2 HAND OPERATION

(a)

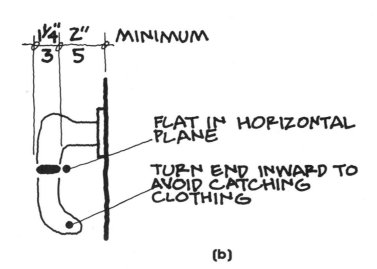

$1\frac{1}{4}$" 2" MINIMUM

3   5

FLAT IN HORIZONTAL PLANE

TURN END INWARD TO AVOID CATCHING CLOTHING

(b)

DETAIL 5.14a   Door and lock/latchset criteria
DETAIL 5.14b   Door handle

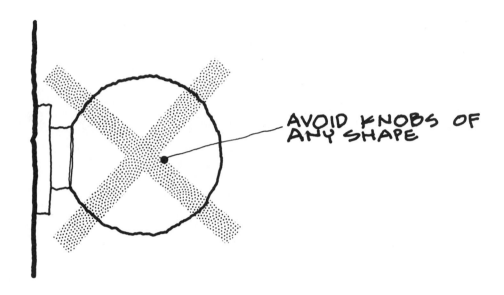

AVOID KNOBS OF
ANY SHAPE

DETAIL 5.15   Door knobs

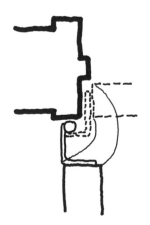

PREFER OFFSET HINGE TO
THROW DOOR OUT OF
OPENING:

· PROVIDES LARGER
OPENING FOR A GIVEN
DOOR SIZE

· REDUCES DAMAGE
FROM WHEELCHAIR

DETAIL 5.16   Door butts

Hardware

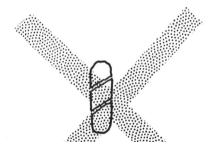

AVOID RISING PIVOT SELF CLOSING
HINGES EXCEPT ON VERY LIGHT DOORS

PROVIDE RISING PIN BUTTS, OR EXTERIOR
OPENABLE LOCKS WHERE EPILEPTICS
ARE PRESENT

DETAIL 5.17 Hinges

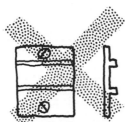

AVOID MAGNETIC CATCHES (EXCEPT LIGHT KITCHEN CABINETS AND FIRE DOOR ELECTRO-MAGNETIC HOLD OPEN)

(a)

AVOID RECESSED HARDWARE

(b)

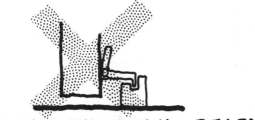

AVOID LOW MANUAL RELEASE DOOR HOLD OPEN

(c)

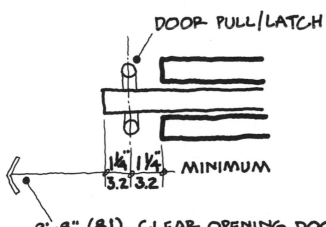

DOOR PULL/LATCH

1¼" / 1¼"
3.2 / 3.2 MINIMUM

2'-8" (81) CLEAR OPENING, DOOR IN FULL POSITION

(d)

DETAIL 5.18a **Magnetic catch**   DETAIL 5.18c **Manual hold-open**
DETAIL 5.18b **Recessed pulls**   DETAIL 5.18d **Sliding-door access**

Handrails and Grab Bars

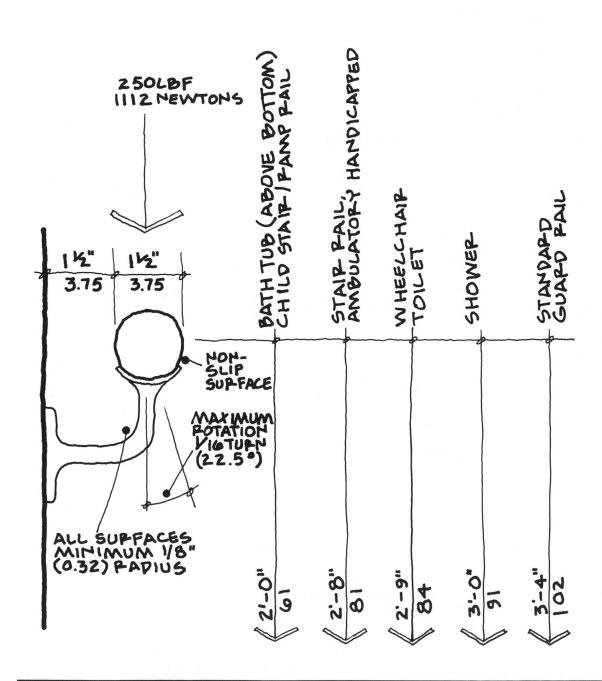

250 LBF
1112 NEWTONS

1½"   1½"
3.75   3.75

NON-
SLIP
SURFACE

MAXIMUM
ROTATION
1/16 TURN
(22.5°)

ALL SURFACES
MINIMUM 1/8"
(0.32) RADIUS

BATH TUB (ABOVE BOTTOM)
CHILD STAIR / RAMP RAIL
2'-0" 61

STAIR RAIL;
AMBULATORY HANDICAPPED
2'-8" 81

WHEELCHAIR
TOILET
2'-9" 84

SHOWER
3'-0" 91

STANDARD
GUARD RAIL
3'-4" 102

DETAIL 5.19   Typical handrails

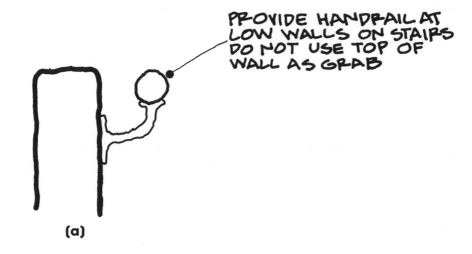

PROVIDE HANDRAIL AT LOW WALLS ON STAIRS DO NOT USE TOP OF WALL AS GRAB

(a)

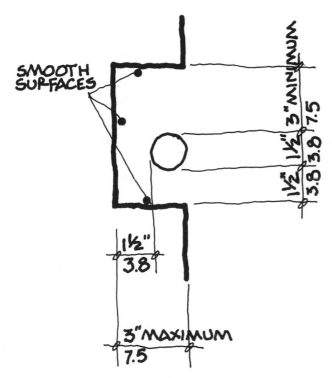

SMOOTH SURFACES

1½" 1½" 3" MINIMUM
3.8 3.8 7.5

1½"
3.8

3" MAXIMUM
7.5

AVOID RECESSED HANDRAILS WHEREVER POSSIBLE

(b)

DETAIL 5.20a Handrail and low wall
DETAIL 5.20b Recessed handrails

Handrails and Grab Bars

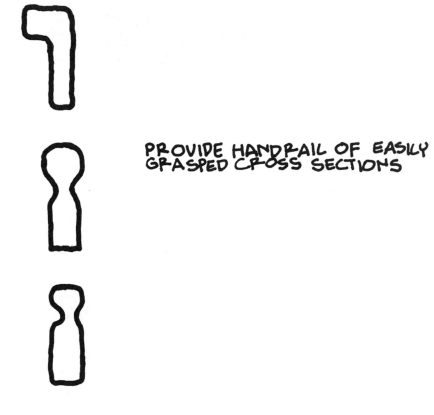

PROVIDE HANDRAIL OF EASILY
GRASPED CROSS SECTIONS

ACCEPTABLE

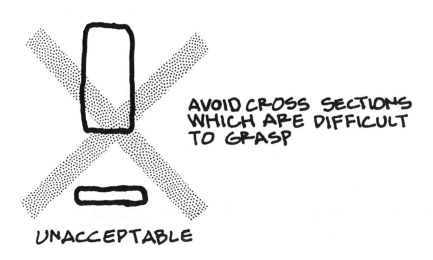

AVOID CROSS SECTIONS
WHICH ARE DIFFICULT
TO GRASP

UNACCEPTABLE

DETAIL 5.21   Handrail shapes

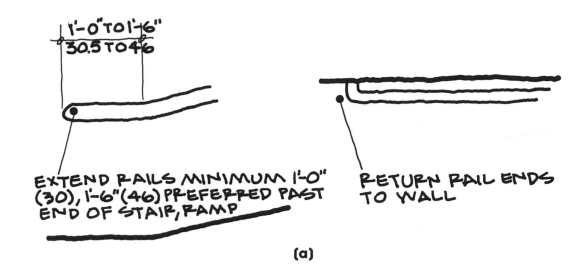

EXTEND RAILS MINIMUM 1'-0"
(30), 1'-6"(46) PREFERRED PAST
END OF STAIR, RAMP

RETURN RAIL ENDS
TO WALL

(a)

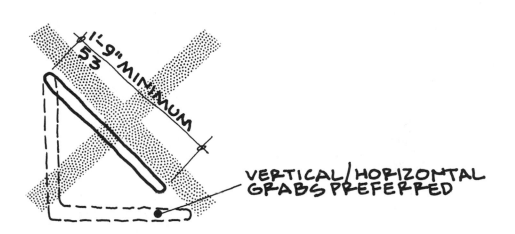

VERTICAL/HORIZONTAL
GRABS PREFERRED

AVOID DIAGONAL GRABS; THEY ARE A
COMPROMISE BETWEEN VERTICAL AND
HORIZONTAL GRABS

DIAGONAL GRABS REQUIRE SIMULTANEOUS
PUSH AND PULL BY HAND AND ELBOW,
AND ARE <u>DANGEROUS</u>

IF DIAGONAL GRABS MUST BE USED, THEY
MUST BE LONG ENOUGH, 1'-9"(53) TO FIT
ENTIRE FOREARM

IF DIAGONAL GRABS ARE USED, THEY
<u>MUST</u> BE LOCATED ON <u>BOTH</u> SIDES

(b)

DETAIL 5.22a   **Handrail ends**
DETAIL 5.22b   **Diagonal grabs**

Handrails and Grab Bars

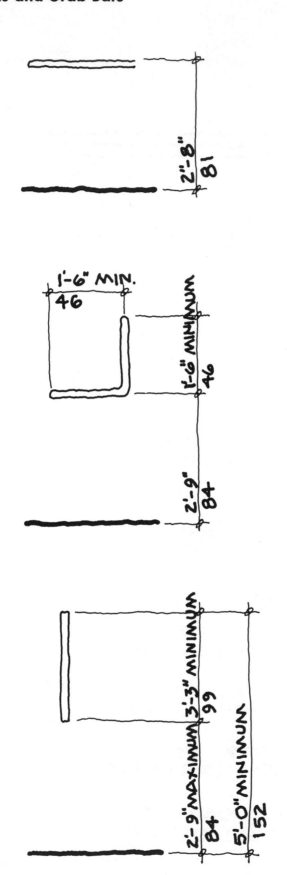

DETAIL 5.23   Toilet grab bars

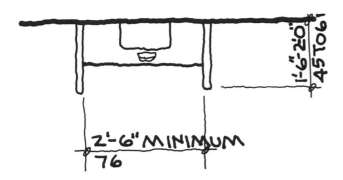

2'-6" MINIMUM
76

1'-6"-2'-0"
45 TO 61

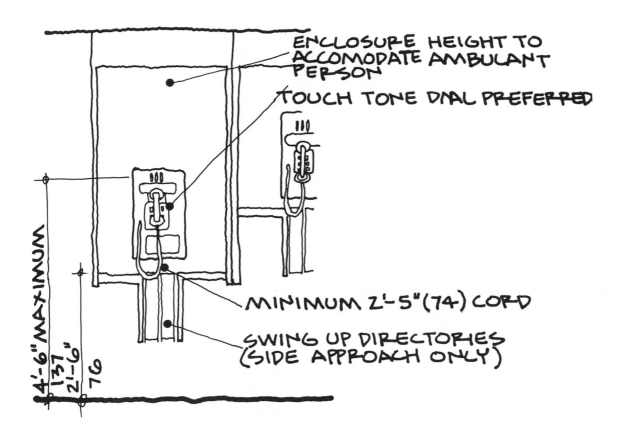

ENCLOSURE HEIGHT TO ACCOMODATE AMBULANT PERSON

TOUCH TONE DIAL PREFERRED

MINIMUM 2'-5"(74) CORD

SWING UP DIRECTORIES (SIDE APPROACH ONLY)

4'-6" MAXIMUM
137

2'-6"
76

FOR SHALLOW ENCLOSURE, BOOKS MAY HANG BELOW PHONE

FOR DEEP ENCLOSURE OR BOOTH WHICH REQUIRES 'HEAD IN' APPROACH, SEAT, SHELF, AND/OR DIRECTORIES MUST NOT EXTEND BELOW 2'-5" (74)

DETAIL 5.24 Telephone enclosure

Telephones

ONE SET OF SEPARATE DIRECTORIES
SHOULD BE ACCESSABLE FROM WHEELCHAIR

LOOSE BOOKS MUST BE ON A TETHER

DETAIL 5.25   Directory shelf

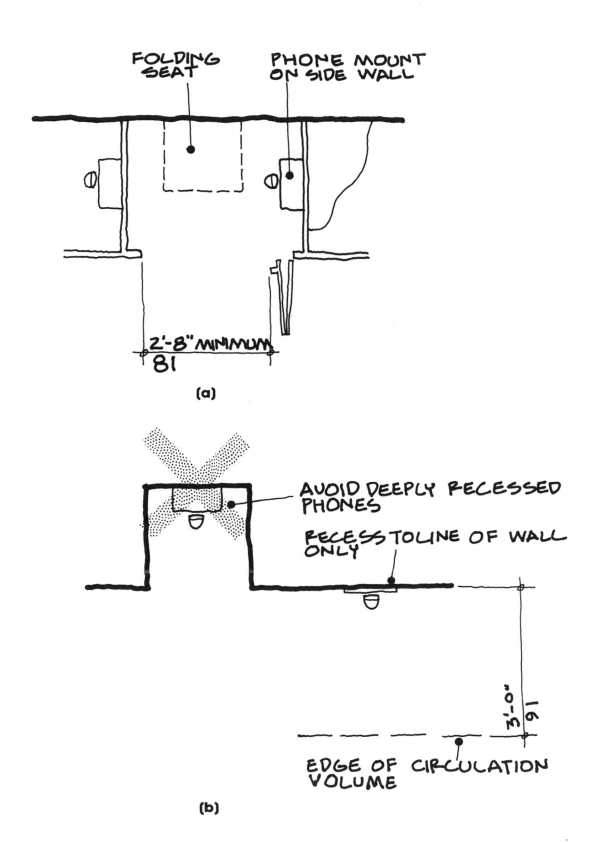

FOLDING SEAT

PHONE MOUNT ON SIDE WALL

2'-8" MINIMUM
81

(a)

AVOID DEEPLY RECESSED PHONES

RECESS TO LINE OF WALL ONLY

3'-0"
91

EDGE OF CIRCULATION VOLUME

(b)

DETAIL 5.26a   Telephone booth
DETAIL 5.26b   Recessed telephones

Telephones

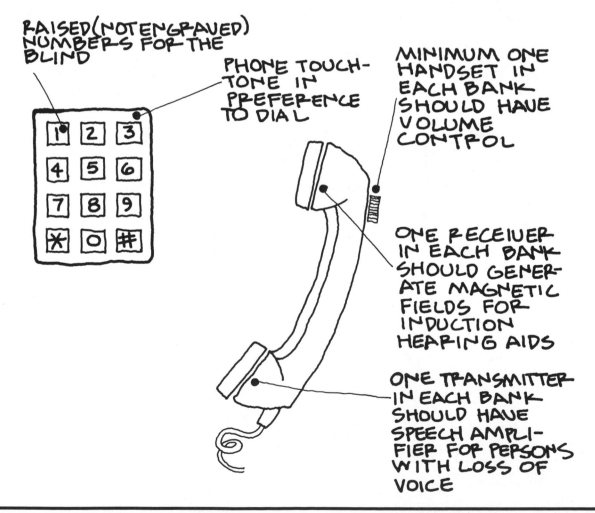

RAISED (NOT ENGRAVED) NUMBERS FOR THE BLIND

PHONE TOUCH-TONE IN PREFERENCE TO DIAL

MINIMUM ONE HANDSET IN EACH BANK SHOULD HAVE VOLUME CONTROL

ONE RECEIVER IN EACH BANK SHOULD GENERATE MAGNETIC FIELDS FOR INDUCTION HEARING AIDS

ONE TRANSMITTER IN EACH BANK SHOULD HAVE SPEECH AMPLIFIER FOR PERSONS WITH LOSS OF VOICE

DETAIL 5.27   Telephone instruments

Drinking Fountains

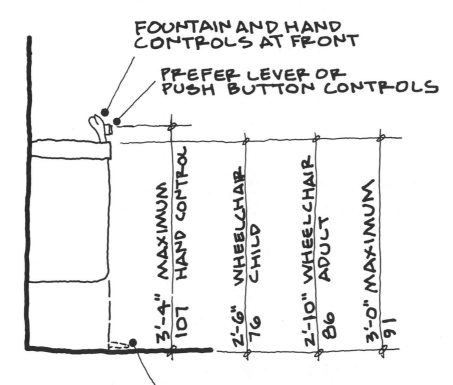

FOUNTAIN AND HAND CONTROLS AT FRONT

PREFER LEVER OR PUSH BUTTON CONTROLS

3'-4" MAXIMUM HAND CONTROL 107

2'-6" WHEELCHAIR CHILD 76

2'-10" WHEELCHAIR ADULT 86

3'-0" MAXIMUM 91

FOOT OPERATED FOUNTAINS MUST ALSO HAVE HAND CONTROL

PROVIDE ALTERNATE FOUNTAINS WHERE RIM OF EXISTING FOUNTAIN IS HIGHER THAN 3'-0" (91)

(a)

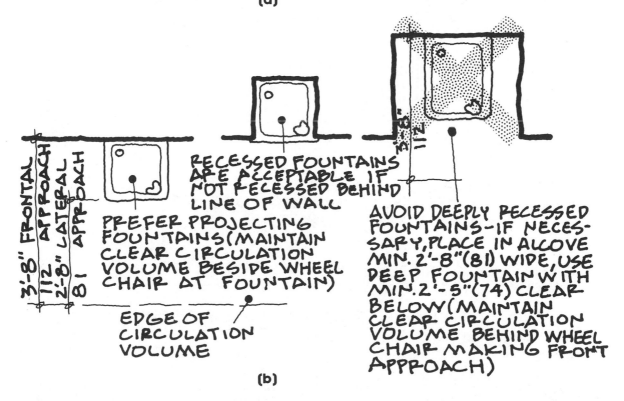

3'-8" FRONTAL APPROACH 112

2'-8" LATERAL APPROACH 81

PREFER PROJECTING FOUNTAINS (MAINTAIN CLEAR CIRCULATION VOLUME BESIDE WHEEL CHAIR AT FOUNTAIN)

EDGE OF CIRCULATION VOLUME

RECESSED FOUNTAINS ARE ACCEPTABLE IF NOT RECESSED BEHIND LINE OF WALL

AVOID DEEPLY RECESSED FOUNTAINS—IF NECESSARY, PLACE IN ALCOVE MIN. 2'-8" (81) WIDE, USE DEEP FOUNTAIN WITH MIN. 2'-5" (74) CLEAR BELOW (MAINTAIN CLEAR CIRCULATION VOLUME BEHIND WHEEL CHAIR MAKING FRONT APPROACH)

(b)

DETAIL 5.28a   Drinking fountain height
DETAIL 5.28b   Access to fountains

Drinking Fountains

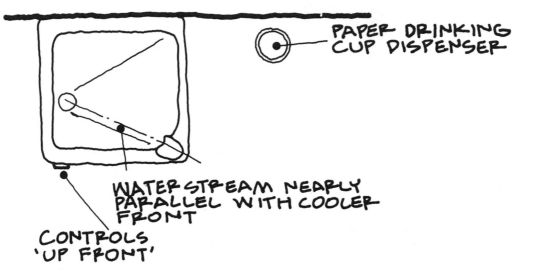

PAPER DRINKING
CUP DISPENSER

WATER STREAM NEARLY
PARALLEL WITH COOLER
FRONT

CONTROLS
'UP FRONT'

SPOUT LOCATION, HEIGHT, DIRECTION
SUCH AS TO ALLOW FOR USE OF
4"(10) HIGH PAPER CUPS

CONTROLS SHOULD BE AT FRONT OR
FRONT SIDE OF FOUNTAIN

AVOID CONTROLS REQUIRING GRASPING,
PINCHING OR TWISTING

DETAIL 5.29   Spout, control location

Accessories

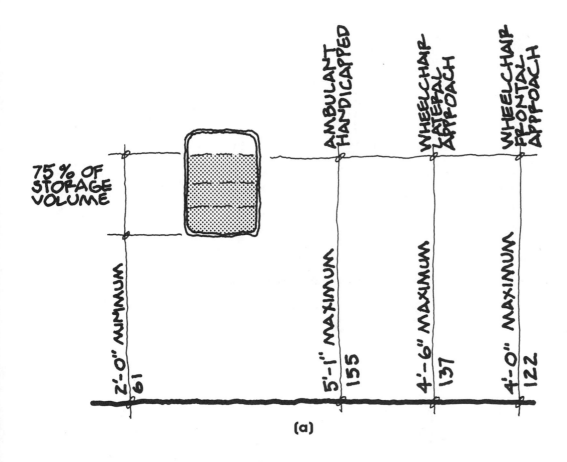

75% OF STORAGE VOLUME

2'-0" MINIMUM
61

AMBULANT HANDICAPPED

WHEELCHAIR LATERAL APPROACH

WHEELCHAIR FRONTAL APPROACH

5'-1" MAXIMUM
155

4'-6" MAXIMUM
137

4'-0" MAXIMUM
122

(a)

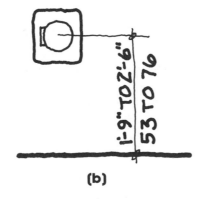

1'-9" TO 2'-6"
53 TO 76

(b)

DETAIL 5.30a   Medicine cabinet
DETAIL 5.30b   Vacuum outlet

Accessories

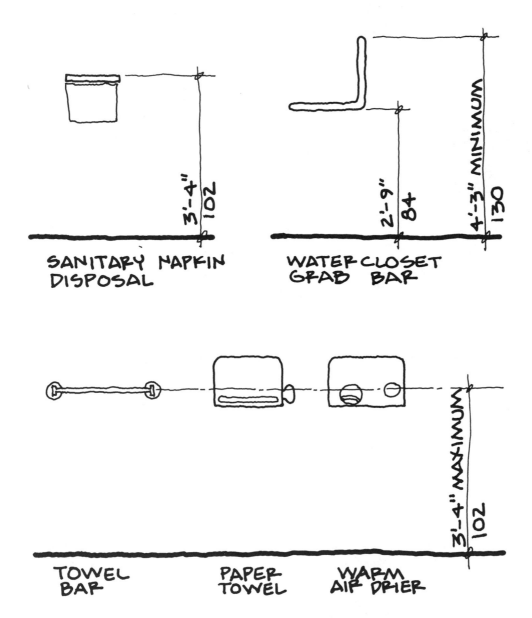

SANITARY NAPKIN
DISPOSAL

3'-4"
102

WATER CLOSET
GRAB BAR

2'-9"
84

4'-3" MINIMUM
130

TOWEL
BAR

PAPER
TOWEL

WARM
AIR DRIER

3'-4" MAXIMUM
102

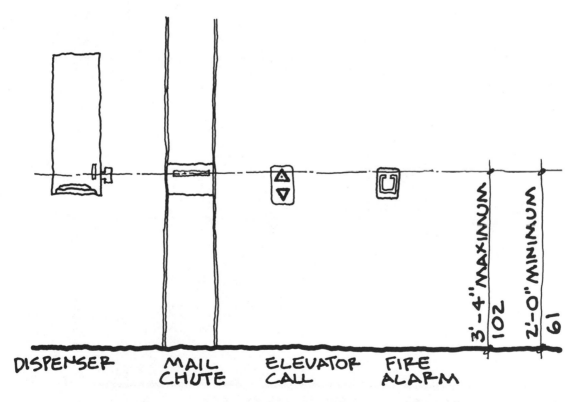

DISPENSER   MAIL   ELEVATOR   FIRE
            CHUTE   CALL   ALARM

NO ACCESSORY ELEMENT SHOULD REQUIRE
MORE THAN 8 LBF (35.5 NEWTONS) TO OPERATE

3'-4" MAXIMUM 102

2'-0" MINIMUM 61

DETAIL 5.32

Accessories

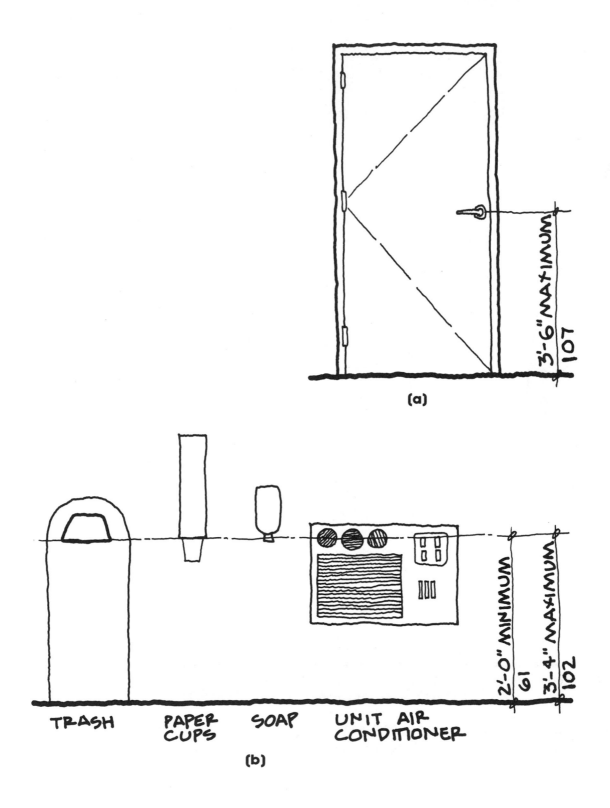

(a)

TRASH PAPER CUPS SOAP UNIT AIR CONDITIONER

(b)

DETAIL 5.33a Latch height
DETAIL 5.33b

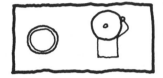 

PROVIDE LIGHT WITH AMPLIFIED ALARM BELL FOR DOOR, TELEPHONE, FIRE ALARM IN RESIDENTIAL FACILITIES FOR THE DEAF

(a)

PROVIDE REMOTE INTERCOM, DOOR LOCK IN RESIDENTIAL FACILITIES FOR THE HANDICAPPED

(b)

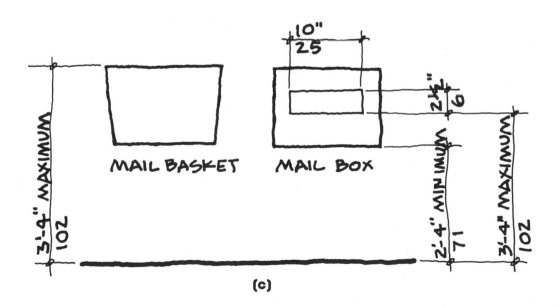

(c)

DETAIL 5.34a   Hearing-impaired alarm
DETAIL 5.34b   Door intercom, control
DETAIL 5.34c   Mail receptacles

Accessories

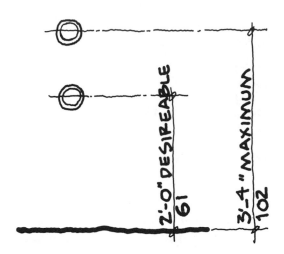

LOW THERMOSTAT DESIREABLE TO SET
WARM AIR TEMPERATURE NEAR FLOOR

(a)

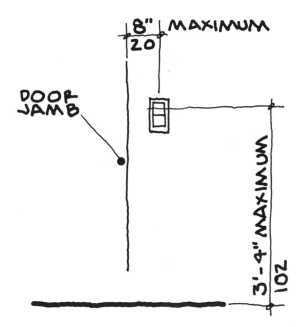

ALIGN SWITCH FOR LIGHT TO DOOR
LATCH HEIGHT

(b)

DETAIL 5.35a   Thermostat height
DETAIL 5.35b   Switch height

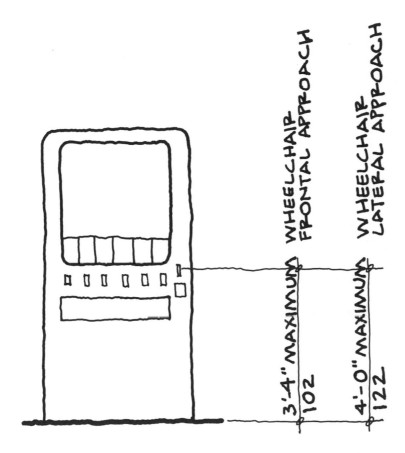

WHEELCHAIR
FRONTAL APPROACH

WHEELCHAIR
LATERAL APPROACH

3'-4" MAXIMUM
102

4'-0" MAXIMUM
122

AVOID VENDING MACHINES WHICH REQUIRE
GRASPING OR PINCHING TO OPERATE
CONTROLS

PREFER PUSH BUTTON TYPE SELECTION

IF PULLING REQUIRED, MAXIMUM 3LBF
(13 NEWTONS) TO OPERATE

DETAIL 5.36 Vending machines

Accessories

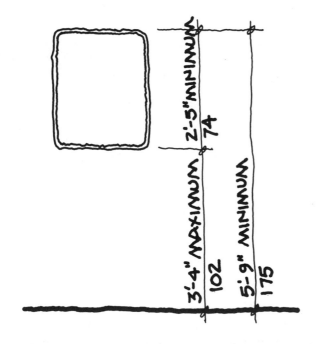

2'-5" MINIMUM
74

3'-4" MAXIMUM
102

5'-9" MINIMUM
175

BOTTOM OF MIRROR DOWN TO 3'-0" (90)
DESIRABLE

ONE FULL LENGTH MIRROR DESIRABLE

MIRROR TILT/SWING TYPE DESIRABLE

DETAIL 5.37   Mirrors

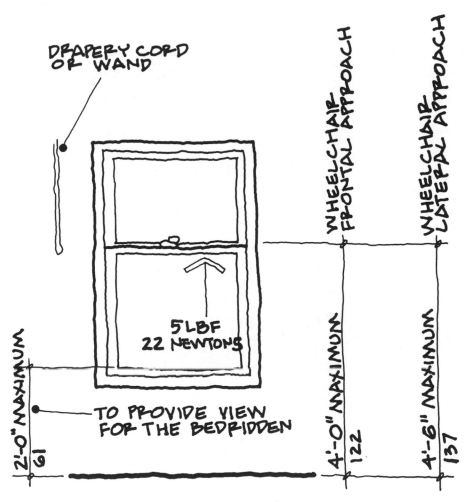

DRAPERY CORD OR WAND

WHEELCHAIR FRONTAL APPROACH

WHEELCHAIR LATERAL APPROACH

5 LBF 22 NEWTONS

2'-0" MAXIMUM 61

TO PROVIDE VIEW FOR THE BEDRIDDEN

4'-0" MAXIMUM 122

4'-6" MAXIMUM 137

MAXIMUM 5 LBF (22 NEWTONS) TO OPERATE ANY PART OF ANY WINDOW

DETAIL 5.38   Windows

Accessories

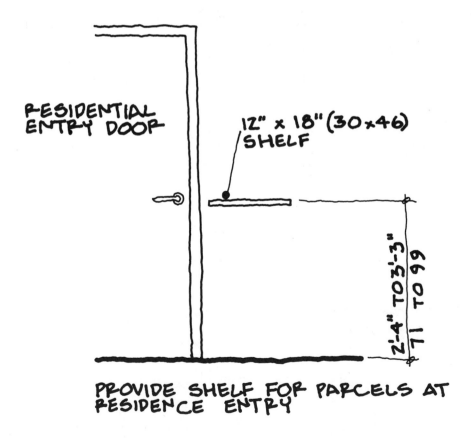

RESIDENTIAL
ENTRY DOOR

12" x 18" (30x46)
SHELF

2'-4" TO 3'-3"
71 TO 99

PROVIDE SHELF FOR PARCELS AT
RESIDENCE ENTRY

DETAIL 5.39 Entry shelf

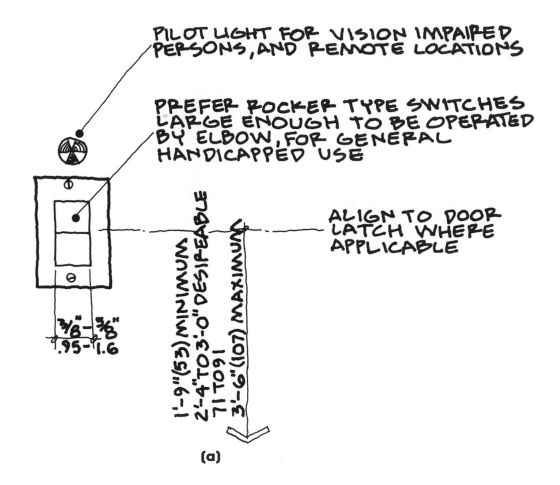

PILOT LIGHT FOR VISION IMPAIRED PERSONS, AND REMOTE LOCATIONS

PREFER ROCKER TYPE SWITCHES LARGE ENOUGH TO BE OPERATED BY ELBOW, FOR GENERAL HANDICAPPED USE

ALIGN TO DOOR LATCH WHERE APPLICABLE

3/8" - 3/8"
.95 - 1.6

1'-9"(53) MINIMUM
2'-4" TO 3'-0" DESIREABLE
71 TO 91
3'-6" (107) MAXIMUM

(a)

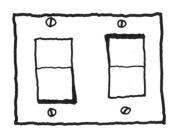

MAXIMUM GANG TWO SWITCHES (LARGER GANGS ARE CONFUSING TO THE ELDERLY AND RETARDED)

(b)

DETAIL 5.40a   Switches
DETAIL 5.40b   Switch gangs

Electrical Devices

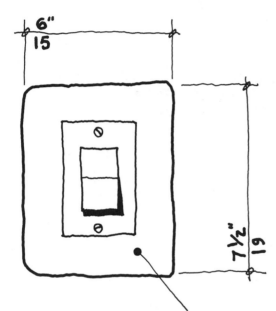

6"
15

7½"
19

PROVIDE WALL GUARDS WHERE SWITCHES
ARE USED BY PALSIED OR INCOORDINATE
PERSONS

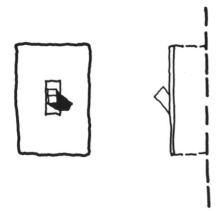

PROJECTING TYPE SWITCHES
(MOUNTED ON PROJECTING
BOXES WHERE POSSIBLE)
ARE BEST FOR THE PALSIED
AND INCOORDINATE

DETAIL 5.41   Switches

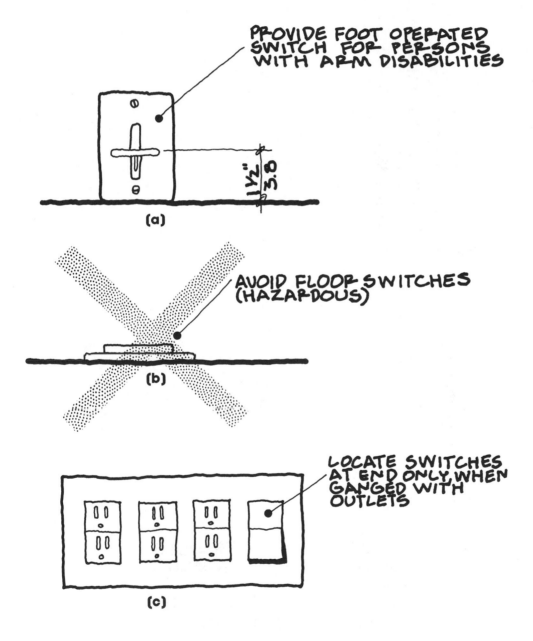

PROVIDE FOOT OPERATED
SWITCH FOR PERSONS
WITH ARM DISABILITIES

1½" / 3.8

(a)

AVOID FLOOR SWITCHES
(HAZARDOUS)

(b)

LOCATE SWITCHES
AT END ONLY WHEN
GANGED WITH
OUTLETS

(c)

DETAIL 5.42a Foot switch
DETAIL 5.42b Floor switch
DETAIL 5.42c Switch/outlet gangs

Electrical Devices

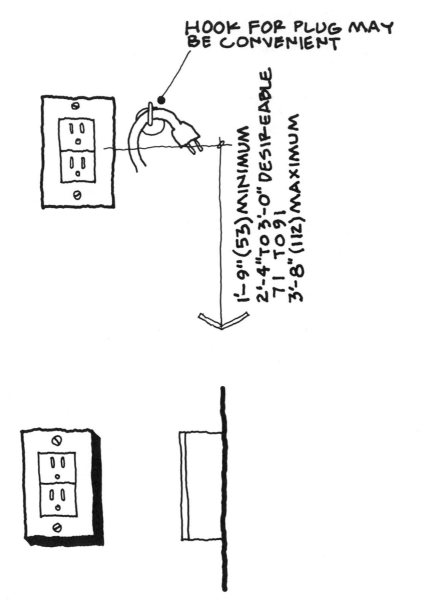

HOOK FOR PLUG MAY
BE CONVENIENT

1'-9" (53) MINIMUM
2'-4" TO 3'-0" DESIREABLE
71 TO 91
3'-8" (112) MAXIMUM

PROJECTED SURFACE OUTLETS ARE DESIREABLE
FOR THE PALSIED AND INCOORDINATE, ESPECIALLY
WHERE MOUNTED LOW

AVOID LOW OUTLETS WHERE USED BY THE
ELDERLY AND THOSE PRONE TO DIZZINESS

DETAIL 5.43 Outlets

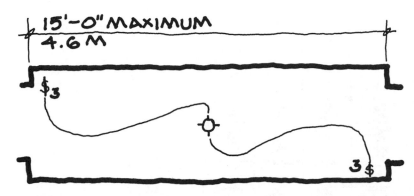

PROVIDE 3 WAY SWITCHES IN ROOMS,
PASSAGES 15'(4.6) AND GREATER ACROSS

(a)

PREFER WALL BRACKET LIGHTING IN
INDIVIDUAL HANDICAPPED LIVING UNITS

(b)

DETAIL 5.44a   Maximum switch distance
DETAIL 5.44b   Light types

Finishes

	AMBULANT	WHEELCHAIR	BLIND	ELDERLY
DEEP PILE CARPET	—	✗	✗	—
LOW PILE CARPET	O	—	—	O
RESILIENT	O	O	O	—
HARD	—	O	O	—
GLOSSY (NOT SLIPPERY)	✗	—	—	✗
SLIPPERY	✗	✗	✗	✗

O GOOD
— ACCEPTABLE
✗ POOR

AVOID CARPET OR USE VERY LOW, DENSE
CARPET IN HIGH MOBILITY AREAS

AVOID SURFACES WHICH MAY APPEAR
SLIPPERY; SUCH SURFACES CAUSE
ANXIETY AMONG THE AMBULANT
HANDICAPPED AND ELDERLY

DETAIL 5.45   Floor surfaces

	RUBBER		LEATHER	
	DRY	WET	DRY	WET
STEEL PLATE, PHENOLIC RESIN/ALUNDUM GRIT SURFACED	0.69	0.45	0.64	0.47
CONCRETE, CARBORUNDUM GRIT	0.65	0.60	0.37	0.43
SMOOTH PAVING BRICK	0.68	0.38	0.27	0.27
SMOOTH TERAZZO	0.53	0.25	0.35	0.16
TERAZZO, ALUNDUM GRIT	0.74	0.33	0.44	0.18
SMOOTH QUARRY TILE	0.69	0.28	0.31	0.20
WHITE OAK, WAXED AND POLISHED	0.49	0.19	0.24	0.17
LINOLEUM				
CLEAN	0.68	0.19	0.32	0.10
SOLVENT WAX, POLISHED	0.62	0.19	0.25	0.13
WATER EMULSION WAX, POLISHED	0.71	0.16	0.34	0.10
RUBBER TILE				
SOLVENT WAX, POLISHED	0.61	0.17	0.29	0.16
WATER EMULSION WAX, POLISHED	0.80	0.32	0.42	0.20
ASPHALT TILE				
WATER EMULSION WAX, POLISHED	0.72	0.22	0.37	0.15
VINYL, SMOOTH	0.47	0.22	0.25	0.21

FOR INTERIOR SURFACES, DRY RUBBER (SHOES, HEELS, WHEELCHAIR TIRES, CRUTCH TIPS), WILL BE THE USUAL CONDITION

COEFFICIENT OF FRICTION OF LESS THAN 0.40 SHOULD BE CONSIDERED SLIPPERY AND DANGEROUS

ADOPTED FROM NATIONAL BUREAU OF STANDARDS, RESEARCH PAPER RP 1879

DETAIL 5.46   Friction of surfaces

Finishes

PREFER SLIGHTLY ROUGH
NON-SKID SURFACES

AVOID SMOOTH,
POLISHED SURFACES

AVOID LOOSE MATS, AREA RUGS

PREFER DIRECT GLUE DOWN INSTALLATION
PREFER HIGH DENSITY LOW PILE CARPET
AVOID INDOOR/OUTDOOR CARPET, ESPECIALLY THAT OF WIDE (SLIPPERY) FILAMENT

AVOID ANY TYPE OF DEEP, THICK OR LOOSE PILE

AVOID DEEP OR SOFT PADDING AND UNDERLAYMENT

INSET OR RAMP UP TO CARPET (MAXIMUM ½" (1.25) INSET); (RAMP AT MAXIMUM 1:12)

NOISY, RESONANT SURFACES ARE BEST FOR THE BLIND

DETAIL 5.47   Floor surfaces

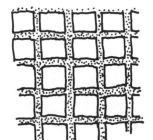

CERAMIC MOSAIC JOINTS PROVIDE GOOD FRICTION FOR WHEELCHAIRS (TILE AREA MUST BE LEVEL; AVOID WIDE OR DEEP JOINTS)

(a)

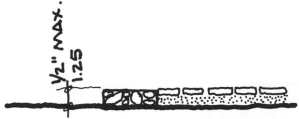

AVOID LEVEL CHANGE MORE THAN ½" (1.25)

AVOID LEVEL CHANGES OF ANY HEIGHT (EVEN IF RAMPED) WHEN FLOOR ON LOW SIDE IS SLIPPERY

AVOID GRILLES IN FLOOR WHERE EVER POSSIBLE; WHERE USED, MAXIMUM OPENING ½" (1.25) IN ANY DIRECTION

ONE DIRECTION GRATES SHOULD HAVE BARS PERPINDICULAR TO DIRECTION OF TRAVEL

(b)

AVOID MATS, RUGS THICKER THAN ½" (1.25), OR WHICH ARE RECESSED MORE THAN ½" (1.25)

(c)

DETAIL 5.48a   **Ceramic floors**
DETAIL 5.48b   **Entry grille**
DETAIL 5.48c   **Entry mat**

Finishes

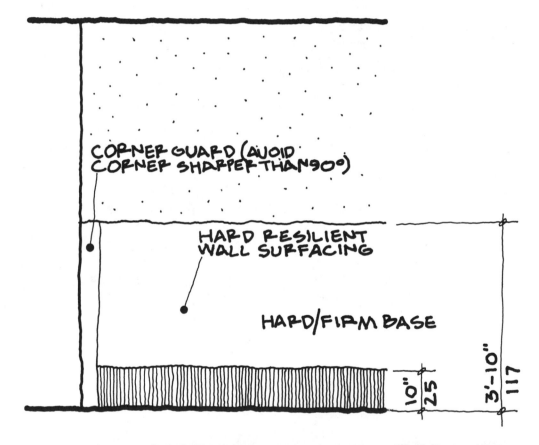

CORNER GUARD (AVOID CORNER SHARPER THAN 90°)

HARD RESILIENT WALL SURFACING

HARD/FIRM BASE

10"
25

3'-10"
117

HIGH BASE APPEARS INSTITUTIONAL, IS PSYCHOLOGICALLY BAD — USE ONLY WHERE MOST DAMAGE WILL OCCUR (RESTRICTED SPACES WHERE WHEELCHAIRS MUST MANEUVER)

DETAIL 5.49   Wall surface protection

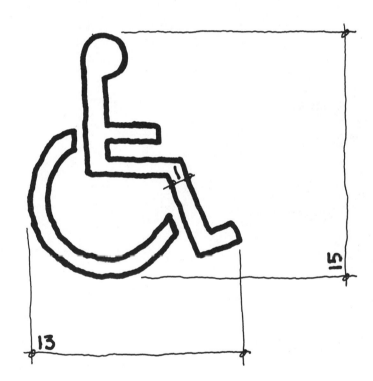

DISPLAY SYMBOL AT: ACCESSIBLE ENTRANCES
ACCESSIBLE TOILETS
ORIGINS OF ACCESSIBLE
PATHS OF TRAVEL
ON MAPS AND BUILDING
DIAGRAMS
AT HANDICAPPED PARKING
SPACES

DETAIL 5.50   Access symbol proportion

Identification/Signage

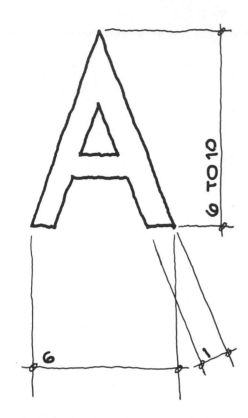

LETTER SIZE[2]	READING DISTANCE[1]
½" (1.25)	25' (7.6M)
1" (2.5)	50' (15M)
1½" (3.75)	75' (23M)
2" (5)	100' (30.5M)
3" (7.5)	200' (61M)
4" (10)	300' (91.5M)

1 HIGH CONTRAST, NORMAL VISION, HELVETICA TYPE FACE

2 USE LETTERS 25—50% LARGER FOR SIGHT IMPAIRED PERSONS

USE CLEAR, EASILY IDENTIFIABLE TYPE FACES WHERE SIGHT IMPAIRED PERSONS ARE PRESENT (HELVETICA IS EXCELLENT)

PROVIDE MAXIMUM CONTRAST IN COLOR AND VALUE

DETAIL 5.51   Letter size, proportion

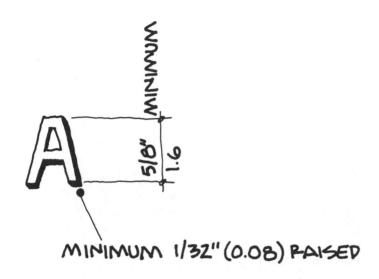

MINIMUM 1/32" (0.08) RAISED

PROVIDE RAISED LETTERS/NUMBERS FOR
IDENTIFICATION FOR THE BLIND

AVOID RECESSED LETTERS (MORE DIFFICULT
TO READ, FILL WITH DIRT)

PROVIDE RAISED NUMBER/LETTER IDENTIFI-
CATION AND SIGNS FOR ROOM IDENTIFICATION,
ROUTE MAPS, LOCATION INSTRUCTIONS,
CULTURAL DESCRIPTIVE MATERIAL

PROVIDE RAISED CHARACTER SIGNS/MAPS/
DIRECTORIES WHERE A PERSON WOULD
ORDINARILY BE EXPECTED TO FIND HIS
OWN WAY

AVOID LOWER CASE LETTERS (THEY ARE
BE MORE DIFFICULT TO IDENTIFY BY
TOUCH)

BRAILLE LETTERS, NUMBERS MAY BE ADDED
TO RAISED LETTER/NUMBER SIGNS; AVOID
USE OF BRAILLE ALONE (MAJORITY OF BLIND
CAN NOT READ BRAILLE

DETAIL 5.52 Sight-impaired lettering

Identification/Signage

	ASPHALT	BRICK	CARPET	CONCRETE	TILE CERAMIC	QUARRY	RESILIENT	RUBBER	VINYL	WOOD	TERRAZZO
ASPHALT	–	O	O	O	O	O	X	O	–	O	O
BRICK	O	–	O	X	X	X	O	O	O	O	X
CARPET	O	O	–	O	O	O	O	–	O	O	O
CONCRETE	O	X	O	–	X	X	O	O	O	O	X
TILE CERAMIC	–	X	O	X	–	X	O	O	O	O	X
QUARRY	O	X	O	X	X	–	O	O	O	O	X
RESILIENT	–	O	O	O	O	O	–	O	X	O	O
RUBBER	O	O	–	O	O	O	O	–	O	O	O
VINYL	–	O	O	O	O	O	X	O	–	O	O
WOOD	O	O	O	O	O	O	O	O	O	–	O
TERRAZZO	O	X	O	X	X	X	O	O	O	O	–
EARTH	O	O	–	O	O	O	O	–	–	O	O

O GOOD
X POOR
— NOT GIVEN

DETAIL 5.53   Difference in hardness perceivable to blind

PREFER WHITE LETTERS ON BLACK BACKGROUND FOR BETTER CONTRAST/LEGIBILITY

 PLACE BRAILLE EXPLANATORY STRIPS ON UPPER LEFT CORNER OF LONG TEXTUAL SIGNS

 AVOID GRAPHIC SYMBOLS AS THE ONLY FORM OF SIGNAGE— THEY ARE CONFUSING, HARD TO 'FEEL' FOR THE BLIND

DETAIL 5.54 Signs

BRAILLE 'CELL'

ALL BRAILLE LETTERS AND
NUMBERS ARE MADE USING
DOTS ARRANGED IN THE
STANDARD 'CELL', DOTS
NUMBERED FOR REFERENCE

CAPITAL SIGN

PLACED IN FRONT OF ANY
LETTER INDICATES A
CAPITAL LETTER

NUMBER SIGN

PLACED BEFORE A NUMBER OR
GROUP OF NUMBERS INDICATES
THAT NUMBERS FOLLOW
(SOME NUMBERS DUPLICATE
LETTERS)

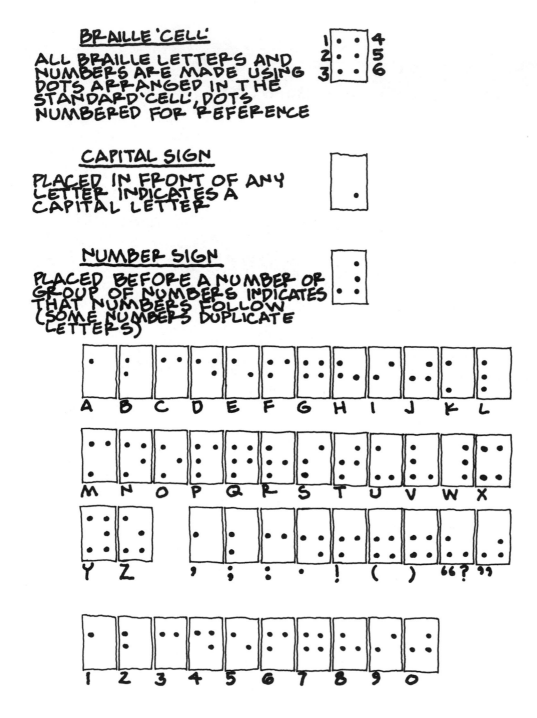

DETAIL 5.55   Braille alphabet

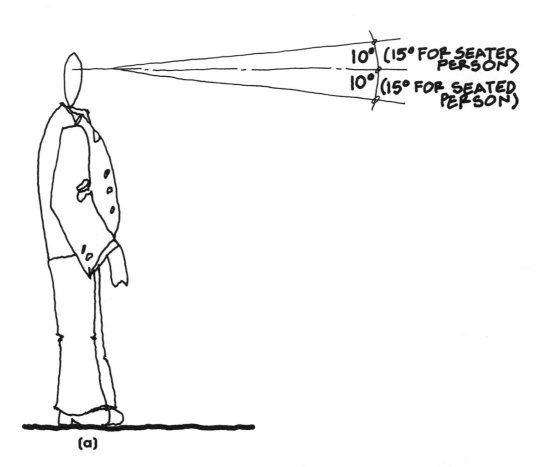

(a)

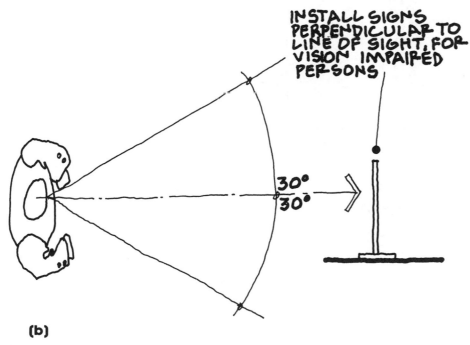

(b)

DETAIL 5.56a   Vertical angles of vision
DETAIL 5.56b   Lateral angles of vision

Identification/Signage

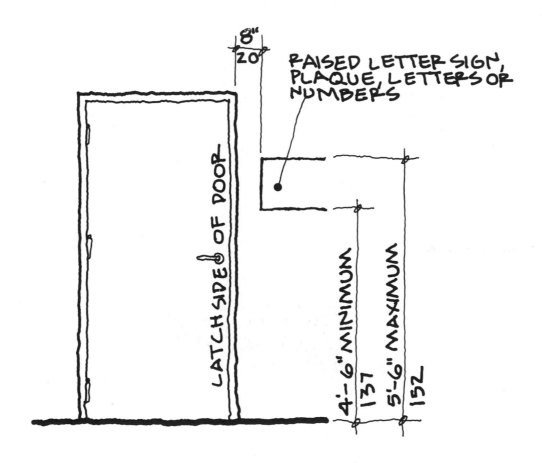

8"
20"

RAISED LETTER SIGN,
PLAQUE, LETTERS OR
NUMBERS

LATCH SIDE OF DOOR

4'-6" MINIMUM
137

5'-6" MAXIMUM
152

ROOM IDENTIFICATION SHOULD BE RAISED
LETTERS AND NUMBERS (FEW AS POSSIBLE)

BRAILLE IDENTIFICATION MAY/SHOULD BE
ADDED TO LETTERS AND NUMBERS

AVOID USE OF BRAILLE ALONE (MAJORITY
OF THE BLIND CAN NOT READ BRAILLE)

DETAIL 5.57   Room identification

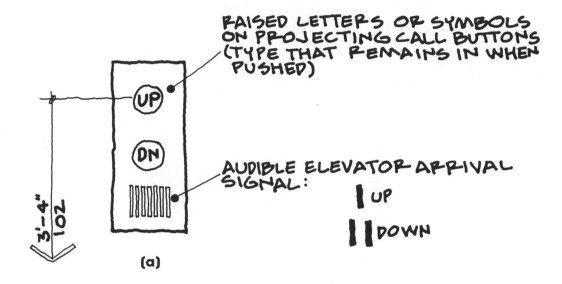

RAISED LETTERS OR SYMBOLS ON PROJECTING CALL BUTTONS (TYPE THAT REMAINS IN WHEN PUSHED)

AUDIBLE ELEVATOR ARRIVAL SIGNAL:

| UP

|| DOWN

(a)

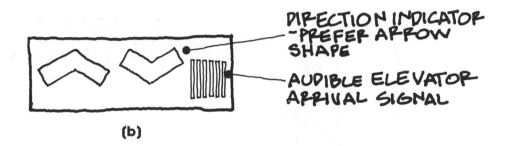

DIRECTION INDICATOR - PREFER ARROW SHAPE

AUDIBLE ELEVATOR ARRIVAL SIGNAL

(b)

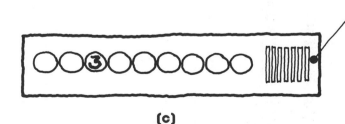

AUDIBLE LEVEL INDICATOR (TAPE LOOP WITH FLOOR NUMBER SPOKEN)

(c)

DETAIL 5.58a   Elevator call
DETAIL 5.58b   Elevator arrival signal
DETAIL 5.58c   Elevator floor indicator

Identification/Signage

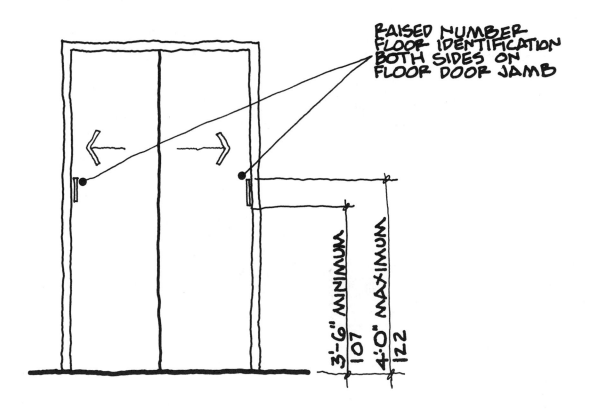

RAISED NUMBER
FLOOR IDENTIFICATION
BOTH SIDES ON
FLOOR DOOR JAMB

3'-6" MINIMUM
107

4'-0" MAXIMUM
122

DETAIL 5.59   Tactile floor indication

ABRASIVE COAT, KNURL OR
ROUGHEN HARDWARE ON
DOORS LEADING TO AREAS
WHICH ARE DANGEROUS TO
THE BLIND:

STAIRS
LOADING PLATFORMS
MECHANICAL ROOMS
STAGES
PITS
LOFTS
FIRE ESCAPES
ETC.

DETAIL 5.60   Warning hardware

Identification/Signage

ILLUMINATED EXIT SIGN SHOULD FLASH
OR BLINK WHEN AUDIBLE ALARM
SOUNDS

BLINKING TO BE 5 HZ. OR LESS

FLASHING ILLUMINATED EXIT SIGNS
SHOULD BE POWERED FROM EMERGENCY
POWER SYSTEM

(a)

AUDIBLE EMERGENCY SIGNALS SHOULD
EXCEED AVERAGE AMBIENT SOUND LEVEL
BY MINIMUM 15 db ; EXCEED 30 SEC. OR
LESS DURATION AMBIENT NOISE BY
MINIMUM 5db

MAXIMUM AUDIBLE EMERGENCY
SIGNAL 120 db

(b)

DETAIL 5.61a   Exit sign
DETAIL 5.61b   Audible emergency signal

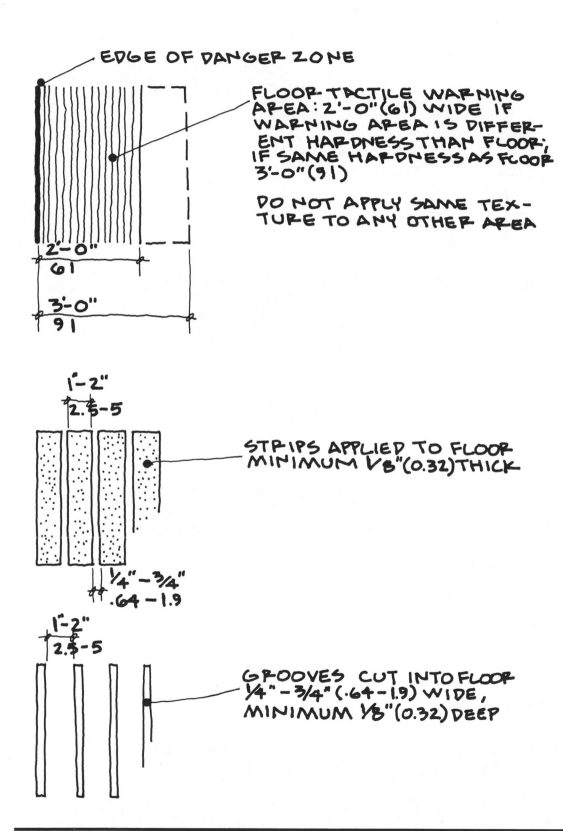

EDGE OF DANGER ZONE

FLOOR-TACTILE WARNING AREA: 2'-0" (61) WIDE IF WARNING AREA IS DIFFERENT HARDNESS THAN FLOOR; IF SAME HARDNESS AS FLOOR 3'-0" (91)

DO NOT APPLY SAME TEXTURE TO ANY OTHER AREA

2'-0"
61

3'-0"
91

1"-2"
2.5-5

STRIPS APPLIED TO FLOOR MINIMUM 1/8" (0.32) THICK

1/4" - 3/4"
.64 - 1.9

1"-2"
2.5-5

GROOVES CUT INTO FLOOR 1/4" - 3/4" (.64-1.9) WIDE, MINIMUM 1/8" (0.32) DEEP

DETAIL 5.62   Floor warning textures

Identification/Signage

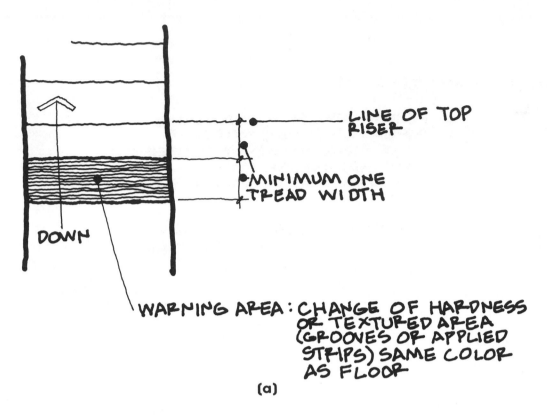

LINE OF TOP RISER

MINIMUM ONE TREAD WIDTH

DOWN

WARNING AREA : CHANGE OF HARDNESS OR TEXTURED AREA (GROOVES OR APPLIED STRIPS) SAME COLOR AS FLOOR

(a)

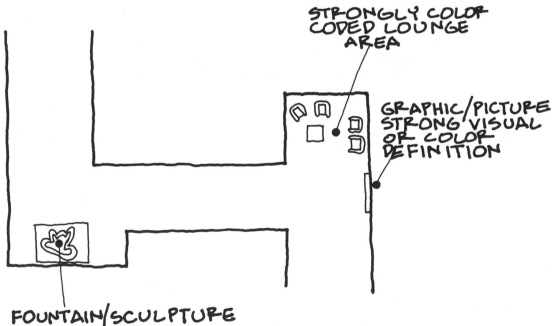

STRONGLY COLOR CODED LOUNGE AREA

GRAPHIC/PICTURE STRONG VISUAL OR COLOR DEFINITION

FOUNTAIN/SCULPTURE

PROVIDE VISUAL 'LANDMARKS' FOR THE ELDERLY AND VISUAL HANDICAPPED

(b)

DETAIL 5.63a   **Hall stair warning**
DETAIL 5.63b   **Orienting "landmarks"**

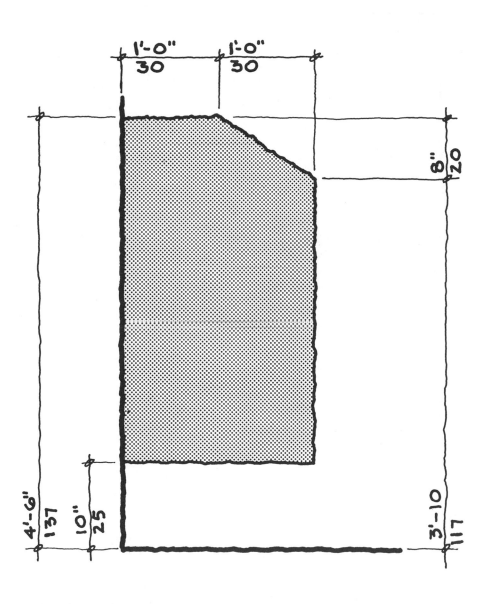

DETAIL 5.64 Accessible storage volume

Storage

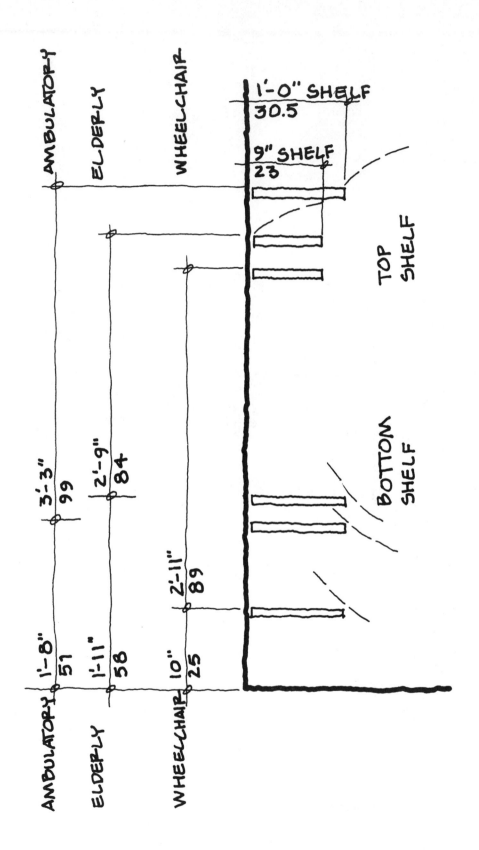

DETAIL 5.65   Storage shelving

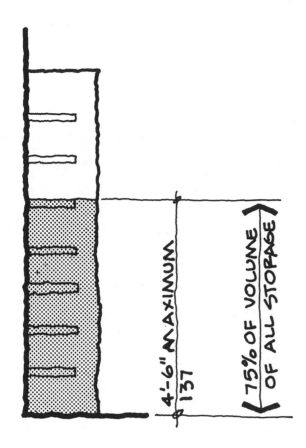

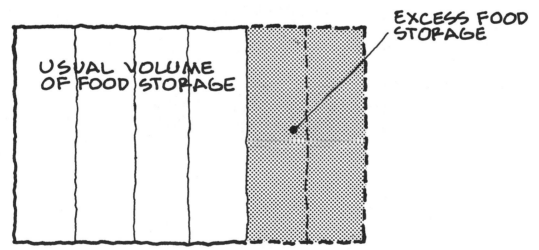

EXCESS FOOD STORAGE

USUAL VOLUME OF FOOD STORAGE

PROVIDE EXCESS FOOD STORAGE IN RESIDENCES, APARTMENTS FOR THE HANDICAPPED. (THE HANDICAPPED DEPEND ON DELIVERIES OR DIFFICULT, INFREQUENT SHOPPING TRIPS)

DETAIL 5.66   Kitchen storage volume

Storage

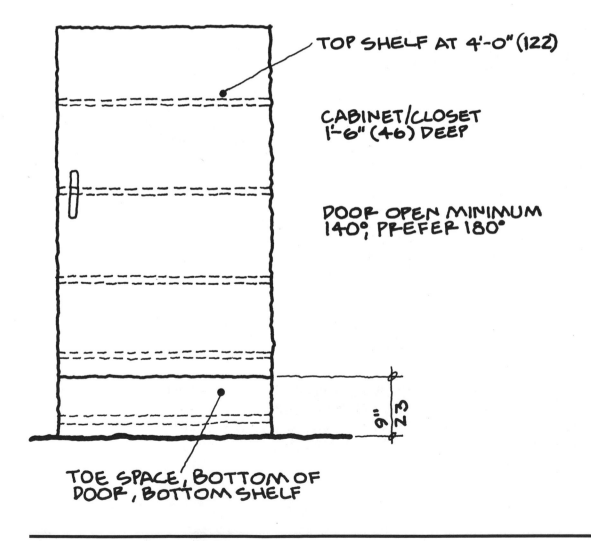

TOP SHELF AT 4'-0" (122)

CABINET/CLOSET
1'-6" (46) DEEP

DOOR OPEN MINIMUM
140°, PREFER 180°

9" / 23

TOE SPACE, BOTTOM OF
DOOR, BOTTOM SHELF

DETAIL 5.67   Storage cabinet

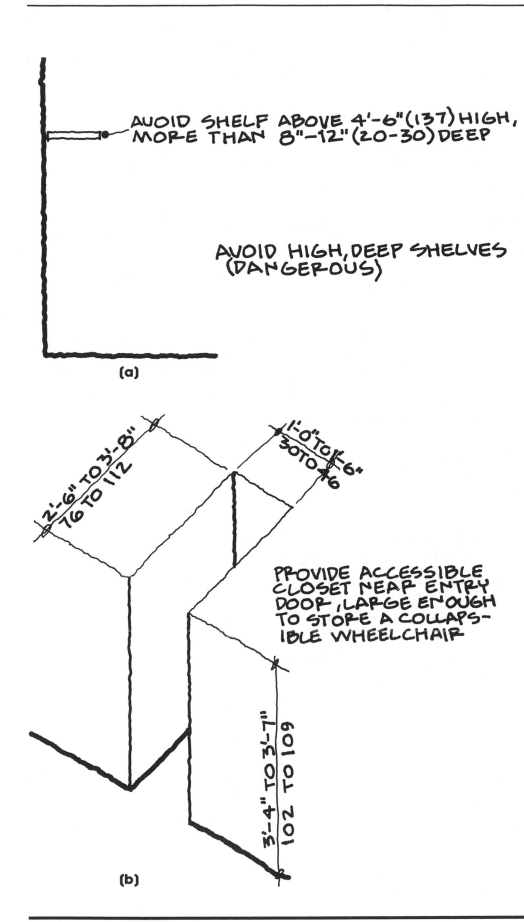

AVOID SHELF ABOVE 4'-6"(137) HIGH,
MORE THAN 8"-12"(20-30) DEEP

AVOID HIGH, DEEP SHELVES
(DANGEROUS)

(a)

2'-6" TO 3'-8"
76 TO 112

1'-0" TO 1'-6"
30 TO 46

PROVIDE ACCESSIBLE
CLOSET NEAR ENTRY
DOOR, LARGE ENOUGH
TO STORE A COLLAPS-
IBLE WHEELCHAIR

3'-4" TO 3'-7"
102 TO 109

(b)

DETAIL 5.68a   Shelf
DETAIL 5.68b   Wheelchair storage

Storage

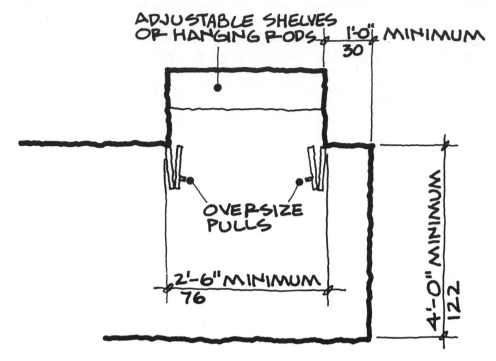

ADJUSTABLE SHELVES
OR HANGING RODS

1'-0" MINIMUM
30

OVERSIZE
PULLS

2'-6" MINIMUM
76

4'-0" MINIMUM
122

PREFERABLY EACH HALF OF A BIFOLD
PAIR SHOULD BE 2'-6" (76) WIDE

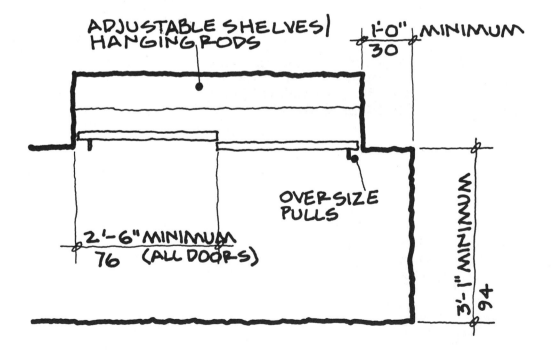

ADJUSTABLE SHELVES/
HANGING RODS

1'-0" MINIMUM
30

OVERSIZE
PULLS

2'-6" MINIMUM
76 (ALL DOORS)

3'-1" MINIMUM
94

DETAIL 5.69   Accessible closets

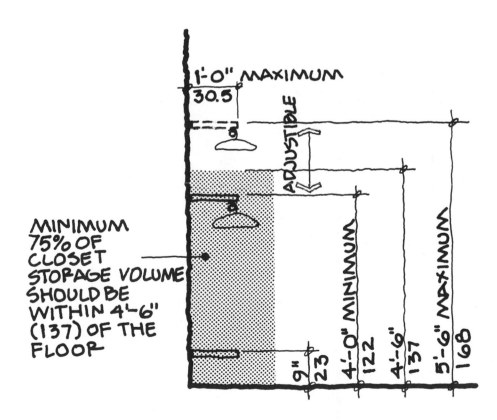

1'-0" MAXIMUM
30.5

ADJUSTABLE

MINIMUM 75% OF CLOSET STORAGE VOLUME SHOULD BE WITHIN 4'-6" (137) OF THE FLOOR

9" 23

4'-0" MINIMUM 122

4'-6" 137

5'-6" MAXIMUM 168

DETAIL 5.70   Closets

Storage

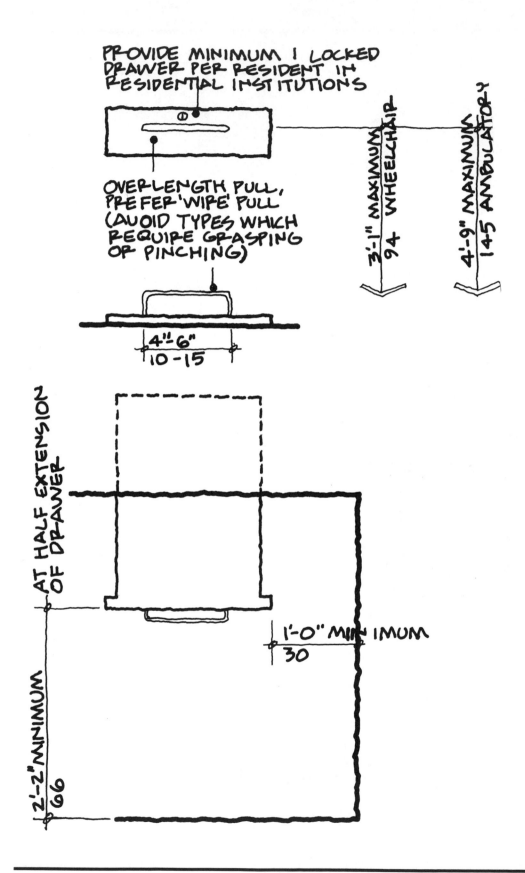

PROVIDE MINIMUM 1 LOCKED DRAWER PER RESIDENT IN RESIDENTIAL INSTITUTIONS

OVERLENGTH PULL, PREFER 'WIRE' PULL (AVOID TYPES WHICH REQUIRE GRASPING OR PINCHING)

4"-6"
10-15

3'-1" MAXIMUM WHEELCHAIR
94

4'-9" MAXIMUM AMBULATORY
145

AT HALF EXTENSION OF DRAWER

1'-0" MINIMUM
30

2'-2" MINIMUM
66

DETAIL 5.71   Drawers

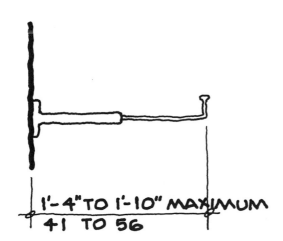

1'-4" TO 1'-10" MAXIMUM
41 TO 56

PREFER LINEN STORAGE ON PULLOUT
BARS WHERE POSSIBLE

DETAIL 5.72 Linen storage

Part Six
Furniture

It must be recognized that furniture for the mobility handicapped, in addition to its usual function, will in almost all cases be used also as support for persons raising, lowering, or steadying themselves. For this reason, the weight and especially the stability of all furniture should be carefully considered.

For all persons, elderly and able-bodied as well as the physically handicapped, chair arms are useful and comfortable. Arms are, of course, highly desirable for the physically disabled as an aid in raising themselves from a sitting position.

Chair seats should be at the 19 to 20″ (48 to 51) height; seats which are deep, soft, or much lower should be avoided.

The provision of high extensions or backs on (fully stable) furniture, as a high footboard on beds is useful as an aid for the mobility handicapped.

For persons with lesser vision and less ability to avoid occasional collisions with furniture, all corners and edges should be rounded. Where many vision-impaired persons will be present, the use of padded furniture may be worthy of consideration.

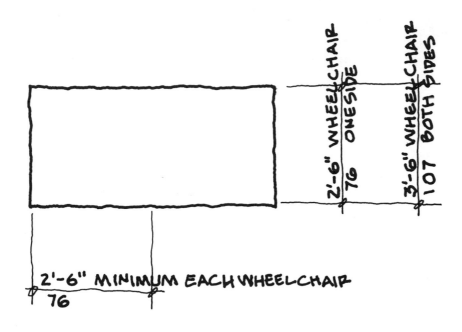

2'-6" WHEELCHAIR 76 ONE SIDE

3'-6" WHEELCHAIR 107 BOTH SIDES

2'-6" MINIMUM EACH WHEELCHAIR
76

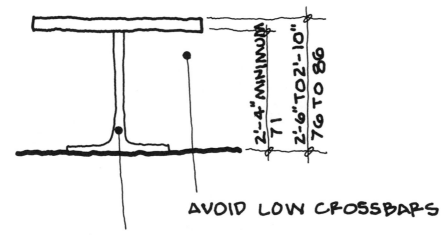

2'-4" MINIMUM 71

2'-6" TO 2'-10" 76 TO 86

AVOID LOW CROSSBARS

AVOID CORNER LEGS, PREFER CENTER PEDESTAL

CENTER PEDESTAL SHOULD BE HEAVILY WEIGHTED TO OFFSET USE OF CORNERS OF THE TABLE AS SUPPORT POINTS BY THE HANDICAPPED

DETAIL 6.1 Accessible table

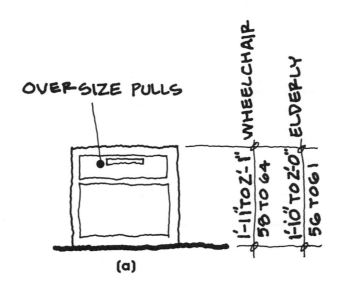

OVERSIZE PULLS

1'-1" TO 2'-1" WHEELCHAIR
58 TO 64

1'-10" TO 2'-0" ELDERLY
56 TO 61

(a)

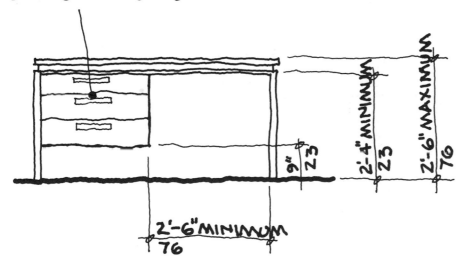

OVERSIZE PULLS

9"
23

2'-4" MINIMUM
23

2'-6" MAXIMUM
76

2'-6" MINIMUM
76

PREFER RELATIVELY HEAVY, WIDE, STABLE
FURNITURE FOR THE AMBULATORY HANDICAPPED
AND ELDERLY, SINCE THE FURNITURE WILL BE
USED FOR SUPPORT

(b)

DETAIL 6.2a   Bedside table
DETAIL 6.2b   Accessible desk

OVERSIZE PULLS

DRAWERS NARROW ENOUGH TO REQUIRE ONLY ONE PULL

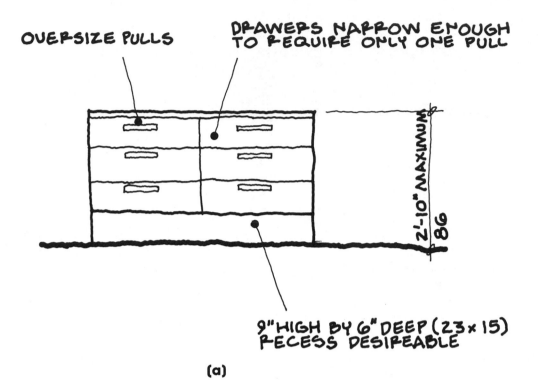

2'-10" MAXIMUM
86

9"HIGH BY 6"DEEP (23×15) RECESS DESIREABLE

(a)

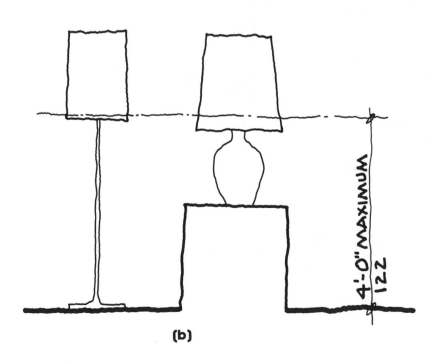

4'-0" MAXIMUM
122

(b)

DETAIL 6.3a   Dressers
DETAIL 6.3b   Lamps

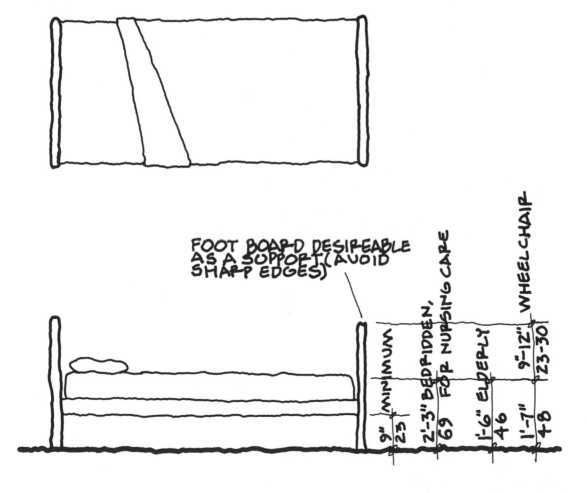

FOOT BOARD DESIREABLE
AS A SUPPORT (AVOID
SHARP EDGES)

9" MINIMUM
25

2'-3" BEDRIDDEN,
69 FOR NURSING CARE

1'-6" ELDERLY
46

1'-7" 9"-12" WHEELCHAIR
48   23-30

DETAIL 6.4   Beds

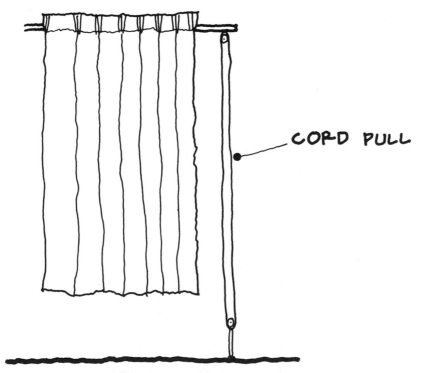

CORD PULL

PREFER CAPTIVE CORD DRAW DRAPES
AVOID LOOSE END CORDS AND WAND PULLS

DETAIL 6.5 **Draperies**

Part Seven
Planning

FIRE SAFETY

- Provide exit signs set to flash (less than 5 hertz) when a fire alarm sounds; power from the emergency power system.
- Audible fire signals should exceed the average ambient sound level by a minimum of 15 decibels (15 phones); they should exceed a noise of 30 seconds or less duration by a minimum of 5 decibels (5 phones); the maximum audible emergency signal should not exceed 120 decibels (120 phones).
- Provide visual/light alarm signals in all areas occupied by the deaf.
- Provide under-pillow vibrating alarm signals in bedrooms for the deaf.
- Provide a minimum of two accessible exits or horizontal exits for all accessible areas of all buildings.
- Where there is only one accessible exit, provide a minimum of one fireproof refuge area (fire-rated enclosed elevator lobby preferred, or enlarged landing area in a fire-rated stair enclosure).
- A fire refuge area should be a minimum of 16 square feet (1.5 square meters) outside of exit circulation paths. Provide an occupancy/call system from refuge areas to fire department annunciator location, or entrance vestibules.
- Open fireplaces can be hazardous to the disabled; they should be covered with tempered glass doors, and guarded by a 9 to 18" high (23 to 46) raised hearth.
- Provide fire detectors, especially in institutions, as follows:

	Rate of temperature rise detector	Fixed temperature detector, adjustable	Fixed temperature detector, permanent setting 175 to 240°F (79 to 116°C)	Smoke / products of combustion detector (ionization type preferred)
Kitchen	●			
Basement	●	○		
Storage	●	○		
Soiled linen	●	○		
Trash	●	○		
Garage		●		
Accessible attic			●	
Residential sleeping area				●

Preferred ●
Acceptable ○

HEATING

- Provide for a general ambient temperature of 75°F (24°C) in habitable areas used by the nonambulatory handicapped.
- Provide supplementary heat for paraplegics and the elderly. Radiant floor or ceiling heat is good. Quick-reaction types are desirable. Avoid hot surfaces in locations where they would be exposed to touch.
- Avoid drafts from forced-air or convection heating systems.

PUBLIC BUILDINGS

- *All* entrances should be accessible if possible.
- Minimum of two entrances should be accessible for use as fire exits.
- All accessible entrances should be marked.
- Accessible entrances should be at or near the main public entrances, *not* at loading areas or the rear of the building.
- Provide an information phone at accessible entrances if possible.
- Provide tactile information signs, directories, and maps at accessible entrances.
- All lobbies, offices, toilets, cafeterias, public lounges, and vending areas should be accessible.
- In buildings with elevators, accessible toilets should be no more than two stories away from any floor (provide directory of accessible toilets in elevator cab).
- No toilet should be more than a 5-minute (travel time) round trip from any location in the building.

APARTMENTS, BOARDING HOUSES, HOTELS, AND INSTITUTIONS

- Provide a minimum of 4 percent of dwelling units as handicapped accessible in apartments.
- Provide 4 to 10 percent of rooms as handicapped accessible in boarding houses.
- Provide 10 percent of rooms as handicapped accessible in hotels.
- Prefer to locate accessible rooms/units on the entrance level (to maintain access in case of elevator failure).
- Provide access to all cooking, eating, sleeping, toilet, storage, and laundry areas.
- Units for families should have at least two bedrooms accessible.
- All walks, parking, patios, playgrounds and recreation facilities, common areas, mail, trash disposal, lobby, and lounge areas should be handicapped accessible.
- In apartments, provide excess food storage volume.
- No toilet should be located more than 30' (9 meters) from any bedroom.
- Provide 4 percent of individual dwelling units as handicapped accessible.
- Provide access to all cooking, eating, sleeping, toilet, storage, and laundry areas.
- The kitchen of each accessible dwelling unit should provide space for a table and two wheelchairs (eating space in the kitchen reduces the need to carry food into another room in a wheelchair).

PUBLIC BUILDINGS

All entrances should be accessible if possible.

Appendix 1

Federal
Laws

Architectural Barriers Act of 1968

Public Law 90-480

August 12, 1968

AN ACT

To insure that certain buildings financed with Federal funds are so designed and constructed as to be accessible to the physically handicapped.

Be it enacted by the Senate and House of Representatives of the United States of America in Congress assembled, That, as used in this Act, the term "building" means any building or facility (other than (a) a privately owned residential structure and (b) any building or facility on a military installation designed and constructed primarily for use by able bodied military personnel) the intended use for which either will require that such building or facility be accessible to the public, or may result in the employment or residence therein of physically handicapped persons, which building or facility is---

(1) to be constructed or altered by or on behalf of the United States;

(2) to be leased in whole or in part by the United States after the date of enactment of this Act after construction or alteration in accordance with plans and specifications of the United States; or

(3) to be financed in whole or in part by a grant or a loan made by the United States after the date of enactment of this Act if such building or facility is subject to standards for design, construction, or alteration issued under authority of the law authorizing such grant or loan.

SEC. 2. The Administrator of General Services, in consultation with the Secretary of Health, Education, and Welfare, is authorized to prescribe such standards for the design, construction, and alteration of buildings (other than residential structures subject to this Act and buildings, structures, and facilities of the Department of Defense subject to this Act) as may be necessary to insure that physically handicapped persons will have ready access to, and use of, such buildings.

SEC. 3. The Secretary of Housing and Urban Development, in consultation with the Secretary of Health, Education, and Welfare, is authorized to prescribe such standards for the design, construction, and alteration of buildings which are residential structures subject to this Act as may be necessary to insure that physically handicapped persons will have ready access to, and use of, such buildings.

SEC. 4. The Secretary of Defense, in consultation with the Secretary of Health, Education, and Welfare, is authorized to prescribe such standards for the design, contruction, and alteration of buildings, structures, and facilities of the Department of Defense subject to this Act as may be necessary to insure that physically handicapped persons will have access to, and use of such buildings.

SEC. 5. Every building designed, constructed, or altered after the effective date of a standard issued under this Act which is applicable to such building, shall be designed, constructed, or altered in accordance with such standard.

SEC. 6. The administrator of General Services, with respect to standards issued under section 2 of this Act, and the Secretary of Housing and Urban Development, with respect to standards issued under section 3 of this Act, and the Secretary of Defense with respect to standards issued under section 4 of this Act, is authorized---

(1) to modify or waive any such standards, on a case-by-case basis, upon application made by the head of the department, agency, or instrumentality of the United States concerned, and upon a determination by the Administrator or Secretary, as the case may be, that such modification or waiver is clearly necessary, and

(2) to conduct such surveys and investigations as he deems necessary to insure compliance with such standards.

Public Law 91-205

March 5, 1970

AN ACT

To amend the Act of August 12, 1968, to insure that certain facilities constructed under authority of Federal law are designed and constructed to be accessible to the physically handicapped.

Be it enacted by the Senate and House of Representatives of the United States of America in Congress assembled, That the first section of the Act entitled "An Act to insure that certain buildings financed with Federal funds are so designed and constructed as to be accessible to the physically handicapped", approved August 12, 1968 (42 U.S.C. 4151), is amended—

(1) by striking out "or" at the end of paragraph (2);

(2) by striking out the period at the end of paragraph (3) and inserting in lieu thereof: ";or"; and

(3) by adding at the end thereof the following:

(4) to be constructed under authority of the National Capital Transportation Act of 1960, the National Capital Transportation Act of 1965, or title III of the Washington Metropolitan Area Transit Regulation Compact.

Public Buildings Cooperative Use Act of 1976

Public Law 94–541

October 18, 1976

AN ACT

To amend the Public Buildings Act of 1959 in order to preserve buildings of historical or architectural significance through their use for Federal public building purposes, and to amend the Act of August 12, 1968, relating to the accessibility of certain buildings to the physically handicapped.

Be it enacted by the Senate and House of Representatives of the United States of America in Congress assembled,

TITLE II

Sec. 201. The Act entitled "An Act to insure that certain buildings financed with Federal funds are so designed and constructed as to be accessible to the physically handicapped", approved August 12, 1968 (42 U.S.C. 41514156), is amended as follows:

(1) The first section is amended by inserting after "structure" the following: "not leased by the Government for subsidized housing programs"; and by striking out in paragraph (2) the following: "after construction or alteration in accordance with plans and specifications of the United States".

(2) Section 2 is amended—

(A) by striking out "is authorized to prescribe such" and inserting in lieu thereof "shall prescribe";

(B) by striking out "as may be necessary to insure" and inserting in lieu thereof "to insure whenever possible"; and

(C) by inserting immediately after "Department of Defense" the following: "and of the United States Postal Service".

(3) Section 3 is amended—

(A) by striking out "is authorized to prescribe such" and inserting in lieu thereof "shall prescribe"; and

(B) by striking out "as may be necessary to insure" and inserting in lieu thereof "to insure whenever possible".

(4) Section 4 is amended—

(A) by striking out "is authorized to prescribe such" and inserting in lieu thereof "shall prescribe"; and

(B) by striking out "as may be necessary to insure" and inserting in lieu thereof "to insure whenever possible".

(5) Immediately after section 4 insert the following new section:

"Sec. 4a. The United States Postal Service, in consultation with the Secretary of Health, Education, and Welfare, shall prescribe such standards for the design, construction, and alteration of its buildings to insure whenever possible that physically handicapped persons will have ready access to, and use of, such buildings.".

(6) Section 6 is amended—

(A) by inserting immediately after "section 4 of this Act," the following: "and the United States Postal Service with respect to standards issued under section 4a of this Act";

(B) by striking out "is authorized";

(C) by inserting immediately after "(1)" the following: "is authorized"; and

(D) by striking out all that follows "(2)" and inserting in lieu thereof "shall establish a system of continuing surveys and investigations to insure compliance with such standards.".

(7) By adding at the end thereof the following new section:

"Sec. 7.(a) The Administrator of General Services shall report to Congress during the first week of January of each year on his activities and those of other departments, agencies, and instrumentalities of the Federal Government under this Act during the preceding fiscal year including, but not limited to, standards issued, revised, amended or repealed under this Act and all case-by-case modifications, and waivers of such standards during such year.

"(b) The Architectural and Transportation Barriers Compliance Board established by section 502 of the Rehabilitation Act of 1973 (Public Law 93-112) shall report to the Public Works and Transportation Committee of the House of Representatives and the Public Works Committee of the Senate during the first week of January of each year on its activities and actions to insure compliance with the standards prescribed under this Act.".

Sec. 202. The amendment made by paragraph (1) of section 201 of this Act shall not apply to any lease entered into before January 1, 1977. It shall apply to every lease entered into on or after January 1, 1977, including any renewal of a lease entered into before such date which renewal is on or after such date.

Sec. 203. Section 410(b) of Title 39, United States Code, is amended by adding at the end thereof the following:

"(8) The provisions of the Act of August 12, 1968 (42 U.S.C. 4151–4156)."

Explanation: Title II of Public Law 94-541 brings buildings and facilities under the jurisdiction of the U.S. Postal Service into the realm of compliance with PL 90-480. Moreover, PL 94-541 now makes it obligatory rather than optional, for the Administrator of GSA, the Secretary of HUD, the Secretary of Defense, and the Postal Service to prescribe standards for access and use by disabled. Also, this law now mandates that these Federal department heads must institute ongoing internal Department compliance review systems. This is another provision which was previously only allowed, but now is mandated by law.

Rehabilitation Act of 1973

Public Law 93-112

September 26, 1973

ARCHITECTURAL AND TRANSPORTATION BARRIERS COMPLIANCE BOARD

Sec. 502. (a) There is established within the Federal Government the Architectural and Transportation Barriers Compliance Board (hereinafter referred to as the "Board") which shall be composed of the heads of each of the following departments or agencies (or their designees whose positions are Executive Level IV or higher):

(1) Department of Health, Education, and Welfare;

(2) Department of Transportation;

(3) Department of Housing and Urban Development;

(4) Department of Labor;

(5) Department of the Interior;

(6) General Services Administration;

(7) United States Postal Service; and

(8) Veterans' Administration.

(b) It shall be the function of the Board to: (1) insure compliance with the standards prescribed by the General Services Administration, the Department of Defense, and the Department of Housing and Urban Development pursuant to the Architectural Barriers Act of 1968 (Public Law 90-480), as amended by the Act of March 5, 1970 (Public Law 91-205); (2) investigate and examine alternative approaches to the architectural, transportation, and attitudinal barriers confronting handicapped individuals, particularly with respect to public buildings and monuments, parks and parklands, public transportation (including air, water, and surface transportation whether interstate, foreign, intrastate, or local), and residential and institutional housing; (3) determine what measures are being taken by Federal, State, and local governments and by other public or nonprofit agencies to eliminate the barriers described in clause (2) of this subsection; (4) promote the use of the International Accessibility Symbol in all public facilities that are in compliance with the standards prescribed by the Administrator of the General Services Administration, the Secretary of Defense, and the Secretary of Housing and Urban Development pursuant to the Architectural Barriers Act of 1968; (5) make to the President and to Congress reports which shall describe in detail the results to its investigations under clauses (2) and (3) of this subsection; and (6) make to the President and to the Congress such recommendations for legislation and administration as it deems necessary or desirable to eliminate the barriers described in clause (2) of this subsection.

(c) The Board shall also (1) (A) determine how and to what extent transportation barriers impede the mobility of handicapped individuals and aged handicapped individuals and consider ways in which travel expenses in connection with transportation to and from work for handicapped individuals can be met or subsidized when such individuals are unable to use mass transit systems or need special equipment in private transportation, and (B) consider the housing needs of handicapped individuals; (2) determine what measures are being taken, especially by public and other nonprofit agencies and groups having an interest in and a capacity to deal with such problems, (A) to eliminate barriers from public transportation systems (including vehicles used in such systems), and to prevent their incorporation in new or expanded transportation systems and (B) to make housing available and accessible to handicapped individuals or to meet sheltered housing needs; and (3) prepare plans and proposals for such further actions as may be necessary to the goals of adequate transportation and housing for handicapped individuals, including proposals for bringing together in a cooperative effort, agencies, organizations, and groups already working toward such goals or whose cooperation is essential to effective and comprehensive action.

(d) In carrying out its functions under this section, the Board shall conduct investigations, hold public hearings, and issue such orders as it deems necessary to insure compliance with the provisions of the Acts cited in subsection (b). The provisions of subchapter II of chapter 5 and chapter 7 of title 5, United States Code, shall apply to procedures under this section, and an order of compliance issued by the Board shall be a final order for purposes of judicial review.

(e) The Board is authorized to appoint as many hearing examiners as are necessary for proceedings required to be conducted under this section. The provisions applicable to hearing examiners appointed under section 3105 of title 5, United States Code, shall apply to hearing examiners appointed under this subsection.

(f) The departments or agencies specified in subsection (a) of this section shall make available to the Board such technical, administrative, or other assistance as it may require to carry out its functions under this section, and the Board may appoint such other advisers, technical experts, and consultant as it deems necessary to assist it in carrying out its functions under this section. Special advisory and technical experts and consultants appointed pursuant to this subsection shall, while performing their functions under this section, be entitled to receive compensation at rates fixed by the Secretary, but not exceeding the daily pay rate, for a person employed as a GS-18 under section 5332 of title 45, United States Code, including traveltime, and while serving away from their homes or regular places of business they may be allowed travel expenses, including per diem in lieu of subsistence, as authorized by section 5703 of such title 5 for persons in the Government service employed intermittently.

(g) The Board shall, at the end of each fiscal year, report its activities during the preceding fiscal year to the Congress. Such report shall include an assessment of the extent of compliance with Acts cited in subsection (b) of this section, along with a description and analysis of investigations made and actions taken by the Board, and the reports and recommendations described in clauses (5) and (6) of subsection (b) of this section. The Board shall prepare two final reports of its activities under subsection (c). One such report shall be on its activities in the field of transportation barriers to handicapped individuals, and the other such report shall be on its activities in the field of the housing needs of handicapped individuals. The Board shall, prior to January 1, 1975, submit each such report, together with its recommendations, to the President and the Congress. The Board shall also prepare for such submission an interim report of its activities in each such field within 18 months after the date of enactment of this Act.

(h) There are authorized to be appropriated for the purpose of carrying out the duties and functions of the Board under this section $1,000,000 each for the fiscal years ending June 30, 1974, and June 30, 1975.

Amendments to Rehabilitation Act of 1973

Public Law 93-516

December 7, 1974

Sec. 100. This title shall be known as the "Rehabilitation Act Amendments of 1974.".

EXTENSION OF AUTHORIZATION OF APPROPRIATIONS FOR ARCHITECTURAL AND TRANSPORTATION BARRIERS COMPLIANCE BOARD

Sec. 110. Section 502(h) of such Act is amended by inserting before the period at the end thereof a comma and "and $1,500,000 for the fiscal year ending June 30, 1976".

Sec. 111. (n) (1) Section 502(a) of such Act is amended by redesignating clauses (6), (7), and (8) thereof as clauses (7), (8), and (9), respectively, and by inserting immediately after clause (5) the following new clause:

"(6) Department of Defense;"

(2) Section 502(a) of such Act is further amended by adding at the end thereof the following new sentence: "The Secretary of Health, Education, and Welfare shall be the Chairman of the Board, and the Board shall appoint, upon recommendation of the Secretary, a Consumer Advisory Panel, a majority of the members of which shall be handicapped individuals, to provide guidance, advice, and recommendations to the Board in carrying out its functions.".

(o) (1) Section 502(d) of such Act is amended by striking out "section, the Board" in the first sentence and inserting in lieu thereof "Act, the Board shall, directly or through grants to or contracts with public or private nonprofit organizations, carry out its functions under subsections (b) and (c) of this section, and".

(2) Section 502(d) of such Act is further amended by adding at the end thereof the following new sentences: "Any such order affecting any Federal department, agency, or instrumentality of the United States shall be final and binding on such department, agency, or instrumentality. An order of compliance may include the withholding or suspension of Federal funds with respect to any building found not to be in compliance with standards prescribed pursuant to the Acts cited in subsection (b) of this section."

(p) Section 502(e) of such Act is amended by adding before the first sentence the following new first sentence: "There shall be appointed by the Board an executive director and such other professional and clerical personnel as are necessary to carry out its functions under this Act.".

(q) Section 502(g) of such Act is amended by striking out in the penultimate sentence "prior to January 1" and inserting in lieu thereof "not later than September 30".

(**Editor's Note:** In addition, two other provisions of the Rehabilitation Act Amendments of 1974 expand the involvement of the A&TBCB under separate areas of PL 93-112. Section III (k) of PL 93-516 amends Section 304(e) (1) of PL 93-112 concerning special projects. The initial legislation under PL 93-112 mandates technical assistance to rehabilitation facilities and to other facilities under the jurisdiction of the Vocational Rehabilitation program for the purpose of the removal of architectural and transportation barriers. The amendment of PL 93-516 requires that such technical assistance be provided only with the concurrence of the A&TBCB; this should ensure compliance with ANSI 117.1-1961 in such rehabilitation and other installations. Section III (I) of PL 93-516 amends Section 306 (b) of PL 93-112 concerning the general grant and contract requirements as they relate to an application for assistance for a construction project. The amending provisions of PL 93-516 are twofold: it is now required that the plans and specifications of such construction which is assisted by a grant under Section 306 (b) of PL 93-112 have the full concurrence of the A&TBCB; it is further required that this new responsibility of the A&TBCB be extended as well to all general construction project requirements in section 306(b) to an application for any project which involves construction. To our understanding, the A&TBCB must concur with any and all construction under section 306(b) of PL 93-112, whether it be construction of a new facility or alteration, renovation, or remodeling of an existing structure.)

Appendix 2
State Laws

State	Statute	Adopts ANSI 117.1	Publ. funded bldg.	Pvt. funded bldg. open to public	Pvt. bldg.	Remodelling	Waivers/ variances	Information
ALABAMA	State Act 224, 1965 amended State Act 1210	No	Yes	No	No	More than 50% of value	Yes	
ALASKA	State Laws 1976 35.10.015	No	Yes	No	No	Yes		State Dept. of Transportation & Public Facilities, Division of Design Review & Constr. Pouch 6900, Anchorage, AL 99501
ARIZONA	Ariz. Rev. Statutes Title 34, Chapt. 4	No	Yes	Yes	No	No	No	State Dept. Administration Finance Division, Planning Office, 605 West Wing, Capital Bldg., Phoenix, AZ 85007
ARKANSAS	Arkansas Act 122, 1967	Yes	Yes	No	No	Yes	No	Arkansas Dept. Health, 4815 W. Markham St., Little Rock, AK 72201
CALIFORNIA	California Govt. Codes 1968 Section 4450	No	Yes	Yes	Yes	Yes	Specified items	Office of the State Architect, 1500 5th St., Sacramento, CA 95814
COLORADO	CRS 1973, Vol. 3, Title 9, Article 5 Rev.; CRS 1973, 1976 Annual Suppl. Vol. 3, Art. 5	No	Yes	Yes	No	More than 25% of value	No	State Buildings Division, State Service Bldg., 1525 Sherman St., Room 617, Denver, CO 80203

State	Statute	Adopts ANSI 117.1	Publ. funded bldg.	Pvt. funded bldg. open to public	Pvt. bldg.	Remodelling	Waivers/ variances	Information
CONNECTICUT	State Bldg. Code Article 21	No	Yes	Yes	Yes	More than 25% of value	Specified items	Dept. Administrative Services, Bureau of Public Works, Room 523, State Office Bldg., Hartford, CT 06115
DELAWARE	Delaware Laws Title 29, Chapt. 69, Section 6917	No	Yes	No	No	No	No	Dept. of Administrative Services, Division of Facilities Management, O'Neil Building, P.O. Box 1401, Dover, DE 19901
DISTRICT OF COLUMBIA	None							Bureau of Bldg. and Zoning, Administration, 614 H. Street N.W., Washington, DC 20001
FLORIDA	Florida Statutes Chapt. 553, Part 5	Yes	Yes	Yes	Yes	Yes	No	Department of Community Affairs, Division of Technical Assistance, 2571 Executive Ctr. Circle, East Tallahassee, FL 32301
GEORGIA	Senate Bill 412 House Bill 91	No	Yes	Yes	Yes	More than 20% of value	Yes	Georgia State Fire Marshal's Office, 7 Martin Luther King Drive S.W., Atlanta, GA 30334
HAWAII	Hawaii Rev. Statutes 103-50-1969	Yes	Yes	No	No	No	No	State Department of Accounting & General Services, 1151 Punchbowl St., P.O. Box 119, Honolulu, HI 96810
IDAHO		Yes 1976	Yes	Yes	No	More than 25% of value	Yes	Department of Labor & Industrial Services, Safety Division, 317 Main Street, Room 400, State House, Boise, ID 83720
ILLINOIS	Ill. Rev. Statutes 1975 Public Act 79-978	No	Yes	Yes	Yes	Yes	Local appeal	Capitol Development Board, Wm. Stratton Office Bldg., Springfield, IL 62706
INDIANA	I.C. 2211-1 1971 Rev.	No	Yes	Yes	Yes	Yes	Yes	State Building Commissioner, 215 N. Senate Ave., Room 300, Graphic Arts Building, Indianapolis, IN 46204
IOWA	104 Codes of Iowa	No	Yes	Yes	Yes	More than 25% of value	Yes	Office of Planning and Programming, Building Code Commission, 523 E. 12th St., Des Moines, IA 50319
KANSAS	Kansas Statutes 58-1301; 31-150	Yes 1961	Yes	Yes	Yes	More than 25% of value	Historical bldg. by written application	State Department of Administration, Division of Architectural Services, State Office Bldg., Topeka, KS 66612
KENTUCKY	Kentucky Rev. Statutes 227-030	Yes	Yes	Yes	No	In public accessible areas	No	State Fire Marshal's Office, 127 Building, Frankfort, KY 40601
LOUISIANA	Act 625 1977	Yes: 1977 Draft copy	Yes	Yes	Yes	Govt. buildings	No	Department of Public Safety Office of Fire Protection, 9131 Interline Dr., Baton Rouge, LA 70809

State	Statute	Adopts ANSI 117.1	Publ. funded bldg.	Pvt. funded bldg. open to public	Pvt. bldg.	Remodelling	Waivers/ variances	Information
MAINE	Maine Statutes, Title 25, Part 7 Chapt. 331	No	Yes	No	No	Any cost exceeding $100,000	No	Bureau of Public Improvements, Room 119, State Office Building, Augusta, ME 04333
MARYLAND	Annotated State Code, Art. 78A, 51; Art. 41, 257 JK	No	Yes	Yes	Yes	Pvt. bldg. only, more than 50% of market value	No	Governor's Office for the Handicapped, Old Armory Building, 11 Bladen Street, Annapolis, MD 21401
MASSACHUSETTS	528 Acts 1974 amending Chap. 22 General Laws 13A	No	Yes	Yes	Yes	More than 5% of value	Petition	Architectural Barriers Board, McCormick State Office Building, #1 Ashburten, Room 1319, Boston, MA 02108
MICHIGAN	Public acts 1972 230	No	Yes	Yes	Yes	Yes	Yes	Michigan Department of Labor, Bureau of Construction Codes, State Secondary Complex, 7150 Harris Drive, P.O. Box 30015, Lansing, MI 48909
MINNESOTA	MS 16.83 to .87	No	Yes	Yes	Yes	Yes		State Department of Administration, Building Code Office, 408 Metro Square, St. Paul, MN 55101
MISSISSIPPI	1972 Codes 43-6-101 to 43-6-125	No	Yes	No	No	Yes	Yes	Mississippi State Board of Health Division of Food and General Sanitation, P.O. Box 1700, Jackson, MS 39205
MISSOURI	L 1975 HB 270	No	Yes	No	No	Yes	No; schools exempted	Office of Administration, Division of Design and Construction, P.O. Box 809, Jefferson City, MO 65101
MONTANA	Revised Codes of Montana 1947 Title 69, Chapter 21	Yes	Yes	Yes	Yes	More than 25% of value	Yes	State Building Code Office, 1509 6th Avenue, Capitol Station, Helena, MT 59601
NEBRASKA	LB 602 1974; RRS 72-1101 to RRS 72-1124	No	Yes	Yes	No	More than 50 % of value	Yes	State Fire Marshal's Office, Public Building Safety Advisory Committee, 301 Centennial Mall South, 6th Floor, Lincoln, NE 68509
NEVADA	NRS 338.180 State Building Code	Yes (1971)	Yes	No	No	No	No	State Public Works Board, 505 E. King St., Carson City, NV 89710
NEW HAMPSHIRE	N.H. Laws 1977, Chap. 269	No	Yes	No	No	No		State Dept. Public Works, Public Works Architect, John O. Morton Building, 85 Loudon Road, Concord, NH 03301
NEW JERSEY	Senate Bill 1252	No	Yes	Yes	Yes	More than 25% of value	Written applications; bldg. on Nat. Register	State Dept. of Treasury, Div. of Bldg. & Constr., P.O. Box 1243, Trenton, NJ 08625

State	Statute	Adopts ANSI 117.1	Publ. funded bldg.	Pvt. funded bldg. open to public	Pvt. bldg.	Remodelling	Waivers/ variances	Information
NEW MEXICO	State Laws Chapt. 41	Yes	Yes	No	No	More than 25% of value	No	State Construction Industry Bureau, P.O. Box 5155, Santa Fe, NM 87115
NEW YORK	State Legislative Acts 1972, Chapt. 656	No	Yes	Yes	Yes	Yes	No	Housing & Bldg. Codes Bureau, Div. of Housing & Community Development, #2 World Trade Center, New York, NY 10047
NORTH CAROLINA	General Statutes 1973 168-1 through 168-8	No	Yes	Yes	Yes	Yes	Yes, for industrial buildings only	State Department of Insurance, Engr. & Bldg. Code Div., P.O. Box 26387, Raleigh, NC 27611
NORTH DAKOTA	State Laws 1973, Chapt. 376	Yes (1961)	Yes	No	No	Yes	Yes	State Construction Superintendent, State Capitol Bldg., Bismarck, ND 58505
OHIO	Administrative Code Chapt. 21, 16	Yes (1971)	Yes	No	No	Remodelled area only	No	State Industrial Relations Dept., Division of Factory & Bldg. Inspection, 2323 W. 5th Ave., P.O. Box 825, Columbus, OH 43216
OKLAHOMA		Yes	Yes	No	No	Yes		State Board of Public Affairs, Engineering Division, 306 State Capitol Bldg., Oklahoma City, OK 73105
OREGON	O.R.S. 476-030	No	Yes	Larger than 4000 sq. ft.	No	Yes	Yes	Dept. of Commerce, Bldg. Codes Division, 401 Labor & Industry Building, Salem, OR 97310
PENNSYLVANIA	P.L. Acts 176, 216, 235, 299, Chapt. 34, 37	No	Yes	Yes	Yes	Yes (all work)	Yes	Bureau of Occupational & Industrial Safety, Bldg. Division, Room 1514, Labor & Industry Bldg., 77th & Forster St., Harrisburg, PA 17120
RHODE ISLAND	General Laws 1970, Title 37, Chapt. 17	(1969 ASA Code)	Yes	Yes	Yes	More than 25%	No	State Bldg. Code Commissioner, 12 Humbert St., N. Providence, RI 02911
SOUTH CAROLINA	1976 Codes, 10-5-210 to 10-5-230	Yes 1971	Yes	Yes	Yes	More than 25%	Yes	Chief Engineer, Finance Division, Budget Control Board, P.O. Box 11333, Columbia, SC 29211
SOUTH DAKOTA	SDCL 5-14-12 to 5-14-14 amended	Yes 1971	Yes	No	No	Yes	Yes	State Engineer's Office, Suite 205 Foss Building, Pierre, SD 57501
TENNESSEE	TCA 53-2544	No (N.C. code)	Yes	Yes	No	Yes	Yes	State Architect, Suite 1100, #1 Commerce Place, Nashville, TN 37219

State	Statute	Adopts ANSI 117.1	Publ. funded bldg.	Pvt. funded bldg. open to public	Pvt. bldg.	Remodelling	Waivers/ variances	Information
TEXAS	61st Leg., Senate Bill 111, Art. 678g	No	Yes	Yes	No	Public funded bldg. only	Yes, public-funded bldg.	State Board of Control, Prevention of Architectural Barriers Division, Box 13047, Capitol Station, Austin, TX 78711
UTAH	U.C.A. Chapt. 27	No	Yes	No	No	Yes		State Bldg. Board, Room 124, State Capitol, Salt Lake City, UT 84114
VERMONT	V.S.L. Chapt. 25, Titles 3 and 18	Yes (amended)	Yes	No	No	Yes	Yes	Architectural Barriers Compliance Board, 2 West Ave., Montpelier, VT. 05602
VIRGINIA	Commonwealth Assembly 1970, Chapt. 539	Yes	Yes	Yes	Yes	Yes	Yes	Division of Engineering and Building, 209 9th St. Office Bldg., Richmond, VA 23219
WASHINGTON	Additions to State Building Code 1976	No	Yes	Yes	Yes	Yes	No	State Department of Administration, Engineering & Architecture Division, 106 Maple Parkway, Olympia, WA 98504
WEST VIRGINIA	Senate Bill 372	No	Yes	Yes	Yes	Yes	Yes	Division of Vocational Rehabilatation, 1427 Lee Street East, Charleston, WV 25301
WISCONSIN	W.S. 101.13, IND. 52.04	No	Yes	Yes	Yes	More than 25%	Yes	Safety and Building Division, 201 E. Washington Ave., P.O. Box 7946, Madison, WI 53707
WYOMING	W.S. 35-503 to 506	Yes	Yes	No	No	Yes	No	Department of Fire Prevention & Electrical Safety, 720 W. 18th St., Cheyenne, WY 82002
UNITED STATES	PL 93-112, Section 504, VSC 706; (Federal Register, May 4, 1977, p. 22675)	Yes	Yes	No	No	Yes	Yes	Office of New Programs, Office of Civil Rights, Department of HEW, Washington, DC 20201

NOTES:
1. Many codes which do not adopt ANSI 117.1 are based in part or in whole on the 1961–1973 editions of ANSI 117.1.
2. 'Private Buildings'; when included in the state laws, generally exclude 1- and 2-family dwellings, industrial and some work occupancies.
3. 'Remodelling': when cost of the remodelling work exceeds the percentage of building cost given, some or all of the requirements apply.
4. Waivers and variances when available are generally reviewed on a case-by-case basis.

Bibliography

Access for All, Ohio Governor's Committee on Employment, and Schooley Cornelius Associates; Columbus, Ohio, 1977.

An Illustrated Handbook of the Handicapped Section of the North Carolina State Building Code, North Carolina State Department of Insurance; Raleigh, N.C., 1974.

American Society of Landscape Architects, *Barrier Free Site Design*, U.S. Department of Housing and Urban Development; Washington, 1975.

Arts and the Handicapped, Educational Facilities Laboratories and the National Endowment for the Arts, New York, 1975.

Building Code of the City of New York, City of New York, New York.

Building Construction Code of New York State, State of New York, Albany, N.Y.

Chronic Conditions and Limitations of Activity and Mobility, National Center for Health Statistics; Washington, 1967.

Comprehensive Barrier-Free Standards, New Jersey Easter Seal Society, Trenton, N.J., 1975.

Diffrient, N., *Humanscale 1-2-3*, M.I.T. Press; Cambridge, Mass., 1974.

Goldsmith, S., *Designing for the Disabled*, 2d ed., McGraw-Hill, New York; 1st ed., Royal British Institute of Architects, London, 1963.

Harkness, S., and Groom, J. N., *Building Without Barriers for the Disabled*, Watson-Guptill, New York, 1976.

Housing for the Physcially Impaired, A Guide for Planning and Design, U.S. Department of Housing and Urban Design, Washington, 1969.

HUD and the Handicapped, Minneapolis–St. Paul Area Office, U.S. Department of Housing and Urban Development; Minneapolis, 1975.

Kiewel and Salmon, *Accessible Architecture*, Advisory Committee to the Mayor and the City Council of Minneapolis on the Handicapped, Minneapolis, 1977.

Making Facilities Accessible to the Physically Handicapped, New York State University Construction Fund, Albany, 1967.

Manual of Acceptable Practices to the HUD Minimum Property Standards, United States Department of Housing and Urban Design, Washington, 1973.

Moakley, *Barrier-Free Design: The Law*, Eastern Paralized Veterans' Association, New York, 1976.

National Citizens' Conference, Social and Rehabilitation Service, *The Goal Is Mobility*, HEW SRS-113, U.S. Department of Health, Education and Welfare, Washington, 1969.

Prevalence of Selected Impairments, National Center for Health Statistics, Washington, 1973.

Proposed Specification for Making Buildings and Facilities Accessible to, and Useable by Physically Handicapped Persons (proposed American National Standards Institute document ANSI A117.1, 1977 revision) Syracuse University School of Architecture, Syracuse 1977.

Research Paper RP 1879, National Bureau of Standards, Washington, 1948.

Tice and Shaw, *Barrier Free Design: Accessibility for the Handicapped*, Institute for Research and Development in Occupational Education, New York, 1974.

Index